T0302130

VOICES ON THE GERMAN EDITION

Oliver Schlaudt has written a very readable introduction to the philosophy of economics. Anyone who wants to deal with the subject should pick up this book [...]. With his book, Schlaudt makes an important contribution [to] the formation of a genuine philosophy of economics.

— **Christian Neuhäuser** in *Deutsche Zeitschrift für Philosophie*

Brilliant plea for a political and ecological economy [...]. Sharp, subtle, truly philosophical analysis [...]. Apocalypses can hardly be explained more soberly, and a greater compliment can hardly be paid to a philosopher.

— **Reinhard Mehring** in *Philosophischer Literaturanzeiger*

The more fundamental the problem, the more helpful are specialists on the big issues [...]. Schlaudt explains conclusively why economists find it difficult to analyze conflicts between economic process and ecological sustainability.

— **Norbert Häring** in *Handelsblatt*

PHILOSOPHY OF ECONOMICS

Philosophy of Economics: A Heterodox Introduction provides an introduction to the philosophy of economics through the prism of heterodoxy.

Heterodox economics covers a range of approaches and schools of thought but what they have as a common denominator is the conviction that economic phenomena cannot be understood, and thus must not be studied, in isolation from their relevant context. Conversely, the current form of neoclassical economics emerged from the conviction that there is something like economic rationality sui generis which can be treated independently from all other aspects of our world, social or natural. Heterodox approaches challenge this conviction, from a variety of angles: the economic actor is not isolated, but lives in society which shapes him; market goods are only one kind of goods among others, constituting a larger set with ambiguous and shifting inner frontiers; production of goods takes place within nature, is subjected to physical laws and induces in most cases ecologically problematic fluxes of matter (e.g. waste); finally, the whole economic process in general is not in equilibrium, but shows secular trends through which it is connected to the historical world. This book demonstrates the vitality of these heterodox challenges from a philosophical point of view because not only do they formulate new hypotheses within economics, but they challenge economic theory on a much more fundamental level: how is the economy situated in the world, and which are the right methods for its investigation?

This book is an ideal introduction for anyone seeking alternative or critical perspectives on the philosophy of economics and economic theory.

Oliver Schlaudt teaches philosophy of science and political philosophy at the Philosophy Department of Heidelberg University, Germany, and at SciencesPo Paris, France (Campus Nancy). His main research interests include philosophy of science, philosophy of economics, philosophy of technology and cognitive archaeology.

Economics and Humanities

Series Editor: **Sebastian Berger**, *University of the West of England (UWE Bristol), UK.*

The *Economics and Humanities* series presents the economic wisdom of the humanities and arts. Its volumes gather the economic senses sheltered and revealed by some of the most excellent sources within philosophy, poetry, art, and storytelling. By re-rooting economics in its original domain these contributions allow economic phenomena and their meanings to come into the open more fully; indeed, they allow us to ask anew the question "What is economics?". Economic truth is thus shown to arise from the Human rather than the Market.

Readers will gain a foundational understanding of a humanities-based economics and find their economic sensibility enriched. They should turn to this series if they are interested in questions such as: What are the economic consequences of rooting economic Truth in the Human? What is the purpose of a humanities-based economics? What is the proper meaning of the "oikos", and how does it arise? What are the true meanings of wealth and poverty, gain and loss, capital and productivity? In what sense is economic reasoning with words more fundamental than reasoning with numbers? What is the dimension and measure of human dwelling in the material world?

These volumes address themselves to all those who are interested in sources and foundations for economic wisdom. Students and academics who are fundamentally dissatisfied with the state of economics and worried that its crisis undermines society will find this series of interest.

Capital in the History of Accounting and Economic Thought
Capitalism, Ecology and Democracy
Jacques Richard and Alexandre Rambaud

Economics, Accounting and the True Nature of Capitalism
Capitalism, Ecology and Democracy
Jacques Richard and Alexandre Rambaud

For more information about this series, please visit: www.routledge.com/Economics-and-Humanities/book-series/RSECH

PHILOSOPHY OF ECONOMICS

A Heterodox Introduction

Oliver Schlaudt

Translated from German by Adrian Wilding

Routledge
Taylor & Francis Group

LONDON AND NEW YORK

First published 2022
by Routledge
2 Park Square, Milton Park, Abingdon, Oxon OX14 4RN

and by Routledge
605 Third Avenue, New York, NY 10158

Routledge is an imprint of the Taylor & Francis Group, an informa business

© 2022 Oliver Schlaudt

The right of Oliver Schlaudt to be identified as author of this work
has been asserted by him in accordance with sections 77 and 78 of the
Copyright, Designs and Patents Act 1988.

British Library Cataloguing-in-Publication Data
A catalogue record for this book is available from the British Library

Library of Congress Cataloging-in-Publication Data
Names: Schlaudt, Oliver, author.
Title: Philosophy of economics : a heterodox introduction /
Oliver Schlaudt.
Description: Abingdon, Oxon ; New York, NY : Routledge, 2022. |
Series: Economics and humanities | Includes bibliographical references
and index.
Identifiers: LCCN 2021020286 (print) | LCCN 2021020287 (ebook) |
ISBN 9781032068480 (hbk) | ISBN 9781032068336 (pbk) |
ISBN 9781003204077 (ebk)
Subjects: LCSH: Economics—Philosophy. | Economics—
Methodology. | Economics.
Classification: LCC HB72 .S342 2022 (print) | LCC HB72 (ebook) |
DDC 330.1—dc23
LC record available at https://lccn.loc.gov/2021020286
LC ebook record available at https://lccn.loc.gov/202102028

This work was published originally in the German language under
the title *Wirtschaft im Kontext: Eine Einführung in die Philosophie der
Wirtschaftswissenschaft in Zeiten des Umbruchs,* © Vittorio Klostermann
GmbH, Frankfurt am Main, 2016.

ISBN: 978-1-032-06848-0 (hbk)
ISBN: 978-1-032-06833-6 (pbk)
ISBN: 978-1-003-20407-7 (ebk)

DOI: 10.4324/9781003204077

Typeset in Bembo
by codeMantra

CONTENTS

FIGURES

TABLES

BOXES

ACKNOWLEDGEMENTS AND CREDITS

This book, first published in German under the title *Wirtschaft im Kontext* by Vittorio Klostermann, Frankfurt a.M., is based on the seminar 'Economics and the Real World: Alternative Approaches', which I gave in autumn 2015 at the *Institut d'études politiques de Paris*, SciencesPo, Campus Nancy. I would like to thank my colleagues Malte Faber (Heidelberg), Michael Heinrich (Berlin) and Reiner Manstetten (Heidelberg) for their advice and helpful comments on a first version of the manuscript. Jason W. Moore (New York) patiently answered my questions on 'world ecology'. I am grateful to Chrysostomos Mantzavinos (Athens) for the idea of an English translation. This translation from a revised version of the manuscript was done very thoroughly by Adrian Wilding (Jena). I take sole responsibility for any errors in the presentation.

Reproduction of the illustrations was kindly permitted by:

Figure 2.3: © Springer Nature;

Figure 2.4 a and b: © Cambridge University Press;

Figures 2.5, 2.6a, b, and 4.11: © American Association for the Advancement of Science;

Figure 3.3: © Destatis (Statistisches Bundesamt), Germany;

Figure 4.1 and 5.1: © Thomas Piketty, Paris;

Figure 4.2: © Elsevier;

Figure 4.4: © The Wildlife Society, Bethesda (Maryland, USA)

Figure 4.10: © Department for Environment, Food and Rural Affairs, UK (Open Government Licence, https://www.nationalarchives.gov.uk/doc/open-government-licence/version/3/)

Figure 5.2: © United Nations, New York (creative commons CC BY 3.0 IGO)

INTRODUCTION

The purpose of this book is to introduce the reader to the philosophy of economics in a new and contemporary way that takes into account today's reality: our society is experiencing a major crisis, but the economic sciences, from which we would justifiably hope to learn more about our fate, find themselves caught up in exactly the same situation. They too are undergoing a crisis and are embroiled in a fierce debate about their own methods. For philosophy, however, the awkward moment may be a favourable one, as a rare opportunity is offered to take a look behind the scenes at the now exposed conceptual machinery of economics.

Philosophy of economics and philosophy of science

This philosophical examination of the economic sciences represents – formally speaking – a special instance of the philosophy of science, which generally deals with the foundations, methods and limits of the empirical sciences. In the case of economics, a philosophical analysis sometimes acquires a new, unforeseen relevance, since critics of the prevailing economic doctrines often look to philosophy for guidance and orientation.

But it is questionable whether the philosophical literature of recent decades can really help them. In the 20th century, the philosophy of science suffered from a one-sided orientation towards physics, which was considered the queen of the sciences. This was certainly due to its early success, which destined physics to become the model for the other sciences. At the same time, there is a systematic reason why physics seems to be the most fundamental of the sciences: every social process, along with every chemical or biological process, is also a physical process, but not vice versa.

DOI: 10.4324/9781003204077-1

The economic sciences as we know them today owe a debt of gratitude to the second half of the 19th century with its attempt to take physics as a model and to understand and explain economic processes in the same way that physics does its own. Thus, the economic sciences almost inevitably had to consider themselves as a 'dirty' version of physics – and a philosophy that shares this view of scientificity will surely not be in a position to question the economics' assumptions.

The 'dirty' side of economics consists in humans' peculiar relationship to economic laws, which on the one hand act as coercive regulations *upon* us, but on the other hand only work *through* us and our actions. While the laws of nature, without exception and inexorably, rule over matter on large and small scales, social laws impose themselves on the individual and society in a way that is not easy to grasp. Let us consider two texts from the classical literature in which this issue is problematised.

Kant observes at the beginning of his 1784 essay *Idea for a universal history with a cosmopolitan aim*:

> Thus marriages, the births that come from them and deaths, since the free will of human beings has so great an influence on them, seem to be subject to no rule in accordance with which their number could be determined in advance through calculation; and yet the annual tables of them in large countries prove that they happen just as much in accordance with constant laws of nature, as weather conditions which are so inconstant, whose individual occurrence one cannot previously determine, but which on the whole do not fail to sustain the growth of plants, the course of streams, and other natural arrangements in a uniform uninterrupted course.
>
> *(Kant 2007, p. 108)*

Here social laws are realised with the same relentlessness in terms of averages as natural laws, while leaving the individual to follow their every whim.

This appears quite different in the thought of Karl Marx. He uses an example, which we will return to later, to discuss the fact that the individual entrepreneur is not able to stand up to the market in setting wages, but is instead condemned to adapt to competitors. Here, it seems that social laws are mercilessly enforced precisely upon the individual, whereas society as a whole can easily ignore them. This is because society is free to choose whether there should be a market for labour at all, and Marx, as is well known, favoured a different social and economic arrangement.

Kant thus conceived of social laws *grosso modo* as deterministic macro-laws, which allow individuals their freedom at the micro level, but which are nevertheless realised in the sum of their actions. Marx, however, understood them

as uniformities which are enforced precisely by self-regulating sanction mechanisms at the micro level, whereas at the macro level, they appear more as
rules than as laws, revealing a conventional, historical and changeable character. In any case, what distinguishes social laws from the laws of nature is the
fact that, although they act *on* people as coercive laws, they can also only act
through them, which seems to loosen the 'corset' of determination at one level
or another.

Since they saw this difference as a mere flaw and adhered to the model of
physics, it did not seem necessary for the philosophers of science to develop
their own theory of the social sciences. It was sufficient to simply *transfer* the
knowledge gained in physics to the social sciences, and thus to pose the usual
questions: what is an explanation, what is a model, what are laws and what is
their inductive basis, what role does causality play in this, etc. (to see this, open
the table of contents of any introduction to the theory of science). Any deviation
in the social sciences could simply be attributed to the lack of perfection of these
'dirty' disciplines. In fact, this corresponds fairly closely to the attitude and the
self-understanding which the influential philosophers of science of the post-war
period displayed towards the social sciences.

It is these philosophers, of all people, who critics of the prevailing economic
doctrines seek advice from today. The *transfer* from physics to the social sciences
is a heavy burden. First, one can already have doubts as to whether the classics
of the philosophy of science have even developed an adequate concept of science in physics. They tended to reduce science to theory, and accordingly the
concepts of hypothesis and law took a central position in their conceptions. This
picture has been shaken up in recent decades and has given way to a view that
gives much more space to the practical, local and historical aspects of research,
but is also more cautious in the distinction between science and non-science.
This is quite a valid point, as critics of economics often measure it against a
strong normative ideal of science which, in turn, stems from an unrealistic and
sometimes somewhat clichéd image of physics. By contrast, one of the aims of
this book is to work with more realistic and cautious assumptions about science.

Second, as the picture of physics research changed, it also became clear that
physics was by no means the fundamental science it was thought to be. The fact
that every social or biological process is always a physical one does not logically
guarantee that it can ultimately be explained by its physical properties alone.
This was a mere promise. In the Vienna Circle, for example, which is still influential today, this promise was embodied in the assertion that physical language is
the *universal* language. The promise, however, has never been fulfilled.

The great methodological debates, then and now

Philosophers of science – and even more so historians – are today more inclined
to accept a multiplicity of sciences, each of which can claim to be understood

independently and in its own specificities. For the social sciences, there is even a historical blueprint for this, in particular the German-language literature of the late 19th and the early 20th centuries, because these sciences have undergone certain major methodological debates in their development that hold out the prospect of accessing their specificity:

- the dispute between Carl Menger and Gustav Schmoller in Economics during the 1880s, known as the Historicism Dispute (*Historismusstreit*), which concerned the importance of a genuine historical method for the study of economic processes;
- the Value Judgement Dispute (*Werturteilsstreit*) between Schmoller and Max Weber around 1900 on the question of whether social scientific research can legitimise sociopolitical measures;
- the debate between Theodor W. Adorno and Karl Popper in the mid-1960s – more staged than carried-through – known as the Positivism Dispute (*Positivismusstreit*) concerning the interpretation of empirical data, in which the fundamental questions of the Value Judgement Dispute about the relationship between theory and practice, subject and object were taken up again;
- finally, one would have to mention the Individualism Dispute (*Individualismusstreit*) over whether the characteristics of society can be explained by those of individuals or rather vice versa. This dispute, although already present in the 18th century with Jean-Jacques Rousseau's criticism of Thomas Hobbes, always smouldered without ever coming to a head (Freudenthal 1986).

But even the most recent of these debates dates back decades, and thus falls far short of the emergence of the individual facets of the *multiple crisis* that is gradually taking shape and making economics interesting to a more general public today. The economic sciences today display a lively discussion of methods. Nevertheless, this discussion, which is now conducted almost exclusively in English, has hardly moved beyond the scope of the four old major debates, even if it presents the old problems freed from the dust of past decades.

Outsiders, who have a certain basic trust in the sciences, may even be surprised by the harsh tone of today's criticism, which does not question individual hypotheses but essentially the entirety of textbook knowledge. In 1982, Wassily Leontief, Nobel Laureate and former president of the *American Economic Association*, criticised an "aversion for systematic empirical inquiry" in his subject, which relies solely on mathematical models: "Page after page of professional economic journals are filled with mathematical formulas leading the reader from sets of more or less plausible but entirely arbitrary assumptions to precisely stated but irrelevant theoretical conclusions" (Leontief 1982, p. 104). Thomas Piketty recently voiced the same idea, which has not lost its relevance 30 years on, in a

more charming way. Looking back on his beginnings as a doctoral student researching the American economy, he notes:

> To be sure, they [the US economists] were all very intelligent, and I still
> have many friends from that period of my life. But something strange
> happened: I was only too aware of the fact that I knew nothing at all
> about the world's economic problems. My thesis consisted of several
> relatively abstract mathematical theorems. Yet the profession liked my
> work.
>
> *(Piketty 2014, p. 31)*

In the end, he comes to the same conclusion as Leontief:

> To put it bluntly, the discipline of economics has yet to get over its childish
> passion for mathematics and for purely theoretical and often highly ideo-
> logical speculation, at the expense of historical research and collaboration
> with the other social sciences. Economists are all too often preoccupied
> with petty mathematical problems of interest only to themselves. This ob-
> session with mathematics is an easy way of acquiring the appearance of sci-
> entificity without having to answer the far more complex questions posed
> by the world we live in.
>
> *(Ibid. p. 32)*

With this attitude, the economists finally embarrassed themselves thoroughly
in the face of the financial crisis of 2008, especially among a wider public. Even
Queen Elizabeth II felt compelled to ask during a visit to the London School
of Economics why nobody had noticed that a credit crisis was looming on the
horizon. The answer from the leading economists at the British Academy speaks
volumes. At the end of two or three pages of meaningless statements, their response comes down to the argument that there was "a failure of the collective
imagination of many bright people", whereby by "bright people" they mean
themselves, individuals who apparently still cannot grasp the scale of their failure
(Besley and Hennessy 2009, p. 10).

Leontief's image of the unworldly and somewhat naive lover of mathematical models may itself be misleading, of course, since economists do play a
very concrete role in the real world. When they turn the crank and start up
their complicated formal models, one knows in advance with absolute cer-
tainty what the result will be: that only the free, unregulated market will lead
to optimal social results. Every intervention is repulsed like a reflex, whether
it is the minimum wage, environmental protection measures or the action
of trade unions. Joseph Stiglitz sums up contemporary economics as having
moved "from being a scientific discipline into becoming free market capitalism's biggest cheerleader" (Stiglitz 2010, p. 238). The French philosopher

Grégoire Chamayou goes one step further: "Some economists have blood on their hands" (Chamayou 2018, p. 173).

The concept of 'economics in context'

Economists, who, in the hard struggle with facts, models and colleagues, are concerned with the everyday life of scientific work, may consider this representation to be a caricature. Above all, they will probably not want to have the foundations of their work nullified by a philosopher who has nothing to offer but second-hand insights.

But this is not the intention of this book. Rather, this book is based on the observation that the economic sciences today are gradually shifting in their research and perhaps also in their teaching. Numerous alternative approaches have emerged and some of them have even become institutionalised. These include ecological economics, new institutional economics, a historical macroeconomics, feminist economics and approaches that incorporate current research findings from other empirical human sciences (behavioural economics, neuroeconomics, evolutionary economics). The present book takes up this multitude of alternatives and tries to get a picture of the economic sciences in their specificity. It is therefore not a criticism of orthodoxy but a philosophical reading of heterodoxy. (We will see in a moment that such a reading is almost inevitable today.)

The talk of "orthodoxy" and "heterodoxy" adopted here has developed informally in recent years (cf. Mearman, Berger and Guizzo, 2019). The basic thesis of the book, which also shapes its structure, is that the many critiques and alternatives that are summarised here as heterodoxy, most of them formulated independently of each other, also have a common core: from different perspectives, they question the basic assumption that economic processes are *autonomous* processes. Against this assumption, critics argue that economic processes are in fact *embedded in the world* in several respects: the market actor is embedded in a social world with fellow human beings, institutions and shared resources; production, distribution and consumption of goods are embedded in the physical world (at times, economists even have to be reminded of the validity of the laws of nature!) and in a finite natural world, whose reserve of raw materials and capacity to absorb pollutants and waste are exhaustible; the life and reproduction processes of society are only partially organised in the form of a market and depend in part on non-market organised activities (family, education, care, culture, law, etc.); the entire economic process is part of a global history, i.e. it takes place in a certain global constellation (in which, for example, centre and periphery can be distinguished), participates in major global changes (such as urbanisation), is subject to contingent political influences, and even produces them.

In sum, according to the emerging consensus of heterodoxies, economic processes are embedded in other processes with which they form a series of interfaces. These boundaries are crossed in both directions; the spaces external to the economy shape and influence the economy just as much as it has a shaping effect on them. The central concept of this book will therefore be the *boundary* (also 'limit' or 'interface'). From a scientific-philosophical perspective, we are interested in what happens at such a boundary and what *conceptual* resources are needed to adequately describe this event (Figure I.1).

Of course, there are possible responses to this argument. A priori, we can distinguish three possible responses: (1) that the economic process does indeed take place independently of other (social and, in the narrower sense, natural) processes, (2) that a dependency exists, but that the respective external spaces can be adequately captured in economic vocabulary, in particular the concept of economic *value* and (3) that a dependency exists and that this dependency requires a corresponding new vocabulary at each border. The last of these responses can be further nuanced to determine whether the classical vocabulary of economics needs merely to be enriched with new elements (such as finiteness and power relations) or whether even its core vocabulary must be replaced. The boundaries or 'limits' of which we will speak are thus twofold: first, real, material and causal limits of a real process, and second also limits of concepts whose investigation is the task of philosophy in the form that Immanuel Kant gave it and baptised with the name of critique.

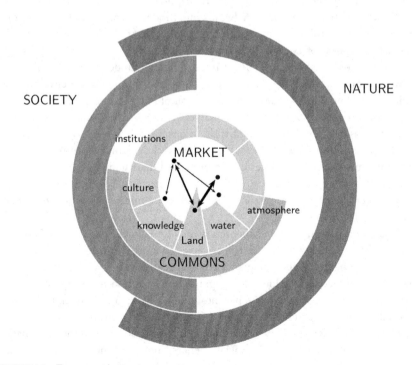

FIGURE I.1 Economy in context.

The fundamental question, which is becoming acute today in the economic sciences and which the philosopher must actually only take up more than work out himself, is therefore: *Which is the right basic vocabulary to adequately grasp economic processes as an integrated part of the social life process?* Obtaining this basic vocabulary requires 'work on the concept', and this will be the task of the present book. In particular, we will see that the questions about models, experiments, explanations, etc., that are often posed in the philosophy of economics and taken over from the philosophy of physics are not mistaken, but are premature. In fact, the more fundamental question of what is in principle the correct vocabulary for the economic sciences is still unresolved.

Economics – descriptive or normative?

We will therefore be concerned with investigating concepts, which is not surprising for a philosophy of science perspective, but at the same time it should be noted that the concepts and theses of the economists make it somewhat difficult for a philosophical analysis, since in discursive terms these have a peculiarly 'opaque' character. One never knows exactly whether one is dealing with a *descriptive* and neutral or a *normative* and politically demanding discourse. This is also a consequence of the 'dirty' character of economics described above, i.e. the strange fact that its 'atoms', namely individuals, understand themselves as free and thus as objects of *both* descriptions *and* prescriptions.

We will see that from the very beginning, modern economics has been concerned with the problem of not only *investigating* free trade, but also *justifying* it. The same applies, of course, to economics' critics. The creators of ecological economics, for instance, not only wanted to better understand what humans do in economic activity, but also genuinely wanted to protect the environment (Chapter 4). The same is true in the discussion of common property as the limit of private property (Chapter 3): for Garrett Hardin, the boundary of private property was also the boundary of the responsibility that each of us bears and should therefore be widened as far as possible. When Elinor Ostrom countered him with functioning examples of self-organised management of the commons as an alternative to the dichotomy of market or centralised power, it seemed obvious to her that the practical success of such economic practices justified them as a political demand.

This descriptive–normative, theoretical–practical double-facedness takes on a characteristic shape at the boundary between economy and context in which we are interested here. On the one hand, we observe historically an expansion of the market into the context. Not only geographically, but also in its core countries, the market is penetrating ever deeper into people's lives, and more and more human relationships are being transformed into those between market actors. This phenomenon is often collectively referred to as "imperialism". On the other hand, one can also observe that in the social sciences, more and more phenomena are described and analysed in economic vocabulary. In view of this development, one often speaks of "economics imperialism" (Boulding 1969). Gary S. Becker, winner of the Nobel Prize for Economics, is a representative of this trend. At one point in his Nobel Lecture, he describes human partnerships as "efficient bargaining":

> [When] men and women decide to marry or have children or divorce, they attempt to maximize their utility by comparing benefits and costs. So they marry when they expect to be better off than if they remained single, and they divorce if that is expected to increase their welfare. [...] According to this theory, richer couples tend to gain a lot from remaining married, whereas many poorer couples do not. A poor woman may well doubt whether it is worth staying married to someone chronically unemployed.
>
> *(Becker 1997, p. 46)*

This phenomenon of economic imperialism certainly demands careful evaluation. Clearly, Becker's analysis provokes unease or even outrage, and he is probably deliberately playing with such reactions. But is this really due to an improper expansion of economic vocabulary? In 1975, the French sociologist Pierre Bourdieu proposed, in a related sense, that science be described not as a disinterested search for truth but as a struggle for the monopoly of authority, which he understood as a form of "symbolic capital". Accordingly, he presented the behaviour of the researcher as an "investment strategy" with "profit motives" (Bourdieu 1975). This is far less likely to provoke moral outrage. In a later study, the sociologists of science Bruno Latour and Steve Woolgar emphasised that scientists actually use such economic terms themselves when reflecting on their behaviour (Latour and Woolgar 1986, p. 189).

Without going further into the issue here, we can at least express the reservation that the problematic aspect of Becker's analysis is not necessarily his use of economic terminology. His approach suffers less from an inadequate vocabulary than from the fact that he hopelessly underestimates the complexity of his subject. Nevertheless, precisely because of the clearly noticeable shortcomings of his analysis, the normative undertone becomes more apparent: Becker legitimises capitalist profit motives by 'naturalizing' them, i.e. by presenting them as a natural phenomenon and a natural state of human being. For him, all life is a market, and the extension of market vocabulary indicates that no legitimate limits can be drawn to the market's practical expansion.

It may be enough here to merely mention this double-facedness; the reader is thereby forewarned of an almost omnipresent peculiarity of economic thinking.

Structure of the book

Chapter 1 briefly presents economic 'orthodoxy', explaining its account of economic events as autonomous processes and the laws which determine them. The key problems around economics that have recently become well known in public debates are mentioned at this point. In Chapters 2–4, a 'limit' or 'boundary' in the sense specified above is the focus: in Chapter 2, the limits of individualism in collective phenomena, in Chapter 3, the limits of private property and market in a jointly shared world, and finally in Chapter 4, the limits set by a finite nature. In the fifth (and final) chapter, we attempt to extract the essential arguments from these three perspectives. A minimal consequence of this is the broadening out of the science of economics by means of a historical dimension, which is at the same time also understood to be a global, i.e. world-historical dimension. But we will also explore current approaches that try to fill out this formal framework with a unifying theory. Whether these approaches will be successful is still an open question, but they nevertheless already allow us to take a new look at the current, multisystemic crisis.

1

ORTHODOX ECONOMICS

The illusion of autonomy

1.1 Economics – an overview

An introduction to the philosophy of economics does not replace an introduction to economics. But, since this book is aimed at a general audience interested in economics and philosophy, neither should it presuppose that the reader is already familiar with economic theory. Without making the audacious claim to provide an introduction to neoclassical economics in this chapter, the fundamentals of this discipline shall be presented in such a way that the layperson in the field of economics can gain a sufficiently clear picture of its conceptual machinery. A reader looking for an introduction to economics will find that there are already a number of works available today that take the heterodox approaches fully into account (see e.g. Bowles 2004; Gowdy 2010; Daly and Farley 2011; Goodwin et al. 2014).

1.1.1 Prefatory note on terminology: economics and economy

The economists have named their research field after "the economy". We do not use this term to refer to the entirety of businesses (organised under private or public law), as is often the case in politics and the daily press when, for example, the "interests of the economy" are mentioned. Rather, the entirety of the economic actions of people is meant. One could perhaps speak less ambiguously of "the organisation of production and consumption". It has become a common practice to define economic decisions and actions as those that serve the intended satisfaction of needs with the given resources and technical possibilities:

> Economics is the study of how men and society choose, with or without the use of money, to employ scarce productive resources which could have

DOI: 10.4324/9781003204077-2

alternative uses, to produce various commodities over time and distribute them for consumption now and in the future amongst various people and groups of society.

(Samuelson 1967, p. 5)

Although this definition is often accepted, even by critics of the prevailing doctrine, one should nevertheless mistrust it, since it is not neutral but rather is already tailored to the programme of the neoclassical approach (Screpanti and Zamagni 2005, esp. p. 185). In speaking of the satisfaction of needs, it is first of all one-sidedly committed to the perspective of the *consumer*, second, it encourages us to take the consumer's needs as *given* (as an "exogenous variable", more on this later) and third it tends to reduce the economic process to the *market* as a mechanism of efficient resource allocation. We should ask ourselves whether the focus should not instead be placed on the social process as a whole, and in such a way that the economy's interaction with the environment is not obscured.

In this sense, some authors have suggested that we once again characterise economic processes as the social "metabolism" that was self-evident for Karl Marx (Fischer-Kowalski 1998; Fischer-Kowalski and Hüttler 1998; Moore 2015a, Chap. 3). This way of speaking takes advantage of a biological analogy that allows us to highlight certain characteristics which economic processes share with the organism: in both cases, we are dealing with an open, dynamic and self-regulating system. The 'life process' of society consists in reproducing its essential structure in a self-organised way in its metabolism with the environment, with the given resources and technical possibilities. Another author suggests that we talk about the economy in a more general way as an "autopoietic system", which helps us identify the differences that separate the economy from the biological organism. Unlike the latter, the mode of organisation of the economic process is based, for example, on communicative processes and the purposeful actions of individuals (De Angelis 2013, p. 607).

This broader notion of economic activity also allows one to capture the impact of collective processes on the needs of individuals (i.e. to treat needs as 'endogenous' variables), which will prove useful and perhaps even necessary.

Among the 'economic' activities, one traditionally distinguishes between production, distribution (especially money-mediated exchange) and consumption of goods. If the goods and other factors flow back into production instead of being consumed, one speaks of allocation instead of distribution. In addition to these classical activities, the handling of resources and waste is also emphasised today. The economic actors include not only private individuals or private households but also companies, governments and central banks, as well as the sometimes extremely powerful corporations (on the latter, see Nace 2003).

1.1.2 Economics

If we stick to the self-conception of the discipline, we can say the following about economics in advance. Economics is largely divided into the two branches

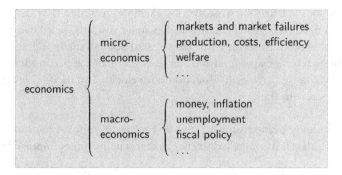

FIGURE 1.1   Micro- and macroeconomics.

of micro- and macroeconomics. The former starts with the various economic entities, while macroeconomics is devoted to aggregate economic processes, drawing on macroeconomic variables such as national budgets. Gross national product, unemployment rate and inflation rate are typical macroeconomic variables that are defined and measured by the so-called econometrics. One area of microeconomics that will be of particular interest to us is welfare economics, which studies the impact of microeconomic variables on the economic welfare of society. Monetary economics, on the other hand, which has also attracted the occasional attention of philosophers and, in the wake of the financial crisis, for example, with David Graeber's influential book *Debt* (Graeber 2011), has also aroused more general interest, belongs to macroeconomics (Figure 1.1).

Micro- and macroeconomics do not examine different objects in the sense of a division of labour, but rather look at the same set of objects from different perspectives, from the 'small' and the 'big', respectively. This can create tensions. While microeconomics, for example, sees unemployment as the result of a deviation from the norm of the ideal market, macroeconomics is much more willing to understand it as an empirically established normality (Stiglitz 1991, p. 7). The conflict arises from the fact that the reductionist programme of microeconomics is committed to attributing macroeconomic phenomena to interactions at the microeconomic level. This programme is called 'microfoundation'. We will come back to the problems associated with it (but see, for example, Bergh and Gowdy 2003).

1.2 The theory of general equilibrium

1.2.1 First of all: what is an explanation?

Let us now look at how microeconomics tries to explain economic processes. Without getting too involved in the difficult and controversial philosophical question of what an explanation actually is, we can at least state that every explanation implicitly involves two steps. First, we must agree on what needs to be explained and what does not. And second, it must be determined what is considered an explanation. Aristotle, for example, regarded it as "natural" and thus not in need of explanation, that things strive towards their "natural place", i.e. heavy things fall to earth, while the celestial bodies remain in their heavenly sphere. In Newton's classical physics, on the other hand, it is considered natural that a body changes neither its direction nor velocity "by itself". Newton's first law of motion runs thus:

> Every body perseveres in its state of rest, or of uniform motion in a right line, unless it is compelled to change that state by forces impress'd thereon.
> *(Newton 1729, p. 19)*

Uniform motion is defined as the base line. Deviations are in need of explanation. For example, when planets in space are pushed into an elliptical orbit, "forces" are accepted as explanation, even if their origin is not yet known, as in the case of gravitation.

We can draw from this that a phenomenon, e.g., a property, is always explained by something else, which itself is accepted without explanation, at least temporarily. As Immanuel Kant already pointed out, it is an inherent problem in scientific explanation that it tends to lead to an infinite regress, insofar as x which was used to explain y itself demands explanation (Kant 1998, B536). Every science has to deal with this problem, and it goes without saying that economic science must not be measured by a standard that even physics does not meet. At any given moment, every science must begin with certain presuppositions. These can of course change over time, and in the controversy over methods, it always remains a legitimate question what is actually to be explained by what, provided that all parties to the controversy accept that there is no such thing as an unconditional explanation.

The classical explanatory model of physics consists in a certain reductionism, namely that of *mechanism*: the properties of a system are explained by those of its parts and in this sense are traced back to them, but never vice versa. Physics explains the properties of solids and molecules in terms of the properties of atoms and the properties of atoms in terms of the properties of their components, electrons and nuclei. Electrons are considered elementary particles, while the atomic nucleus has a structure and consists of protons and neutrons.

A problem arose for this 'mechanistic' thinking early on, especially in the 18th century, in the form of the *organism*, whose character seems to be just the opposite: its organs are arranged for the purposes of the organism. Here, it seems as if it is the system, the living being, which determines which properties the parts must have, and these are, in turn, 'holistically' explained by the whole that the parts form (on this, see McLaughlin 1990 and Box 1.1). It was the great achievement of Darwin's theory of evolution to name the mechanisms that can explain the purposefulness of the parts without having to seek a being – some Creator God – that arranges those purposes.

BOX 1.1 MECHANISM VERSUS HOLISM IN THE EXPLANATION OF COMPLEX SYSTEMS

Mechanism is a method which tries to trace back the properties of complex systems to the properties and interactions of its parts. The parts themselves may be complex systems. In any case, mechanism presupposes that the parts exist and have their properties independently of their relationship to a whole. Physics is mechanistic. It derives, for example, the properties of gases, liquids and solid states from the properties and interactions of atoms.

There are systems that escape the mechanistic approach. In organisms (in particular in our own body) and ecosystems, the parts do not exist independently from the whole, and each seems mutually adapted to the other such as to result in a stable, living and reproducing whole. The explanation of such systems has to make a detour. We have to give an evolutionary account of how they came into being and how they reproduce.

Are societies more like the ideal gas or more like an organism or an ecosystem? The majority of economists vote for the former approach; sociologists and anthropologists tend to take the latter view. "What individuals are, think, or do comes to them, to a very large extend, from their man-made (cultural) environment", K. William Kapp insisted (Kapp 1961, p. 131).

In social philosophy, there are conflicting views on the relationship between system (society) and part (individual). There is no question that a society exists only through and within individuals: no society without people. But this does not answer the question of the *direction* of the explanation. Historically, the following can be stated *grosso modo*: in pre-capitalist social philosophy, e.g., in Thomas of Aquinas, there dominated a holistic explanation, with the organism being used as an analogy: humans are different, and everyone has his or her special place in the whole. Only the whole body of society is capable of survival; none of its specialised parts can survive outside it. In the epoch of capitalism, this changes. Social philosophy adopts the reductionist method of natural philosophy (Freudenthal 1986), and its view of society fits in well with the liberal worldview of the rising bourgeoisie: society is no longer a hierarchically structured creature with a divinely sanctioned head, but results from the movements and interactions of single, free and equal individuals. With the 19th century, the holistic way of explaining things is revived. Karl Marx and Émile Durkheim deserve special mention here. Although each is far from proclaiming a natural hierarchy of individuals, each certainly assumes, in a sense unspecified, that society has a life of its own that can prevail over the individual. Since then, the social sciences have been divided over this question of methodological individualism.

1.2.2 Homo œconomicus

The general equilibrium theory of microeconomics, known as neoclassical economics, stands unambiguously in the mechanistic, viz., individualistic tradition.
It seeks to explain social phenomena as the overall result of the decisions of individual actors. The decisions of actors are, in turn, based on an individual order
of preference. This order is *assumed* but not *explained*. Economics regards it as a
so-called exogenous variable:

> 1 Preferences are exogenous.

Subsequently, a number of further assumptions about the economic actor are
made, which are summarised in the image of *homo œconomicus*. 'Economic man'
is characterised by two features, summarised in the axiom of rationality:

> 2 *Homo œconomicus* strives to maximise his utility or well-being.
> 3 His behaviour is rational.

The 'rationality' of behaviour essentially means that in the face of two alternatives, the actor always has a preference (the postulate of *completeness*) and that his
(*homo œconomicus* emerged from a social imaginary that presumed the rational
economic actor to be male) preferences are consistent, in particular that the order of preference is *transitive*: if he prefers A to alternative B and the latter to C,
he also prefers A to C. In particular, "rational" does not mean that the actor
acts prudently and on the basis of consideration, but only that his behaviour –
thoroughly spontaneous and dictated by preferences – is judged from the outside to be rational in the sense of the formal criteria mentioned. We should
already note here that the relationship between preference, behaviour and utility
is a purely analytical one: it is a conceptual not an empirical part of the theory.
A given preference leads, under given circumstances, to a specific behaviour
which results in a specific well-being – this is so by definition, not on the basis
of experience (cf. Brandstätter, Güth and Kliemt 2003, pp. 319–320). In fact,
behaviour is the only directly observable variable in this theory, and the notions
of preference and utility are solely a matter of theorising about behaviour. We
will return to this issue in Chapter 2.

A further important clarification is required here. It is often claimed that
homo œconomicus is *selfish*. It is important to be very precise on this issue, because
this common assumption is often latched on to by critics (again see Chapter 2).
For the sake of precision, we should emphasise two things. First, the principle
of making decisions according to individual preferences and for the purpose of

maximising utility is not – or is only in a trivial sense – synonymous with a selfish actor, because, as we have just emphasised, it makes no empirical claim about the actors themselves and their motives but simply follows from the definitions. But even if, as is sometimes the case, the individual's order of preferences is restricted by the additional requirement that his preferences and the benefits resulting from his goods need not depend on the context, especially not on the distribution of goods to other individuals–even then, second, we are not dealing with a selfish

4 Independence: the preferences of *homo œconomicus* are unaffected by other individuals.

actor in the true sense of the word. It is true that altruistic action, whether out of compassion or ethical duty, is often used as a counter-example. But to *homo œconomicus* as defined in neoclassical theory, actions out of antipathy or bad faith are just as alien. *Homo œconomicus* not only does not share, he also knows no envy or rancour, which are normally the province of egoists. It is thus more correct to speak of a *self-regarding* than a *selfish* actor, one who follows the maxim of utility maximisation regardless of his fellow humans and his environment (see Bowles and Gintis 2000; Gowdy 2010, p. 130).

1.2.3 Utility and the subjective concept of value

The maximisation of utility is both a subtle and completely trivial demand on *homo œconomicus*. The latter, because in the economically relevant situation of the distribution of goods it translates into a simple "more is better":

5 Postulate of non-satiation: greater consumption brings ever greater utility to *homo œconomicus*.

The actor will always strive for a larger quantity of a good and prefer the larger quantity to the smaller. The only qualification to this rule consists in the fact that utility is not simply proportional to the quantity of the good consumed:

6 Law of decreasing marginal utility: the greater the already existing ownership of a good, the smaller the benefit of each additional unit.

This brings us to the more subtle side of maximising utility and the concept of value. The subjective concept of utility, especially marginal utility, is at the core of the neoclassical theory of value (as we will see in more detail shortly). Value, one might say, is not seen as something objective, independent of the will or desire of the actor, but is related to his 'valuation'. This has enormous consequences. Marx, in *Capital*, had pondered how it is possible to compare and exchange in the market things that are essentially incomparable. Modern economists simply shift this capacity onto people. However, the human being is thereby implicitly thought of as a consumer, whose essential action is to compare and choose. The market is thereby naturalised underhand: it is no longer an enigma, but merely an expression of the 'inner' market that makes up our mental state.

The subjective concept of value has another peculiarity, and it is unclear whether it is a strength or a weakness. It can take into account a large number of factors which determine value. The strength lies in the fact that it can also integrate more questionable emotions of the actor, such as envy or affection. No matter how complicated and capricious the preference structure of a given individual may be, the whole range of his attitudes can be integrated into the subjectively conceived concept of value. If he bids at an auction only because he knows it will annoy a rival, this is nevertheless an economic act that will influence the price and thus be included in the value of the goods bidded for; it is not an act that has to be explained with the help of an additional psychological theory. As we have already seen, however, *homo œconomicus* is not supposed to have these questionable tendencies. His decisions are independent of context, especially of competing actors and their goods.

For two reasons, both of which are relevant to the critique of neoclassical theory, this strength may well turn out to be a weakness. First, there is the danger that this integrative theory could become trivialised and empirically vacuous. We will see this in more detail later in the discussion of the concept of preference (↓ 2.1.2). Second, this approach eliminates any possibility of distinguishing between economic and other non-economic values. In the mechanism of individualistic reductionism, every form of value is translated into a subjective valuation, which – according to the approach just outlined – is integrated into the overall subjective attitude that ultimately constitutes economic value. In particular, ethical commitments can no longer be understood as counter-preferential decisions (Sen 1977, p. 328). Everything is reduced to economic benefits. John Bellamy Foster compares economics with the mythical figure of King Midas, who demanded of the god Dionysus that everything he touched would turn to gold – whereupon he was faced with starvation. Likewise, economists can only appreciate what 'turns to gold': whatever can be translated into economic value and measured in money (Foster, Barrett and York 2009). Critics of neoclassical economics like to quote here the definition of the cynic which Oscar Wilde put into the mouth of Lord Darlington in his 1892 drama *Lady Windermere's Fan* (Wilde 1995, p. 45):

LORD DARLINGTON: What cynics you fellows are!
CECIL GRAHAM: What is a cynic?

LORD DARLINGTON: A man who knows the price of everything and the value of nothing.

Sadly, the same critics forget to quote Cecil Graham's glib reply:

CECIL GRAHAM: And a sentimentalist, my dear Darlington, is a man who sees an absurd value in everything, and doesn't know the market price of any single thing.

LORD DARLINGTON: You always amuse me, Cecil. You talk as if you were a man of experience.

In fact, it is this pair of concepts, 'cynic' and 'sentimentalist', which denote the two poles between which the discussion of economic facts and their neoclassical reading oscillates. This is particularly evident in contemporary debates about the valuation of unpaid work and of ecosystems, where the danger of sentimentalism in the critique of the cynical is everywhere (↓ 3.3 and 4.2). This tension is all the more important to register as it will prove impossible to resolve.

1.2.4 Interaction: the market

Things become interesting when at least two of the *homines œconomici* defined in this way meet and form a system of interacting parts. What will happen now? According to the methodological premise, what happens must be predictable from the minimal specifications of the axiom of rationality alone, just as the shape of the solar system can be derived from the properties of the rotating bodies therein.

If both actors have a given set of goods at their disposal, they will consider whether they can improve their respective utility through an appropriately arranged exchange. Tom Sawyer and Huckleberry Finn exchange a tooth for a tick, "and the boys separated, each feeling wealthier than before", as Mark Twain humorously sums up the fundamental neoclassical principle (Twain 1876, p. 68). Those engaging in an exchange will follow this game until a situation is reached in which neither of them can improve their utility without worsening the utility of the other. This is because until such a situation is achieved, there are incentives for each person to exchange, and once such a situation is achieved, the one whose utility would deteriorate will refuse the exchange, which must be based on mutual agreement. A state of equilibrium is reached, just as the planets, in cosmic evolution, eventually attain stable orbits. The equilibrium criterion whereby no one can improve without another deteriorating is called the 'Pareto optimum'.

Equilibrium in this context means merely that certain variables have taken on a constant value, not that the system is at a standstill. The goods are usually consumed and perpetually replaced by new ones. In the described optimum, the distribution of goods among individuals is constant, but the goods flow, albeit in fixed proportions. Nor does optimum mean that the actors are now satisfied – *homo œconomicus* is by definition never satisfied. The equilibrium represents for him an 'optimum' only in the sense that he can no longer increase his utility by free exchange. The same applies to any mechanical system: stability – and in borderline cases standstill – does not mean the absence of forces, but merely the balance of forces. If a cup is placed on the table, gravity continues to pull on it, but is counterbalanced by the elastic forces of the loaded (and imperceptibly deformed) table top. It should also be emphasised that one cannot speak of 'the' Pareto optimum in general. Apart from the fact that there are generally always several optima, it is also true that the optimal final state is determined relative to the given initial state. A Pareto optimum is the ideal state under a given initial distribution of goods. The Pareto criterion thus proves to be particularly conservative. It does not establish a tabula rasa in order to consider the ideal distribution of goods, but accepts the status quo as the initial situation (Self 1975, p. 26).

Admittedly, the market as a place for the exchange of goods, as discussed here, does not readily correspond to the real market, but is instead characterised by a number of key idealising assumptions:

1 *perfect competition* with a decentralised market structure (no monopolies);
2 *complete information* of market participants about supply, demand, quality, etc.;
3 *complete contracts*, in which all conditions are specified.

These idealisations are fully acknowledged and made explicit (Arrow and Debreu 1954). Of course, idealisations are commonplace in all empirical sciences. This part of economic theory is thus not particularly promising for either an intra-disciplinary or a philosophical critique. For our purposes, these idealisations are interesting, as long as they conceal an *interface*. Incomplete information, for example, can be an expression (and means) of power inequalities. However, the concept of power relations is a sociological one, and in this sense the fiction of the perfect market obscures a boundary with the subject matter of sociological investigation (more on this later, ↓ 2.4).

It should be noted in conclusion that in the (ideal) market, the Pareto optimum will always come about automatically and inevitably. This is also the claim of the so-called *First Fundamental Theorem of Welfare Economics*. It is the basis of the deeply rooted belief that any intervention in the market, especially by the state, will inevitably be harmful, because a disturbed market will fail to reach the Pareto optimum and can only lead to a worse situation. The doctrine of the Pareto optimum is the modern version of the "invisible hand", which is how Adam Smith described the mechanism by which the general good is promoted when each person strives for his or her own profit (Smith 1776, Book 4, Chap. 2). Conversely, the role of institutions in this picture must be limited to correcting any market failures that may result from the distortions of the imperfect market.

This doctrine is not based on empirical studies but derives solely from the conceptual design of neoclassical theory. It thus has a fatally ambiguous character: on the one hand, it is not easily justified, but on the other, it cannot be denied by an adherent of neoclassical doctrine, since it is no mere ideological component but is inscribed at the heart of his very models (on this see Gowdy 2010, Chap. 1).

1.2.5 Values and prices: the marginal principle

The notion of the exchange of goods for mutual maximisation of utility implicitly contains an economic theory of value. The older political economy that ran from David Ricardo to Marx assumed a value that is (in a certain sense) objective and intrinsic to goods, namely a value determined by the labour expended in production, which, at least on statistical average, determined the proportions of exchange and thus, in particular, prices. In the image of exchange as we have just traced it, however, such an external constraint is missing. Individuals exchange in proportions that result solely from the pursuit of maximising utility under given quantities of goods and orders of preference. One could say that subjective valuation has taken the place of objective value.

Let us remember that the utility of a good depends on the quantity of such goods the owner already has, i.e. any extra good that is added is of lesser utility. This principle of marginal utility is fundamental to neoclassical economics, and it is also the basis of the neoclassical theory of production and wages (↓ 1.2.6). Its strength is usually demonstrated by the so-called value paradox, which consists in the curious fact that diamonds, which in most circumstances are quite useless, are much more expensive than water, which is essential for survival. The paradox is easily resolved by the marginal principle: the decisive factor for the respective price is not the utility of each good, but the marginal utility, i.e. the benefit of an additional unit of goods over and above what is available. Water is (in many places, supposedly) available in abundance, diamonds, however, are rare. Any additional unit is therefore assessed differently than the practical significance of the good itself. It is certainly not the case that the older economists were helplessly exposed to this paradox, though. On the contrary, the paradox only occurs if economic value is taken to be determined by use value. In Ricardo and Marx, however, these two dimensions were strictly differentiated. Although use value was regarded as a condition for a good to be sold at all, the price was understood to be determined by other dimensions, namely by the labour time needed to produce it.

It remains to be shown how the marginal principle can be used to derive actual consumer behaviour from (fixed) market prices. If a market actor has a given amount of money and can purchase two different products in a freely chosen ratio, he will choose the ratio in such a way that the two quantities of goods x and y result in identical marginal utility for each additional monetary unit spent. For as long as the marginal utility is not the same, the actor could maximise his or her utility by shifting his or her basket of goods in favour of the product with the higher marginal utility. A mechanical equilibrium is thus established in which the relative price of two goods is more accurately determined for the individual as the ratio of their respective marginal utilities. This subjective value theory is the basis of the so-called *marginal utility theory*, which was developed in the 1870s and is associated with the names of William Stanley Jevons, Léon Walras and Carl Menger. The attractiveness of this approach for economists is due not least to the fact that the marginal utility principle has a direct counterpart in the mathematical derivative, which makes it possible to give all the theorems of this theory an elegant mathematical expression.

1.2.6 Production and wages

Whatever is bought or exchanged in the market must of course be produced first. Behind the neoclassical theory of production is the idea that the producer or company basically behaves in exactly the same way as the consumer in the market: he has to buy (usually on credit) the so-called factors of production – mainly machines (= capital, C) and labour (L) – and then put them to work in such a way that he maximises his output $F(C, L)$ and his profit. Marginal utility has given way to *marginal productivity*. Marginal productivity is the additional output obtained by an additional unit of the factors of production. Again, economists can now determine the conditions of a Pareto optimum in which each available resource is optimally distributed among the branches of production and in each firm the given amount of money is optimally distributed among the various resources. As already seen in the market theory of marginal utility, the concept of marginal productivity now allows the formulation of an equilibrium theory.

We need not go into technical details here, but let us note from the outset that the neoclassical "theory of production" actually reveals nothing about production, for example, what happens in production and how value is created. It is a pure theory of resource allocation. Its most important result, that, technically speaking, in equilibrium the prices of the factors of production will eventually be proportional to their respective marginal productivity, has an immediate and concrete meaning, since economists are mainly interested in the two factors of production: capital and labour. But in this theory the price of labour is nothing other than the wage, and the price of capital is the investor's wage, i.e. the return. The neoclassical theory of production thus makes it possible to derive mathematically the distribution of profit between the capitalist and the workers. This result had enormous significance in the situation of systemic competition between Western capitalist economies and the socialist Eastern bloc, since it implies that in the former there is no exploitation. The theory shows that everyone – capitalist, manager, skilled worker, unskilled worker – earns exactly what corresponds to his or her marginal productivity. In other words, that everyone earns what they deserve (cf. Häring and Douglas 2012, pp. 155–156; Binswanger 2013, pp. 167–168).

So is everything for the best in the best of all possible economic worlds? In fact, the neoclassical theory of production has serious defects, the consequences of which eloquently reveal the neoclassical worldview. The first thing you will notice is that only machines and labour are taken into account as factors of production, but land, raw materials and energy are completely absent. One can speculate about the reasons for this. The American social scientist Jason W. Moore sees in this assumption "a metric of wealth premised on labor productivity rather than land productivity" (Moore 2014, p. 306) which reflects the historical shift into the capitalist age. Work is now the source of value and nature has been downgraded to a resource (see Moore's approach, ↓ 5.2.3). Other authors point to the fact that marginal productivity is reflected in prices and that the low prices of raw materials and energy in the 20th century (when the neoclassical theory of production was formulated) was taken as proof of the relative insignificance of these factors. The share of energy costs in production costs is indeed only around 5%–6%, but this is simply because even finite resources are cheap (Hall et al. 2001, p. 666). A third possible reason for the neglect of natural resources may be that the purpose of the theory of production is ultimately to give a justification of income levels in objective terms, and that while nature (land, raw materials, energy) may appear as a factor of production, these cannot be taken into account in the distribution of profit and so nature can be exploited with impunity. Whatever the reason, it is clear that the neoclassical theory of production carries an inherent ecological deficit.

Second, the neglect of land as a factor of production also has direct and fatal technical consequences. It is true, of course, that at different historical times and with different levels of technological development, capital and labour have different shares in production (capital intensity increases with technological progress and the use of sophisticated machinery). But the neoclassical theory of production, in its role as a theory of fixed equilibrium, is in principle unsuitable for analysing such historical change (Robinson 1953–1954, p. 100). If, however, we look at a given point in time, then on the contrary, the relationship between the factors labour and capital cannot be freely chosen, as the formalism of the neoclassical theory of production assumes in its production function $F(C, L)$. In the case of agriculture where soil is a regenerative resource it may still be true that the use of machines and manual labour can be varied quite freely. Ironically, however, this does not apply to industrial production, which neoclassical theory fixes on by overlooking the factor land. Here, the relationship between machine and labour, i.e. the number of workers at a particular machine, is fixed by the organisation of the factory, so that the preconditions for defining a marginal product are not fulfilled at all, which means that neoclassical wage theory collapses (Binswanger 2013, pp. 174 and 192; cf. Screpanti and Zamagni 2005, p. 175; Häring and Douglas 2012, p. 156.). Some have thus argued that we should abandon the entire assumption of equilibrium and regard the relationship between the factors of production as an empirical characteristic of the production technology used (Lindenberger and Kümmel 2002).

1.2.7 Pareto principle and social well-being

In the following chapter we will encounter further criticisms of the concept of the Pareto optimum. But it is important to understand that its formulation in its time was a response to a theoretical problem and that, in certain respects, it represented a clear advance.

We have already seen that a central concept of neoclassical theory is that of utility. With this, the neoclassical thinkers drew upon the philosophy of utilitarianism, which saw in utility the key to normative questions of ethics – these should be answered by means of a 'hedonistic calculus', i.e. a measurement of the utility of each ethical act. One of the central problems of bourgeois social philosophy is the relation between private benefit and the general welfare. If the starving person steals a loaf of bread from the well-fed, does not his profit outweigh the minor loss of the other? One is tempted to affirm this. But to do so, one would have to be able to compare the gain of one person with the loss of another. Precisely, this is prevented by the subjective concept of utility, since it does not know any intersubjective measure. Intersubjective comparisons of utility are excluded in principle, as economists soon found out (Robbins 1938). It is no surprise that within the framework of a strictly individualistic approach, one gets into difficulties as soon as one deals with collective quantities such as overall utility.

This is where the Pareto principle comes into play. The Pareto principle is a way of avoiding this pitfall and speaking instead of an optimum for a collective without having to refer to an aggregate measure of collective well-being. It is true that in a situation where one individual's well-being improves while another's deteriorates, it is in principle impossible to determine whether the gain in utility of one outweighs the loss of the other, so raising well-being overall. However, if one person's utility improves without another's deteriorating, this question can be answered in the affirmative, and when a situation is reached in which no one's utility can improve further without another's deteriorating, an optimum in this sense is achieved.

The Pareto principle is, of course, too restrictive for many economic applications, in particular to be of use for policy proposals, because there are hardly any political measures which do not have negative consequences, at least for some people. Let us look at the example with which these issues were originally discussed, which is interesting because it also reminds us of the original context of the discussion, namely the question of free trade. The abolition of the Corn Laws in 1846, which were intended to protect British agriculture, led on the one hand to a fall in the price of corn, i.e. the entire population could buy a larger quantity of corn for the same amount of money, since the same wage corresponded to a higher real income, but on the other hand it also led to a shift in income, in this case to the disadvantage of the landed gentry, who under the pressure of foreign competition now had to sell their corn at a lower price. What is the overall utilitarian balance? In each case, there is a loser. None therefore represents a Pareto improvement. Then again, we are dealing here with money that can be redistributed by the state through new taxes and compensation payments. And so it is still possible – at least in principle – to say whether a reform is of positive overall benefit: namely, precisely at the point when, after compensating the disadvantaged, the advantaged still enjoy a net profit.

This observation, which was first made by Nicholas Kaldor and John R. Hicks, does, however, have what some would call a cynical punchline. The two economists agree that the question of whether compensation should be paid or not is a question of distributive justice, on which economists, being the scientists they are, have nothing to say (Hicks 1939, p. 711; Kaldor 1939, p. 550). They therefore omitted this aspect and considered only the hypothetical case. A reform is to be welcomed according to this so-called Kaldor Hicks criterion, even if it brings about only a potential Pareto improvement. To put it crudely: any measure that makes us richer is good, even if the wealth is unequally distributed. After all, it is always possible to redistribute wealth.

This generalisation of the Pareto principle is of enormous importance. It gives us the opportunity to carry out a sober cost-benefit analysis without having to deal with questions of justice. Such analyses form the basis for economic policy advice by economists. The decoupling of questions of efficiency and justice is what makes their recommendations 'objective' – in the sense of being free of value judgements (Bromley 1990, p. 93). This view ties in with Max Weber's position in the value judgement dispute. The occasion was a discussion of "value judgments in academic teaching". Weber condemned the "prophecy" of "academic socialists" and countered it with a "cool lack of passion" which intellectual integrity demands. The subject of teaching should only be "facts that are purely empirical or can be deduced logically", not "valuations that are practical, ethical, or based on some world view" (Weber 2012, pp. 304 ff.). For him, the conceptual key to this was the separation of ends and means, onto which the separation of value judgements and factual judgements can then be mapped: the scientist is only justified in making *empirical* judgements about the *suitability* of a means for an end. Whether an end is desirable, however, is a value judgement he must refrain from making. On social issues, this must be decided in political discourse, for example. Society must therefore be clear about what it wants, and the scientist can then advise whether and how these ends can best be achieved. This view is clearly also behind the attempt to separate issues of distribution from issues of efficiency. This attitude was further promoted by the neo-positivist philosophy of science of the Vienna Circle – a strong influence on Lionel Robbins, for example – which declared empirical judgements to be the only meaningful ones, thus not only excluding value judgements from science but making them appear altogether suspect.

But how can economists, on the one hand, identify the issue of distribution as an issue of value and exclude it as such, and, on the other hand, use the criterion of efficiency to decide whether political reform is desirable? Is the latter not a question of value? Economists do not deny this value dimension, but see themselves as mere advocates of the individual. Desirable, therefore, means: desirable for the individuals in whose name the economists claim to speak.

This manoeuvre is problematic, if only because economists do not refer to real individuals but put in their place a model of *homo œconomicus*, who, we have seen, has the 'natural predisposition' to constantly strive for more. In this way, economists can magically 'naturalise' the value system of 'more is better', along with the imperative of economic growth (regardless of its ecological implications) as a consequence and expression of human 'nature' – without ever having asked a single person about it.

But there is a second, more fundamental problem lurking in this move. In the scenario of potential Pareto improvement, the model actor *homo œconomicus* is not confronted with factual circumstances but with purely *hypothetical* situations. The transition from the hypothetical to the factual case – i.e. the compensation payment due – does not interest economists, who instead delegate it to politics and sociology: whether the compensation payment is desirable is a political question, and whether it could be enforced is a sociological one. But the fact is that the powerful have, in principle, more opportunities to assert their interests. The criterion of potential Pareto improvement thus has a practical bias: in the real world, it will tend to work in favour of the privileged. Economists draw their conclusions from a hypothetical case, which they themselves are not supposed to believe in. They then wash their hands of the matter and refer to the benchmarks of science. But we have understood the magic trick: to judge in a value-neutral, strictly scientific and purely economic way – i.e. the "cool lack of passion" – means here de facto taking sides with the rich and powerful. This form of hypocrisy is typical of economics. Certainly, it is not down to a lack of *personal* intellectual honesty; it is rather a *structural* problem inscribed in the fundamental concepts of modern economics.

It is worth digging a little deeper at this point. As early as 1941, the Hungarian economist Tibor de Scitovsky showed that the Kaldor-Hicks criterion can lead to contradictory results because it allows for situations in which the transition from one state X to another state Y is exactly as desirable as the reverse transition (Scitovsky 1941). This paradox can also be illustrated by the example of the Corn Laws, i.e. the dispute over free trade. Figure 1.2 shows the so-called 'utility limit', i.e. the highest possible utility of one actor as a function of that of the other actors. This means that the graph represents the totality of all Pareto-optimal combinations of utility values. Let us focus on a situation in which a consumer and a producer face each other and which currently occupies point X in the graph, say a free trade scenario. A transition from free trade to the protection of the branch of production in question would move the system to point Y, to which a modified utility value is assigned. The producer's utility would improve, while the consumer's would deteriorate. Nevertheless, this political reform would be desirable according to the Kaldor Hicks criterion, since even after the consumer is compensated, i.e. transition on the utility-possibility threshold from Y to Y',

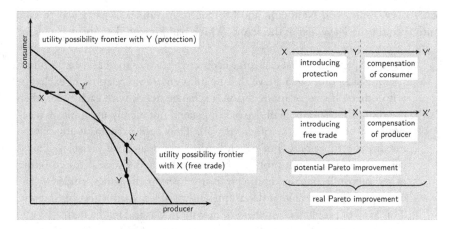

FIGURE 1.2 De Scitovsky's paradox: both the transition from X to Y and its reverse represent a potential Pareto improvement.

the producer would still make a profit. However, the reverse is also true: if the system is at point Y, the transition to free trade (X) represents a potential Pareto improvement, since after the producer is compensated (X to X'), the consumer is still better off.

The root of this problem lies in the fact that compensation does not have to be actually paid. If it does, the paradox disappears – but the whole situation changes fundamentally, because now the choice of the correct solution suddenly depends on the distribution of income: "*if* the consumer is very well off compared with the producer [...], *then* protection is preferable; whilst *if* the producer is well off [...], *then* free trade is better" (Backhouse 1985, p. 303 f., my emphasis). Although the paradox has been resolved, questions of efficiency and distribution prove to be not as neatly separable as economists would have it. This somewhat technical discussion thus shows very precisely the questionable objectivity of economic policy recommendations based on the supposedly value-free criterion of efficiency.

1.2.8 Game theory

The concept of rationality in neoclassical economics as we have encountered it so far lacks any depth. It merely describes the preference structure of the utility maximiser. Neoclassical theory lacks an account of which paths to the optimum are available and which of them the individual takes. In 1944, two American emigrants John von Neumann and Oskar Morgenstern proposed an approach to fill this gap in their now classic book *Theory of Games and Economic Behavior* – in the form of a mathematical formalism where the neoclassical school had provided only a few hints. Von Neumann and Morgenstern wanted in particular to take into account the *interaction* of the actors, which had presented a thorny problem:

> [A participant of a social exchange economy] too tries to obtain an optimum result. But in order to achieve this, he must enter into relations of exchange with others. If two or more persons exchange goods with each other, then the result for each one will depend in general not merely upon his own actions but on those of the others as well. Thus each participant attempts to maximize a function [...] of which he does not control all variables. This is certainly no maximum problem, but a peculiar and disconcerting mixture of several conflicting maximum problems. Every participant is guided by another principle and neither determines all variables which affect his interest. This kind of problem is nowhere dealt with in classical mathematics.
>
> *(Neumann and Morgenstern 1948, p. 11)*

This analysis shares the reductionist individualism of the equilibrium theory, to which the two authors expressly subscribe. However, they add an important aspect which was not foreseen in that theory: *homo œconomicus* is mute and apathetic. In particular, he does not distinguish between variables that describe the unchanging environment and those that depend on the will of other actors, of "motives of the same nature as his own". This distinction changes his behaviour profoundly, as he will form expectations about the behaviour of others and knows that these, in turn, reflect their expectations about his behaviour (Neumann and Morgenstern 1948, p. 12). In a word, his behaviour becomes *strategic*.

The mathematical theory that is referred to here is game theory or the theory of strategy games, which von Neumann had already developed in the 1920s (Neumann 1928). Market events represent the 'game', i.e. they are simply events guided by rules. Where the 'players' have a choice, they make 'moves'. The fixed patterns and principles of their moves form their 'strategy'. What applies to the concept of rational behaviour, applies to the concept of strategy too: its application is not restricted to deliberately planned actions. The behaviour of an actor following his instincts or affects is also described as a strategy. This is particularly important for the application of game theoretical methods to evolutionary research.

The best-known case study of game theory analysis is surely the so-called *Prisoner's Dilemma*. Yet, it is also a problematic case that makes the limits of the individualistic approach tangible, which is why it is of particular interest to us. The Prisoner's Dilemma will be important to the argument later in the book, especially with regard to the question of how to deal with public goods. Let us take a first look at it here.

The Prisoner's Dilemma involves two criminals, A and B, who have been caught by the police and are now being interrogated separately. Their behaviour – confession or denial – will have consequences for the expected length of their sentences. However, the verdict will depend on the behaviour of both, which means that the situation described by Neumann and Morgenstern

		A	
		confesses (defects)	stays silent (cooperates)
B	confesses (defects)	both serve 4 years	A serves 6 years B serves 1 year
	stays silent (cooperates)	A serves 1 year B serves 6 years	both serve 3 years

FIGURE 1.3 The Prisoner's Dilemma.

is prototypically realised: each individual has to deal with a maximisation problem, over whose variables he or she exercises only partial control, as do the other actors (maximising the benefit here naturally means minimising the time in prison). The concrete scenario is the following: everyone faces six years in prison. If both prisoners 'cooperate' and stay silent, they will each be sentenced to three years in prison on the thin evidence. If one of them 'defects' and confesses, he gets off with one year, while the other one has to serve the full six years. If both confess, they are only sentenced to four years (Figure 1.3).

The real difficulty arises from the fact that the two prisoners cannot coordinate their behaviour. It is therefore advisable for each of them to confess, as this is the only way to avoid the maximum penalty regardless of the behaviour of the other. If the second prisoner confesses as well, each has to serve four years; if the second stays silent, this will be just one year. Since the situation is the same for both of them, they should both choose this option and defect. One speaks here of a (strong) *Nash equilibrium*: in this state, each of the players can only worsen their situation by unilateral changes in strategy (Nash 1951, p. 287). Admittedly, this rational strategy leads the players to an inferior Pareto result, because if they had cooperated, they would both have been in a better position! This is the core of the dilemma: the rational strategy from each individual perspective leads to a poor result for everybody. Here we encounter a serious problem inherent in individualistic rationality.

Incidentally, game theory was developed as an instrument of analysis during the Cold War. It is only against this background that the significance of the absolute non-communication between the prisoners, who stand for the nuclear superpowers, becomes clear. The Nash equilibrium is thus specifically the theoretical basis for the "balance of terror". It is interesting to note that in his work Nash once again tightened the assumptions which the model had in Neumann's and Morgenstern's hands. While these dealt intensively with the role of coalition-building in games with more than two players, Nash explicitly excluded this. His players act completely independently, they know neither communication nor coalition. This gloomy picture would subsequently be applied to the analysis of economic and other social processes. Economists thereby understand the whole of society as a kind of generalised Cold War.

Against this background, it is particularly remarkable how the picture changes when the game of the Prisoner's Dilemma is played over several rounds, giving the players the opportunity to react to the behaviour of their fellow players in the preliminary round. The optimal strategy now turns out to be to signal willingness to cooperate in the first turn and then always imitate the other player's move, so that the one's cooperation is rewarded with the other's move, but defection is punished by the other. This strategy is called TIT FOR TAT (in effect: "what you do to me, I will do to you"). When two TIT FOR TAT players meet, they actually reach the Pareto optimum. But even if the other player follows a different strategy, the TIT FOR TAT player remains close to the optimum result. He is not a 'naive' cooperative partner whose strategy could be exploited (Axelrod 1980). It can even be shown that this strategy makes it possible, at least to some extent, to understand the emergence of cooperative behaviour in a purely selfish environment. If only a small cluster of TIT FOR TAT strategists penetrates a population of consistent defectors, it can survive and thrive there (Axelrod 1981; Axelrod and Hamilton 1981).

The question of the evolutionary emergence of cooperation and institutions is a central problem of alternative approaches in economics today. We will come back to this.

1.3 Autonomy, reversibility, infinity

We have now got to know the principles of economics in their most elementary features. Against this background it is striking that economics typically conceptualises market activity along the lines of a physical event. This analogy was not only discovered in retrospect by the historians of economics. The authors of the school of marginal utility in the middle of the 19th century already referred explicitly to the physics of their time, which had just launched one of its most productive concepts with the notion of *energy* (Mirowski 1989). Economics was able to adopt from physics the *extremal principle* which underlies the Pareto principle: according to this, systems left to themselves tend to assume a state in which a characteristic quantity takes on an extreme value. The principle of marginality builds a bridge to mathematics, as it allows the application of analytical methods. Thus, we can finally describe the programme of neoclassical economics in its entirety by the following three elements:

1 Methodological Individualism;
2 Utilitarianism;
3 Paradigm of energetic, mathematical physics.

These three pillars also give rise to the traits which characterise modern economics and which are increasingly being questioned today: mathematical formalism, the claim of scientificity against all alternative approaches, the central concept of utility, the programme of micro-foundation, the assumption of exogenous variables, especially exogenous orders of preference (Mirowski 1984, p. 372).

More important for our question, however, is which characteristics of the object of investigation, the economic process, were already predefined and predetermined by this programme. What only became apparent in retrospect were the barriers that were inscribed in the programme, which at first seemed to promise and guarantee so much success. In this light we can say that the 'mechanistic' economic process, as presented in neoclassical economics, is characterised by the following three features:

1 Autonomy: no dependence;
2 Reversibility: no history;
3 Infinity: no boundaries.

These watchwords refer more specifically to the following:

1.3.1 Autonomy

By autonomy, we mean two specific features. First, the economic process is an autonomous sub-process of the overall social process, i.e. it can be explained solely by the economic spectrum of characteristics of *homo œconomicus*, and there is no dependence on other social sub-processes such as culture, religion, politics and no dependence on nature, which in fact is completely ignored. Second, although there can and will be numerous interferences with other social sub-processes in the real world, these are taken to be mere *disturbances* that reduce market efficiency, i.e. lead to a state that is not Pareto optimal. This autonomy of the economic process is particularly decisive for the self-understanding of economics in relation to the other social sciences. We can thus say that economics is a social science 'against its will', against its own self-conception.

1.3.2 Reversibility

This property is well known from mechanics: mechanical systems, in abstract terms, behave symmetrically under time reversal. In concrete terms, this means that the time-reversed sequence of a given purely mechanical process also corresponds to the laws of mechanics. If one lets the film recording of a shot of two billiard balls or a swinging pendulum run backwards, it shows an event that is permissible according to mechanical laws. (Note that frictional losses, which actually violate the symmetry of time, e.g., by gradually bringing the pendulum's oscillation to a standstill, are not purely mechanical processes, as mechanical energy is converted into heat in the process.) And the same applies in fact to the economic process as understood by microeconomics. Any economic exchange, for example, is also conceivable in reverse.

This characteristic, which we will have to discuss in more detail, is incompatible with the fundamental experience of the directionality of time. But key economic phenomena such as the relationship between debt and profit are also incompatible with the idea of the reversibility of time. Debt is both granted and incurred with a view to future profits (Mirowski 1990, p. 712). But the primary methodological consequence of the notion of reversibility is that all history is excluded from pure economic processes and thus any historical approach in economics is disqualified. The world of market equilibrium knows *no history*, since any disturbance of the equilibrium is assumed to mobilise forces that bring the system back into balance, just as a ball that has been moved in a vessel will always find its way back to the vessel's lowest point.

1.3.3 Infinity

A purely mechanical process, in which the energy content freely floats back and forth between the forms of potential and kinetic energy, knows no inner limit at which it could come to a standstill, and the same applies to the economic process in the neoclassical imagination. Essentially, this is a direct consequence of the principles of autonomy and reversibility. But it is nevertheless worth emphasising infinity separately, because it plays an enormously powerful role in the background of the economist's cosmos of ideas: the economy is a self-sustaining process in a history-less equilibrium that will always be preserved. The significance of this idea can be seen in the fact that it retains its power even when, to take the example of economic growth, a temporally directed quantity occupies a central role and even threatens to tangibly conflict with fundamental facts. As the critics of growth constantly point out, even the lowest constant growth rate leads to exponential growth, which sooner or later must approach the limits of the planet. But economists ignore this by regarding nature as a constantly flowing source that can feed the economic process without itself suffering any change. And where the finite nature of resources becomes a pressing issue, economists focus instead on technological progress, increasing energy efficiency and the substitution of scarce resources with other materials.

1.3.4 The 'system' economy

If we claim here that neoclassical thought views the economy as an autonomous, reversible and infinite process, this is not to say that economists do not know better. But the point is that even if they recognise, as individual persons, the dependence of the economy, for example, on the biosphere, they have, as economists, no language to express this. The *system* economy appears to be autonomous, reversible and unlimited, but 'system' is not to be understood as a construct of causal, spatial or functional unity. 'System' here means instead the totality of what can be described by a particular language. Neoclassical economics speaks only of values and prices. We can say following Luhmann that through the medium of money and the corresponding binary code "to pay or not to pay" the closed, circular and self-referential universe of economics is constituted (Luhmann 1989, p. 52). So when we suggest that economists imagine the economy as an autonomous, reversible and unbounded process, we are not describing a psychological phenomenon but an epistemological one. We name the image inscribed in their concepts. We do not name what they believe, but what their conceptual framework allows them to say.

1.4 A social science despite itself

1.4.1 The 'astronomy of the movement of commodities'

A diagnosis is thus already emerging which will be further substantiated and which we can summarise by saying that the economic sciences have the strange status of social sciences against their will. They are unquestionably a social science, since their subject is a social one, even the most essential in terms of the material life process of societies. At the same time, however, they conceptualise the economic process as a mechanical system, a kind of "astronomy of the movement of commodities" (Albert 1998, p. 153), in which social phenomena no longer have a place. This goes so far that in the neoclassical theory of equilibrium, the market and private property actually play no role. In its pure form (without game theory being applied), this theory knows neither competition nor strategic behaviour, since the actors never meet and are not interested in each other, but silently follow the trajectories of their utility maximisation in the gravitational field of the distribution of goods. This leads to the astonishing situation that this theory, which, as we saw, was also linked to free trade and was intended to provide it with a scientific justification, could easily be read in the 1930s as a theory of allocation in a planned economy (cf. Lange 1936/1937, for a discussion, see Bowles and Gintis 2000, pp. 1427–1428).

1.4.2 Economic laws

The curious status of economics in general and neoclassical economics in particular is well illustrated by the concept of law. Whether there can be laws other than natural laws at all, specifically historical and social laws, is a controversial question, which we will only deal with in more detail at the end of this book (↓ 5.3.2). However, we can determine its relevance and its value to the controversy in advance. It can in any case be stated that the way in which people manage their material life process has changed profoundly several times in human history. Even capitalism has seen many different manifestations in its history (Manchester capitalism, war economy, social market economy, neoliberalism, etc.), and appears today as a heterogeneous system whose fractures and inner tensions cannot be ignored. The phenomenon of monopolies, for example, clearly shows that, of all people, the most successful capitalist actors have a tendency to evade the laws of their own capitalist market and that social institutions have repeatedly to counteract them.

However, economists have drawn different, even opposing conclusions from this undeniable historical diversity. Thomas Piketty, who stepped forth in 2014 with the claim to have revealed the iron economic laws behind history (we will analyse this claim in detail later, ↓ 5.2.1), has made a radical volte-face in his latest book of 2019: economic mechanisms can only work if the corresponding social institutions are in place, first and foremost a tax system and a framework of law, especially inheritance law (he subsumes this under the concept of "ideology"). As Philip Mirowski reminds us, even the neoliberals – despite their own rhetoric to the contrary – know that the market does not exist by itself, but only thanks to its social and cultural frameworks, especially a set of corresponding legal norms (Mirowski 2009, p. 435).

The official neoclassical doctrine gives a different picture of the relationship between historical diversity and the unity of economic laws. The theorist of education Simon Marginson (1993, p. 35) offers an apt analysis:

> The purpose of neoclassical economics was the construction of hypotheses about economic behaviour, in the form of mathematical equations. The ultimate hypotheses were universally valid 'laws' of economics. [...] As the science grew, successive economists added to the stock of laws [...]. However, only propositions that were consistent with the basic axioms of neoclassical economics were considered. In the economists' ideal world, all human behaviour was based on the economic selfinterest of individuals, operating within freely competitive markets. Other forms of behaviour were excluded or treated as 'distortions' of the model.

Marginson makes the important observation here that neoclassical economics does indeed believe in universal laws. But it reconciles them with unruly reality by relating them to an "ideal world" that is purged of all "distortions". His New Zealand colleague Patrick Fitzsimons (Fitzsimons 2000, p. 6) elaborates the "economic fallacy" underlying the notion of an ideal economic world:

> The methodological foundations of neoclassical economics obscure the social, cultural, and political determinants of economic action. [...T]his results in an analysis that is ahistorical and, through a tautological procedure, continually rediscovers the centrality of purely economic notions. Based as it is on the false premise of the 'naturalness' of the pursuit of economic

gain by human inclinations, the 'economic fallacy' imagines that capitalist societies do not have cultures in the way that primitive or pre-modern societies do.

While Piketty sees the "laws of economics" as being bound up with history and culture, the neoclassical economists believe that they are universal and "natural" in a fundamental sense. This does not necessarily mean that they work in all cultures, quite the contrary. In almost all cultures these laws may be distorted or even completely obscured by "interfering factors". But then the material life process of these peoples is treated not as a rational economy but merely as bizarre folklore. Economic laws operate most "naturally" in the capitalist West; yet, the economist views this as an effect not of our culture but of the absence of culturally disruptive factors. We capitalists are the natural human beings who had to endure the whole history of mankind until the "ideal world" of economics finally became reality in the West.

1.4.3 Prospects

We have thus returned to the autonomy of the economic process. It is the core of the neoclassical idea of economic activity and thus the point of attack for the many alternative approaches which are gradually making themselves heard. If one would dare to make a prognosis about the development of the economic sciences, one would certainly arrive at what at first glance seems a rather unspectacular prospect. Should the heterodox approaches really continue to gain in importance and gradually come together to form a new orthodoxy, then economic science may likely become simply a 'normal' social science, i.e. a social science that acknowledges the social and historical character of its subject.

It goes without saying that once the former heterodoxy has become orthodoxy, it must lose its revolutionary charm. But we have not yet reached that point. The economic sciences are in a state of upheaval, and, what makes the situation even more complicated, they are also having to deal with a world in upheaval. The autonomy of the economic process is being questioned from several sides. What happens conceptually at the now revealed interfaces is highly interesting from a philosophical point of view and will be dealt with in the following four chapters. In the next chapter, we will begin with the interface between individual economic actors and society.

2

THE ECONOMY IN A SOCIAL WORLD

'Rational man' in society

2.1 The logical misery of neoclassical economics

We have now at least glanced at the machinery of microeconomic terminology and, in particular, we have learned about the meaning of the concept of *homo œconomicus*. What is noteworthy is that one does not have to wait for the empirical comparison with real people – the first difficulties can already be seen on a purely conceptual level, and are not of a general logical nature but specifically concern the boundary between the individual and society, which is why they lead us directly to this chapter's topic. In the analysis of the prisoner's dilemma, we already got a first impression of this. In contrast to empirical findings, these conceptual problems have been known about for a long time. The classic publications date from the 1950s to the 1970s.

2.1.1 Model Platonism

The first criticism that shall interest us goes back to the essay *Model Platonism: Neoclassical economic thought in critical light* by the philosopher of science Hans Albert, originally published in German in 1963 (Albert 2012). With the suggestive name "Model Platonism", Albert refers *grosso modo* to the attitude of a scientist who encloses himself in his model, moves in purely theoretically circles within the framework of his assumptions and avoids confrontation with the empirical. Such an attitude is made possible by strategies of immunisation against empirical verification. Albert identifies three such strategies in economics. First, the formulation of *ceteris paribus* clauses, which makes an assertion subject to otherwise unchanged circumstances. The law of demand, for example, states that the demand for a good decreases as its price increases, provided that all other variables (in this case the prices and quantities of other goods as well as the

DOI: 10.4324/9781003204077-3

total amount spent) are constant. Insofar as the proviso refers to *all* concomitant circumstances and does not specifically stipulate them, any counter-example to the assertion made can be warded off by assuming that the circumstances have changed. The assertion thus becomes a tautology without any informative value. A second immunisation strategy consists in limiting the scope of a model. The assumptions underlying the model are not interpreted as empirical hypotheses, but as a specification of the scope of its application. Deviations between model and empiricism are attributed to it being applied in the wrong place or manner. A third strategy is to simply leave the scope of a theory open so that one can devote oneself undisturbed to the development of its logical consequences – in the case of economics, with more elaborate mathematical instruments that are supposed to vouch for its scientific character – without worrying about reality any more. This is model Platonism in its purest form.

It should be said that the accusation of immunisation against empiricism should be used circumspectly and is not suitable for criticism 'with a hammer'. This can be seen with the help of a comparison with physics. Galileo almost certainly never carried out his gravitational experiments on the leaning tower of Pisa, and if he had, he would have found the empirical results at odds with the laws still associated with his name today, which predict that all bodies fall at the same rate. The physicist, however, does not care about this discrepancy, because he can attribute it to frictional forces acting in the medium of the surrounding air. The case of the leaning tower of Pisa does not fulfil the conditions of application of the theory. Is it a case of model Platonism? In his famous book on *The Structure of Scientific Revolutions*, the philosopher of science Thomas S. Kuhn described it as a quite common strategy of the sciences to respond to problems as long as possible with *ad hoc* assumptions, as is done here with frictional forces (Kuhn 1962/1996, Chap. 8). Such assumptions are not problematic in themselves. Everything depends on whether they can fruitfully be incorporated into the theory. For frictional forces, which can themselves be studied and described in detail, this is indeed the case.

Model Platonism and immunisation against empiricism are phenomena that affect research in all fields – and, as we have just seen, much more ambiguous phenomena than some critiques of economics assume. They are interesting for us because they are related to the boundary between the individual and society in economics. As we have already seen, for the neoclassical school, this boundary also separates economics from sociology. And this isolation of economics from sociology is a form of model Platonism insofar as it helps economics to preserve its hypotheses by explaining contrary evidence in terms of interfering *social* factors. But we can go one step further in the analysis and ask why social factors *must* necessarily be excluded, i.e. why this is not a reparable error but one that is codified in the model.

The explanation is simply that economics is based on the rational actor and thus assumes an individualistic concept of rationality. The individual is capable of acting rationally on his own, and does so thanks to his natural disposition.

In this view, social factors can only be understood as disruptive factors, as sources of irrational action. Accordingly, social factors must be extra-economic factors and must be excluded as such. The philosopher Alfred Sohn-Rethel has elaborated the resulting tautological framework:

> According to this method, there are for economics no economic problems in the true sense of the word. [... Because insofar as economic phenomena] cannot be subsumed under its explanatory terms, they may have the character of a problem but they are not problems of economics, because their causes are non-economic.
> *(Sohn-Rethel 2012, p. 46)*

What was intended as sharp criticism, some economists have nevertheless been able to adopt as their own self-understanding. It was precisely against the idea of introducing the sociological concept of power relations into economics that a representative of his discipline made the following witty case:

> What I want particularly to stress is that the solution is essentially the transformation of the *conflict* from a political *problem* to an economic *transaction*. An economic transaction is a solved political problem. Economics has gained the title of queen of the social sciences by choosing *solved* political problems as its domain.
> *(Lerner 1972, p. 259, for discussion see Bowles and Gintis 2000, p. 1430)*

Accordingly, the unsolved problems are by definition the subject of the other social sciences, which relate to economics more or less like the engineering sciences relate to physics: the physicist ignores frictional forces and material weaknesses in his idealisations, while the engineer seeks a functioning technical solution from the opposite perspective – that of the dissipative phenomena. (Incidentally, this model of the division of intellectual labour is also no longer suitable for grasping today's research in physics, in whose experiments modelling and simulation are becoming increasingly important and an 'impure' version of experience is becoming the rule, as some philosophers of science have emphasised, e.g. Schmid 2001). Here we see economics confronted for the first time with one of its limits. The strategy it chooses at this moment has been described by Albert as immunisation against reality – to the detriment of economics – while some economists see the same strategy as the secret of their discipline's success – to the detriment of a world that does not want to conform to economic theories. What is important for us to bear in mind is that this tendency towards immunisation – this behaviour in the face of boundaries – is not a contingent phenomenon, nor can it be accounted for in terms of individual scientific misconduct, but is due to an isolation of economics from the other social sciences, which, in turn, is anchored and entrenched in the individualistic concept of rationality. It is the consequence of the very conceptual constitution of the discipline.

2.1.2 *The concept of preference*

We have seen that the rational actors are individualised in terms of their idiosyncratic preferences. The very concept of preference is not as innocuous as it might first seem, both in theoretical and in political terms. Why this is so will become clear in the following paragraphs, in which we will draw upon Amartya Sen's analysis in the 1977 essay *Rational Fools*.

Note that the word "preference" is used ambiguously in everyday life, where two incompatible usages dominate. Consider the case where a person decides to give the last few coins in her pocket to someone in need instead of buying a piece of cake as she had intended. How do we describe the situation with the concept of preference? Has this person acted against her preference? There is one – consistent and legitimate – way of using the concept such that one could reasonably conclude that that the person acted against her preference: the preference is identified with a selfish motive, and it is then an empirical question whether an action was in accordance with or contrary to the preference. One could object to this – and this objection is based on the second use of the word – that it must in fact have been the person's 'real' preference to give the money to the needy person, for otherwise she would not have done so. The conflict between the two descriptions then lies not in the substance but in the definition of the concept of preference. According to the second (and equally valid) definition, it is *impossible* to act *against* one's preferences, since every preference and only one such preference leads to a corresponding action.

It is this second definition that economics has adopted. We have already seen that this conceptual definition has consequences for the scope of theory-building: explanations of actions in terms of preferences risk becoming tautological. This does not mean, of course, that every use of this concept of preference is tautological; a nuanced judgement is required here. Once again, the comparison with physics is illuminating, for in its theories the concept of force as a cause of motion plays an analogous role. The concept of force in use today dates back to the 17th and 18th centuries, and the physicists of that time were well aware of the fact that force only reveals itself in its effects. The explanation that a body moves because a corresponding force has acted on it is therefore also tautological in physics. But where then lies the usefulness of the physical concept of force? The physicist and philosopher Philipp Frank worked out an answer (Frank 1957, p. 109). The concept of force only acquires an empirical meaning when in the purely definitional equation $F = m \cdot a$ (force equals mass times acceleration, which this mass experiences under the designated effect of force) a certain concrete function is used for the force F which makes the force dependent on other variables (e.g. heavy masses and their distance from each other, as in Newton's law of gravitation).

Similarly in economics, the concept of preference can only acquire empirical meaning to the extent that an actor's preferences are subjected to further definitions, such as the formal stipulations of rationality, as we saw in Chapter 1:

transitivity of order of preference, independence from the preferences of other actors, relative temporal constancy. This result does not yet constitute a critique of neoclassical theory, but it does make clear the enormous systematic significance of its concept of rationality: it is the point at which talk of preferences can become empirically meaningful, but it is also the same point, as we have seen, at which the theory can be immunised against counter-evidence.

In addition to these theoretical problems, the concept of preference is also politically charged. We have already seen with the introduction of *homo œconomicus* that preferences are his only motives for action (↑ 1.2.3). On the one hand, the order of preferences thereby proved to be highly inclusive, since it simply absorbs all individual idiosyncrasies (its unconditional respect accordingly expresses the fundamental liberal attitude of economists). On the other hand, however, the preference model also proves to be exclusive, since every other factor guiding action is excluded. This applies in particular to rational argument, as the philosopher John O'Neill emphasised:

> [This is] what appears to me to be the most telling criticism of cost-benefit analysis— that it allows no role for reasoned argument in public policy: it treats all preferences as non-rational wants—political debate is replaced by a surrogate market mechanism [...].
>
> *(O'Neill 1993, p. 67)*

This shift has enormous consequences. According to the French legal scholar Alain Supiot, the entire sphere of politics, the public sphere and the legal sphere, is being obliterated by a purely economic rationality. Our world loses an essential dimension; it becomes flat and two-dimensional, so to speak, reduced to private interests and their interplay (Supiot 2017, 2018). The various facets of this truly cosmological revolution can be easily illustrated:

Reasoned argument	→	preferences
citizen	→	consumer
public sphere	→	market
consensus	→	Pareto optimality (equilibrium)
judgement	→	calculus
justice	→	efficiency
law, politics	→	interests
language	→	money
freedom of speech	→	purchasing power
res publica	→	private utility
solidarity	→	competition

This economisation of the political sphere has often been described. It is important to understand that it is already implicit in the innocuous model of preference-led action and was just waiting to develop.

2.1.3 The impossibility theorems of Arrow and Sen

Having considered preferences, we next take a closer look at what happens in situations involving more than one individual. This question is central to welfare economics, whose purpose is to formulate conclusions about 'societal well-being' as a function of particular circumstances, such as a particular distribution of goods. The problems that exist here are well known. They are the subject of the 'impossibility theorems' of the two Nobel Prize winners in economics, Kenneth J. Arrow and Amartya Sen (Arrow 1950; Sen 1970, 1995). Although these are two quite simple formal theorems with succinct proofs, their actual message and meaning is not so easy to state. The best way to put it is quite broadly: the impossibility theorems indicate a conceptual tension in the attempt to talk about social or collective quantities such as the well-being of a society by means of the Pareto principle. Let us examine the authors' reasoning.

Arrow begins his article by summarising the challenge of a liberal welfare theory: there is no such thing as a 'society' independent of the individuals that make it up. The 'common good' is therefore not to be regarded as a 'Platonic' entity that exists independently of individuals, but must rather be calculated or aggregated 'nominalistically' in some way from individual preferences. As Arrow makes clear, the mechanism that realises the aggregation of individual preferences, whether in the form of a vote or through the market mechanism itself (we have just seen that economists cannot tell the difference between a citizen and a consumer), does not matter. In our societies, both mechanisms coexist, but one can easily imagine models of society in which only one of these mechanisms is present in its pure form.

Let us stick to the 'voting' model, as Arrow and Sen do. In their scenario, individuals are supposed to vote on overall social states, in which every variable for their fellow human beings is determined at the same time as their own state. At first glance, this idea seems strange to us, because we normally entertain the belief that the separation of the market mechanism and majority voting can be mapped onto that of the private and the political: you *vote* for a president who will also be the president of those who did not vote for him or her, but you *buy* the shoes that you alone will wear (even if others have made them, which makes the distinction problematic). Arrow and Sen accordingly also limit the scope of the vote in each case to satisfy liberality. However, both thinkers proceed in a complementary manner: Arrow, on the one hand, demands that the respective individual orders of preference between states of society may only depend on criteria that affect the individual him- or herself (i.e. that no individual makes decisions aimed solely at favouring or disfavouring other persons), but on the other hand rules out the possibility that in decisions which only affect themselves, individuals can prevail over the social preference. Sen, by contrast, allows individual preferences about the distribution of goods whose disparity only affect others, but then concedes that there should be private domains in which society is not obliged to dictate to individuals, i.e. in which individuals can also assert themselves against society in the aggregation of the common good. To put it bluntly: Arrow protects society from the dictatorial tendencies of individuals, Sen grants the individual protection from the dictates of the collective.

Arrow's impossibility theorem states quite firmly that there is no aggregation mechanism that can guarantee that rational – in particular transitive – orders of preference on the part of individuals will result in an equally rational social order of preference. This result is simply a generalisation of Condorcet's paradox of choice formulated in 1785 (Figure 2.1). Sen's impossibility theorem is closely related to Arrow's result, but its derivation is more humorous and catchy. The initial situation differs, as already said, in that individuals now also have an eye on the goods of their fellow human beings. Conversely, liberality is to be guaranteed by a right of veto on the part of the individuals. The theorem is easily understood through Sen's key example, which reflects the author's mischievous aim: to put the liberal, whose mouthpiece the economic sciences appear to be, in a bind.

The question of the case study is: how should a prudish society deal with erotic literature, exemplified here by the novel *Lady Chatterley's Lover*? Two individuals speak out on this. No. 1 prefers that no one reads the book (*A*), but would rather read it himself if necessary (*B*) than see his fellow citizen subjected to the torture of reading it (*C*): $A > B > C$. His dissolute fellow citizen, however, would like above all that the book is read, but finds even greater pleasure than reading it himself in the idea that his prudish neighbour would have to comply with this duty: $B > C > A$. Sen now constructs the collective preference order of the two individuals in two ways, first informally according to liberal principles, then according to the Pareto principle, which is supposed to embody the liberal principle. Considering first the pair (*A*, *B*) – should no one or individual 1 read the book? Individual 1 should get – and would exercise – the right of veto: $A > B$. If, however, one considers the pair (*A*, *C*), i.e. puts the second individual in the place of the first, then the latter should also have the right of

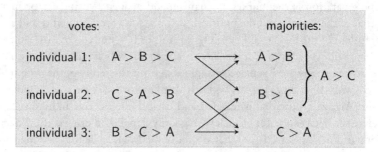

FIGURE 2.1 The choice paradox formulated by Condorcet in 1785: the aggregation of preferences regarding different options according to the majority principle can lead to incoherent results. For example, when applied to the topic of Brexit: A: remain, B: hard Brexit, C: soft Brexit; individual 1: remainer with a preference for clear-cut decisions, individual 2: anxious Brexiteer, individual 3: resolute Brexiteer.

veto – and would claim the reading for himself: $C > A$. The social preference constructed according to liberal values is thus $C > A > B$: individual 2 should be allowed to read the book. Now, according to method 2, this result is obviously not Pareto-optimal, since both individuals would prefer option B to option C, i.e. they would increase their utility by switching from C to B. The result of this method is therefore not Pareto-optimal. "While the Pareto criterion has been thought to be an expression of individual liberty, it appears that [...] it can have consequences that are, in fact, deeply illiberal" (Sen 1970, S. 157).

We have thus encountered a conceptual problem in the attempt to speak about social goods within the individualist framework, i.e. to make statements at the interface between the individual and society. What lesson one should draw from this result is admittedly controversial. It is immediately apparent, for example, that Sen's result is due to the 'pathological' construction of the example: the liberal observer who wants to determine the collective order of preferences has to deal with individuals who do not share his liberal attitude but who are very keen to dictate to each other or even to get one over on each other. But this is precisely the conclusion Sen draws: individual freedom cannot be had with such individuals, but requires "developing individual values that respect each other's personal choices" (Ibid. p. 155 f.). Ironically, these values do not have to be founded in an ethic of mutual benevolence (individual 1 wants to prevent his fellow citizen from reading, or at least pretends to do so), but can also be realised in a higher degree of social indifference – i.e. egoism. But this does not damage the point of Sen's reasoning, since we are still dealing with values for which we have no place in the theoretical framework of the Pareto principle, since they prompt counter-preferential actions.

The consequences of the impossibility theorems for a liberal theory of the common good are unclear. At the time of Arrow's publication – the beginning of the Cold War – the only alternatives were 'freedom or communism'. Put in less dramatic terms, we note a difficulty in talking about collective quantities within an individualist framework. This difficulty can be resolved in two ways. For the influential economist James M. Buchanan, who is certainly representative of his discipline, Arrow's findings meant that it was no longer possible to talk about things like the social good at all. Rousseau's *volonté générale* was summarily dismissed as "mystical" (Buchanan and Tullock 1962, Chaps 2 and 7). Surprisingly, Arrow himself was less clear in his own conclusions:

> The failure of purely individualistic assumptions to lead to a well-defined social welfare function means, in effect, that there must be a divergence between social and private benefits if we are to be able to discuss a social optimum.
>
> *(Arrow 1950, p. 343)*

It seems that Arrow was not prepared to give up talk of the common good so lightly. This commitment is remarkable. We should note that at the time he was writing, Arrow was working for the military-affiliated think-tank the RAND Corporation, where game theory was being pushed as an analysis and predictive tool for the Cold War; his original assignment was to find a mathematical expression for the Soviet Union's collective utility function (Amadae 2003, p. 103). Against this background it is thus surprising that he paved the way for a reading of his theorem that could make him an inspiration for heterodox economics today.

2.2 Empirical pitfalls

After these purely conceptual reflections, we come to the critique from an empirical perspective. There are now a whole series of approaches to test experimentally the assumptions of microeconomics. This *experimental economics*, as is often summarised, is united by the intention to overcome the model Platonism of economic theory and to close the gap with reality. These efforts have fostered a number of fruitful research projects and yielded remarkable results, some of which we will examine in more detail.

It should be said at the outset that the experimental approach does not automatically fulfil its aim of building a bridge to the 'real world'. After all, we are dealing with laboratory experiments under idealised conditions, which themselves have to be reconciled with real conditions. Ironically, a new Platonism seems to loom here. Experimental economics, for example, studies the behaviour of empirical subjects under varied economic conditions. But what counts as an economic condition – and what is to be excluded as an extra-economic condition – is nevertheless unquestioningly prescribed by neoclassical doctrine (Güth and Kliemt 2003). Experimental economics is thus often committed to neoclassical doctrine on the very points which heterodox approaches have placed in question.

The situation is no better for the so-called behavioural economics, which has attracted a lot of attention in recent years and was also awarded the Nobel Prize in Economics in 2019. Its representatives are very proud to leave not only the ivory tower of pure theory, but also the laboratory, in order to carry out the so-called "randomised controlled trials" in the field – in fact, mostly development projects in the Global South – so as finally to do real empirical work. They pose as pragmatists who are primarily interested in the effectiveness of development policy measures (Duflo 2017). As early as 2010, Angus Deaton had accused behavioural economics of being largely useless for precisely this reason: "it focused on *whether* projects worked instead of on *why* they worked" (Deaton 2010, p. 426). His French colleagues Jean-Michel Servet and Bruno Tinel go quite a bit further: the experiments undertaken in behavioural economics do not ask about long-term effects, they ignore the cultural context and only consider individual responsibility, and the development policy measures tested have a conspicuous affinity for the market and financialisation. In short, behavioural economics reproduces the most problematic biases of neoclassical economics (Box 2.1; Servet 2018; Servet and Tinel 2020).

BOX 2.1 SHORTCOMINGS OF BEHAVIOURAL RANDOMISED CONTROLLED TRIALS

- They "ignore contexts and composition effects and reflect the biases of those who perform assessments."
- They "presume without demonstrating that market exchanges are the most effective form of regulation for societies in all situations of social life."
- "The positive or negative incentives ('nudges') offered by behavioral economics aim to normalize the behavior of consumers, users, employees, or small/independent producers. They are part of a set of power devices by which individual behaviors are shaped and forced, without their knowledge, to conform to dominant class interests."

(Servet and Tinel 2020)

In the following, we will take a closer look at the psychological approach of *bounded rationality* and relevant experiments from behavioural science research (not to be confused with behavioural economics). The latter are often casually subsumed under the bounded rationality approach, but there are certain differences, which is why they are presented separately here. These differences may be ones of degree, but they are relevant precisely for methodological questions. The bounded rationality approach is an *individual psychological* one. A single individual is the centre of attention. The fellow human beings who interact with him or her tend to recede and merge with the other peripheral factors into a background 'environment'. The search for explanations of the human actions observed tends to focus on a given, *static* psychological state of the individual, especially on subjective *motives*:

The *bounded rationality* approach:
- individual psychological;
- psychological make-up as an exogenous, static factor;
- explanation of behaviour in terms of motives.

In behavioural science experiments, on the contrary, attention is more focused on groups. Group dynamic effects are distinguished from interactions with the inanimate environment. The individual is thereby conceived not statically but in terms of dynamic developments such as learning processes and conditioning. In the explanation of behaviour, motives become less important than external influences and frameworks, i.e. *structural determinants* (Merton 1939, p. 3):

The approach of the *behavioural sciences*:
- social-psychological/sociological;
- psychological make-up as an endogenous, dynamic factor;
- explanation of behaviour in terms of external influences and structural determinants.

2.2.1 Bounded rationality

The "bounded rationality" approach goes back to the work of the American psychologist Herbert A. Simon in the 1950s, but has only recently attracted wider attention. The Israeli psychologist Daniel Kahneman, who will be the focus of our attention in the following, was even awarded the Nobel Prize in Economic Sciences in 2002. Bounded rationality takes as its subject the mental mechanisms of intuitive judgement and decision-making (Kahneman 2003) and is based on the model of two interacting mental systems.

On the one side there is *intuition*, which, like perception, is a fast, automatic, effortless process and, again like perception, is emotionally influenced and difficult to alter through learning. Unlike perception it typically leads to judgements in the sense of conceptual representations. Intuition essentially has the primary responsibility in our dealings with the world and our decision-making. On the other side stands *reasoning*, which is slow, linear and controlled, requires conscious effort and follows certain rules, but integrates new experiences more easily and flexibly. In this model, reasoning acts as a control mechanism, which, however, only monitors intuition with one eye and only corrects its errors from time to time. The main focus of psychologists is on the heuristic mechanisms according to which the intuition that dominates our actions and decisions functions. This approach promises a more realistic picture of the economic actor. Before we take a closer look at some relevant findings, however, a preliminary remark is in order so that we can better assess these findings' character and scope.

Without looking at any of the experimental results, we can already identify on the basis of this model alone two presuppositions that are inscribed in the programme of bounded rationality and which narrow its horizon. First, rational behaviour is identified with behaviour based on *intellectual effort*, and second, empirical human behaviour is assumed from the outset to *fall short* of optimal rational behaviour, instead of being described more neutrally as a mere deviation from this norm (or as the instantiation of a different kind of rationality).

That these assumptions are not unproblematic can be seen from the results of the experimental testing of economic theories on the behaviour of animals, which can be pointedly summarised in the fact that rats and pigeons often behave – measured by the standards of *homo œconomicus* – more rationally than humans (Kagel 1997). Does this mean that rats and pigeons are intellectually superior to us? Of course not. For one thing, we have already seen that the standards ascribed here to rationality have nothing to do with conscious deliberation and refer just as much to mechanical behaviour and reflexes (↑ 1.2.2 and 2.1.2). Whatever mechanisms may underlie such rational behaviour are irrelevant in the model.

Just as rational behaviour does not have to be deliberate behaviour, deliberate behaviour does not have to be rational. Cognitive complexity in particular can lead to behaviour that contradicts *homo œconomicus'* ideal of rationality (Stanovich 2013). A nice example of this is provided by the independence of preferences from context, as demanded by the rational agent. If you fancy a slice of cake at a coffee party, the rational thing to do is simply to tuck in. However, many people will hesitate if the piece of cake is the last one on the plate – although this is actually an irrelevant contextual feature of the individual-cake system. When people actually evaluate the options open to them in a way that depends on context, this can simply be due to their higher cognitive abilities, which in this case allow them to do justice to a social situation. Amartya Sen was therefore quite right when he spoke of *homo œconomicus* as a "rational fool" (Sen 1977, p. 336).

Admittedly, most researchers would not accept these two problematic assumptions – first, that rational behaviour is necessarily based on conscious deliberation and, second, that 'irrational' behaviour is necessarily deficient. Yet in the experiments conducted by psychologists and behavioural scientists there is nevertheless a tendency to design test situations in which rational behaviour is indeed behaviour based on conscious deliberation, because in these situations the 'rational' behaviour can only be ascertained by an effort of thought, sometimes even basic mathematical reasoning. Consequently, in these situations, the 'irrational' behaviour effectively contradicts the laws of logic or mathematics – it amounts to behaviour that is not simply different but *erroneous*. Outside of these special experimental set-ups, however, neither assumption is generally the case. This is not an objection to the theory of bounded rationality, but a strong indication that it only represents a fragment of the complexity of empirical human beings (cf. Brandstätter, Güth and Kliemt 2003, p. 343). Having said this, we can look at some relevant and striking results of this research approach.

Certain deviations from the postulates of rational choice theory can already be seen in the way risks are dealt with. Intuitive judgements about risky options are the subject of so-called 'prospect theory'. Consider the following example (Figure 2.2, from Kahneman and Tversky 1979, p. 273). Two groups of test persons are asked to choose between two scenarios A and B or C and D, in each of which a bonus is added to the basic salary x and then the option with a 'prospect' of profit can be chosen. The prospect of winning is associated with risk. Group 1, after a bonus of 1,000 monetary units (MU), can choose between the guaranteed payment of another 500 MU and a risky payment of 1,000 MU with a probability of 50%, the latter case being notated hereafter as (1,000,.5). Group 2, after a bonus of 2,000 MU, can choose between a guaranteed deduction of 500 MU and a deduction of 1,000 MU with a probability of 50% (1,000, 0.5).

	initial salary	bonus 1	bonus 2	choice (majority)	standard form
A			$\left\{ \begin{array}{l} \text{+ 500} \\ \\ \text{+(1000, .5)} \end{array} \right.$	X	$\begin{array}{l} 1500 \\ \left(\begin{array}{l} 2000, .5 \\ 1000, .5 \end{array} \right) \end{array}$
	x	+ 1000			
B					
C			$\left\{ \begin{array}{l} -500 \\ \\ -(1000, .5) \end{array} \right.$		$\begin{array}{l} 1500 \\ \left(\begin{array}{l} 2000, .5 \\ 1000, .5 \end{array} \right) \end{array}$
	x	+ 2000			
D				X	

FIGURE 2.2 Bounded rationality: dealing with risks may depend on the way scenarios are presented.

As shown in Figure 2.2, a majority of Group 1 chooses the safe payment, while a majority in Group 2 goes for the risky option. However, the canonical representation of the overall result of the four scenarios in the final column reveals that in fact both groups chose between exactly the same scenarios, only presented in different language. Without delving into the micromechanics of intuitive judgement formation, it can already be seen that the invariance requirement was disregarded, according to which rational choice in particular does not depend on the way alternatives are presented.

However, it is worth taking a closer look at what features of the presentation it was that influenced the evaluation of the options, even if this takes us into more speculative territory. What can be seen in the experiment is a sudden change from risk-averse to risk-taking behaviour. The explanation, as we have already seen, must lie in the presentation. The most striking difference lies in the opposing polarity signs of the prospects of profit: positive in cases A and B, negative in cases C and D. Taking these polarities into account, the decisions follow a familiar pattern: risk aversion for positive prospects and risk taking for negative amounts. This insight, however, has enormous consequences.

The way the subjects of the experiment thought about it must have been as follows: since only one characteristic of the probability of winning was clearly decisive, they must have ignored the amount of the bonus. This is also a well-known mechanism: in the choice between two alternatives, common features are usually bracketed out as irrelevant to the decision ("cancellation"). It follows from the neglect of the bonus that their decision was not guided by the total amount they could gain. In contrast to this key postulate of rationality, it seems to be the *changes* rather than the resulting *states* that determine the subjective evaluation (as we see, losses and gains are generally dealt with differently). This insight represents a deep break with traditional rational choice theory, which always constructs the utility function (especially the indifference curves) in terms of resulting end states and disregards subjects' evaluation of changes. Third and finally, the picture can be further complicated by the fact that gains and losses are always defined relative to a reference point. Most of the time, this is identical with the status quo, so that the gains and losses correspond to the amounts actually paid. But deviations from this are conceivable. For example, a gain that turns out to be smaller than expected may be subjectively evaluated as a loss, because the fact that the gain that was anticipated was already mentally accounted for and the reference point already set higher. Such a shift of reference point can also be induced by the specific description of the scenarios, which can also explain effects like the one observed in the above experiment ("framing effects" in the "coding" of the alternatives).

A second, brief example of bounded rationality mechanisms is offered by the "prototype heuristic", which essentially consists of representing an abstract category by a concrete proxy (Kahneman 2003, pp. 1463 ff.). Making judgements based on the prototype rather than the abstract category may work well in many situations, but it has two typical weaknesses: the so-called "violations of monotonicity" and "extension neglect". Both effects can be illustrated by the example of monetary valuation, especially when dealing with public goods – a case we will encounter again in Chapter 4. In an experiment, collectors valued a set of ten trading cards in mint condition higher than the same set with three additional but defective cards. The price of the latter set should have been at least as high as that of the former, including and exceeding as it does the former's contents. But evidently the flawed cards 'rub off' on the others, thus violating the monotonicity of the prize. A second example is studies of charitable donation. In a Canadian study, the amounts households were willing to donate to save migratory birds threatened by pollution remained constant, regardless of whether the number of birds affected was said to be 2,000, 20,000 or 200,000. The prototype, the image of an oil-slicked bird, completely displaced the information about the number of birds concerned.

These two examples may suffice to give an impression of how remote from real life the postulates of rational choice theory are (for a tabular overview of the heuristics, see Gigerenzer and Brighton 2009, p. 130 f.). However, also the limits of the bounded rationality approach itself are already becoming apparent. Researchers of bounded rationality often present their results in the gesture of 'Behold, this is how the human being really is!'. Depending on how one emphasises this exclamation, the strengths or the weaknesses of this approach become clear. If one puts the emphasis on 'really', this approach releases all its critical potential when it mercilessly allows the assumptions of rational choice theory to fail in the face of reality (or at least in the face of laboratory experiment). However, if one emphasises the 'is' – "that is how the human being really *is*" – it becomes clear that the theory remains trapped in a static framework. It assumes humans have a given and unchanging psychological make-up and addresses neither phylogenetic nor ontogenetic dynamics. Finally, if one emphasises the definite article "the" – "how *the* human being really is" – it is striking that, in addition to historical variation, geographical variation is omitted and the fiction of a universal human being is employed. These are shortcomings that behavioural science research, to which we now turn, is attempting to overcome.

2.2.2 The ultimatum game and its relatives

In behavioural science research, a number of 'games' have been developed to control assumptions about rational behaviour. The concept of a game here is somewhat more general than in game theory, since some of these experiments consist of only one round of the respective game, sometimes even only a single move, so that it is not possible to speak of a pattern of behaviour and hence nor of a strategy. Experimental testing of the postulates of rationality turns out manifestly to their disadvantage. Incidentally, it has long been known that players in the prisoner's dilemma cooperate in ways that run counter to predictions (see, for example, Lave 1962). When two colleagues of the game theorist Nash behaved cooperatively in a game, he is said to have commented: "One would have thought them more rational" (Flood 1952, p. 24a; cf. Field 2001, p. 5).

The Ultimatum Game is an experiment on economic behaviour that was first conducted around 1980 by the German psychologist Werner Güth and his colleagues with students, then repeated 20 years later by a group led by the American anthropologist Joseph Henrich on an international scale, taking particular account of different indigenous communities (Güth, Schmittberger and Schwarze 1982; Henrich et al. 2001, 2005). Both experiments produced remarkable results in their own way. While the first experiment showed a clear deviation in behaviour from the predictions of the *homo œconomicus* model, the second experiment also showed a strong variability among the different communities.

The Ultimatum Game runs as follows. The test persons form pairs of players. They are given a sum of money (at that time between 1 and 10 Deutschmarks) to divide among themselves. Player 1 has the sole right to propose a distribution of the money. Player 2 can accept the proposal, which results in the amounts being paid out, or reject the proposal, in which case both players go away empty-handed. The prediction according to the model of *homo œconomicus* is clear: it is rational in the sense of utility maximisation for Player 1 to offer Player 2 the smallest possible amount greater than zero (10 Pfennig or 1 Deutschmark, with the units of division being clear to the players). Player 2, who also follows utility maximisation, now has a choice between the minimum amount and empty hands, which is why he should accept the minimum amount, in keeping with utility maximisation. The results of the experiment performed with psychology students in Cologne already showed clear deviations from this prediction, on the part of both parties. The players in Role 1 offered significantly higher amounts, on average between 40% and 50% of the total amount. Conversely, offers below 30% were often rejected by players in Role 2, although this gesture came at a 'cost' (the loss of any gain) to them. After a trial round, an almost conflict-free game situation was immediately established, in which rejections of offers were the exception.

It seems obvious to use the concept of fairness in interpreting this data. Players in Role 1 generally make fair offers, while players in Role 2 reject unfair offers, i.e. punish the unfair gesture. (The concept of fairness is used here solely to describe the behaviour, but does not assume that this behaviour is based on a subjective effort to *be* fair – we will come back to this distinction). This interpretation is corroborated by an interesting and – for evolutionary explanation – groundbreaking finding, which admittedly appears somewhat incidentally in the original study. In the original experiment, the consistency of the players' behaviour was tested by finding out whether they would accept the distribution they proposed in Role 1 *if they were in Role 2*. The players' behaviour did prove to be consistent: remarkably, the amounts offered were now higher. The authors took this as an indication that anticipatory role-taking promotes fair behaviour. By conducting a second experiment with a much more complicated design, the psychologists also ensured that the subjects were able to determine the rational solution, so that cognitive failures could be ruled out as an explanation of 'irrational' behaviour. The results of this more complex game pointed in the same direction: balanced distributions were regularly preferred to the Pareto-optimal solution.

The Ultimatum Game was later varied in its structure to better isolate its different aspects (Henrich, Heine and Norenzayan 2010, p. 65; Henrich et al. 2010, p. 1481). In the so-called Dictator Game, Player 2 is deprived of his veto power, Player 1 simply decrees a distribution. While the Ultimatum Game provides a measure of fairness combined with an estimate of the risk of punitive rejection, the punitive aspect is missing in the Dictator Game, which is why its outcomes are considered a pure measure of fairness. If we look at the behaviour of Player 2 in the Ultimatum Game alone, we can regard it conversely as a measure of willingness to punish. Such a measure is also offered by the Third-Party Punishment Game, again a variant of the Dictator Game. Here, Player 1 risks being punished by a newly involved third party for unfair offers. However, since the third party has to do this at his own expense, i.e. should rationally always refrain from doing so, his behaviour also provides a measure of so-called altruistic willingness to punish.

Another important attempt by experimental economics to study punitive behaviour is the so-called Public Goods Game, which will be described in detail because we return to it in Chapter 3. This experiment deals with the social handling of so-called 'free riders' (Fehr and Gächter 2002). The core of the experimental design is as follows. A group of players can voluntarily pay portions of a sum given to each of them into a collective project. For each monetary unit (MU) paid in, each player is paid a certain fraction of it, so that while the investment initially involves a loss, it yields a profit if all the players participate appropriately. For example, if we have four players with 20 MU each and a payout ratio of 0.4, so that for each MU paid in, 0.4 MU is paid out to each player, making a total of 1.6 MU, the following picture emerges:

PUBLIC GOODS GAME, FOUR PLAYERS EACH WITH 20 MONETARY UNITS (MU), REPAYMENT RATE 0.4:

1   *Complete co-operation*: if everyone pays in their entire sum of 20 MU, everyone receives 32 MU back.
2   *Free-riding*: if all but one person pays in their entire sum, but that person pays nothing, 24 MU is paid to each person, but the free rider gets a total of 44 MU.
3   *No co-operation*: if no one donates, everyone is left with the original 20 MU.

The scenario for this experimental set-up is obvious; it is familiar to us from the prisoner's dilemma: free-riding is the strategy that yields the highest profit. However, since 'rationally' every player should choose it, cooperation fails to materialise and everyone is worse off than if they had cooperated. The game can be extended in subsequent rounds to include a punishment option, which, however, is also associated with costs for the punisher, so that exercising the punishment runs counter to utility maximisation – one therefore speaks of "altruistic punishment". As was already evident in the Ultimatum Game, the punishment option is of considerable influence and essential for a deviation from the economic model. Figure 2.3 shows the mean investment amount as a measure of willingness to cooperate in two different courses of the game over 12 rounds. In the first game, the penalty option is deactivated after six rounds; in the second game, it is activated at this point. In each of these variants and further developments of the Ultimatum Game, similar results that are not readily compatible with the model of the rational utility maximiser are replicated.

This brings us to more recent studies in which the Ultimatum Game and its variants were repeated at the international level, in each case in a variant with anonymised playing partners. These experiments have literally added a dimension to the picture, as the old findings now became visible as a point in a spectrum that varies across cultural spheres. The new, more complete picture could hardly have been more surprising. Let us look at it in more detail.

As you can see from Figure 2.4, the model of *homo œconomicus* is nowhere corroborated. It is worth remembering that this model predicts a minimum offer, whereas even the most 'egoistic' societies offer on average around 25% of the total (we must be careful when we speak of egoism, for in fact we know nothing about underlying motives – we will return to this issue in a moment). Furthermore, one immediately sees the enormous range of different behaviours. It is therefore not only necessary to revise the model of *homo œconomicus*, but also to question the assumption of 'the' human as a generalisable, cross-cultural being. The respective behaviour patterns obviously require more local explanations. Before we turn to this, we point out a third surprising feature of the diagram: the population of Western industrialised nations represented by

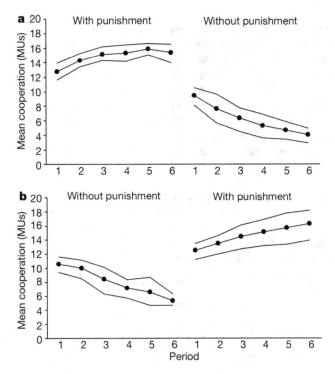

FIGURE 2.3   Chronological course of mean cooperation in two variants of the Public Goods Game. (a) The penalty option is deactivated after six rounds and (b) the punishment option is activated after six rounds. If the altruistic penalty option is activated, the cooperation rate and thus the mean pay-out increase.

Source: Fehr and Gächter (2002, p. 138).

the US city of Pittsburgh is among those with the highest average offers. The very fact that their behavioural pattern is an outlier in terms of the international distribution has led the study's lead author, Joseph Henrich, to a thorough critique of behavioural science (Henrich, Heine and Norenzayan 2010). Behavioural science is consistently based on studies of the population of Western industrialised nations – usually students at the universities of the scientists themselves, with scientists from Western industrialised nations dominating the subject – which have been generalised into statements about 'the' human being. Now, not only does it show a significant variation in behaviour across cultural groups, it also shows that Western industrial societies are among the least representative groups. Henrich et al. were able to demonstrate this for a whole range of characteristics from fairness to spatial perception. Even among industrialised nations, Western countries are consistently an outlier case. For this reason, Henrich et al. speak humorously of the "weirdest" people in the world, where WEIRD is an acronym for "Western, Educated, Industrialised, Rich, and Democratic".

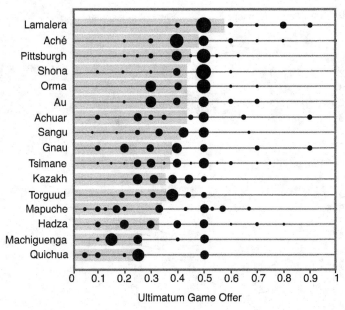

Ultimatum Game Offer

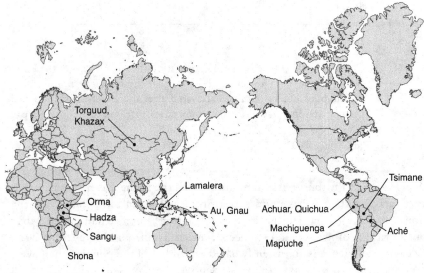

FIGURE 2.4 Frequency chart of the offers in the Ultimatum Game in international comparison. The size of the circular areas reflects the number of corresponding offers, the right edge of the grey bars reflects the average of offers for each group. The population of Western industrialised nations is represented by the city of Pittsburgh (USA).

Source: Henrich et al. (2005).

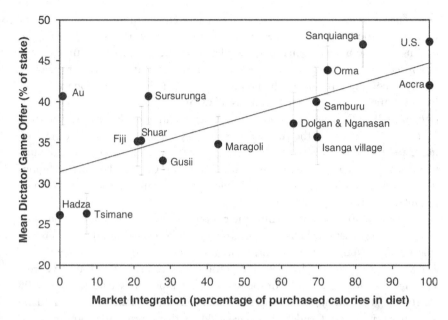

FIGURE 2.5 The average offer in the Dictator Game correlates with the degree of
market integration of a society (measured in terms of the fraction of
calories purchased in the market).

Source: Henrich et al. (2010, p. 1483).

So how do we explain the different patterns of behaviour? First, of course, one
encounters local peculiarities. For example, the Au and the Gnau stand out with
their so-called hyper-fair offers of more than 50%, but also with high rejection
rates of such offers. This can be explained by the local culture of gift-giving, in
which unsolicited gifts in particular oblige the recipient to make a future gift
in return (Henrich et al. 2001, p. 76). Beyond such effects, however, a global
correlation with certain group characteristics can be established. The most important indication is the correlation with the so-called 'market integration' of a
population, which is measured by the fraction of a person's calorie intake that
they purchase in the market (as opposed to from their own production or from
hunting or gathering). Those who cover their entire calorie needs through purchased food are thus 100% market-integrated, while the self-sufficient person has
a market integration of 0% (Figure 2.5). Another positive correlation exists with
membership in one of the world's religions. However, the authors of the study do
not interpret this as an indication of moral action backed up by religion. Market
integration and world religion ultimately point back to a third decisive variable,
namely the size and thus the complexity of populations.

In fact, it seems to be that small societies, as were common in human history until a few thousand years ago, do not know any cultural norm of fairness in dealing with strangers (remember, the players of the Ultimatum Game are anonymised). In fact, the issue of fairness to strangers only arises in larger societies, finally becoming a recurrent theme in the economic life of the modern world. Even the mechanism of 'reputation', as it was used to explain fair behaviour, is only partially effective in large societies. An expanding society in which dealing with strangers becomes the rule must create its own norms in order to stabilise itself, and thus mechanisms to enforce these norms too. The importance of punishment became apparent early on in the Ultimatum Game. The world religions seem to be an important factor that develops with expanding societies, facilitating interactions over greater social distances.

This explanation stands in emphatic contrast to the assumption of evolutionary psychology that our behaviour is explained by a psychological make-up that originated in (and was ideally suited for) small societies and that humanity has, as it were, inadvertently dragged along with it ever since, so that today we treat a stranger as trustingly as if he or she were an acquaintance (see McKinnon 2005 for further discussion). According to Henrich et al.'s explanation, it is actually the other way round. Crudely put, one could say that it was trade and capitalism that 'civilised' us, that is, produced the norms for dealing with strangers that have become the rule in modern society.

2.2.3 Morals and markets

Before we discuss these findings in more detail, let us look at another experiment which complicates the picture further still. "Morals and Markets" is the title of an experiment conducted by two German psychologists on the influence of market interaction on moral behaviour (Falk and Szech 2013). More specifically, the authors follow the thesis that market interaction increases the willingness to put up with serious negative consequences for a third, uninvolved party. Such consequences for third parties are generally referred to in economics as 'externalities'. The third party in the experiment was provided by surplus laboratory mice that would otherwise have been killed. The participants, who were only informed after the experiment of the mice's already certain fate, were to make market decisions – agreeing on a price – which would result either in the killing or safekeeping of the mice. Since the survival of the mice had to be regarded by the test subjects as the normal case, their killing represents the externality. The assumption that the killing of even a small animal as a consequence of an economic exchange represents a moral dilemma for the test subject seems not to be far-fetched and indeed finds confirmation in the experiment.

The thesis of moral erosion by the market is not new, but in a certain version it is all but standard in cultural criticism, uniting authors of politically diverse provenance from Alexis de Tocqueville to Jürgen Habermas (Bowles 2011, p. 48). In the classic version, the thesis is that liberal society is eroding the values on which it itself rests and has thus taken on a "parasitic" relationship to other institutions such as the family or religion that guarantee these social norms, for example, the work ethic and contractual fidelity. We already know from the discussion of the Ultimatum Game that this cannot be the whole truth. But it is interesting to observe this assumption being put to the test in the experiment.

During the experiment, a market-based decision with the morally relevant externality was made in three different scenarios:

1   Individual decision. The subject is offered €10. If she accepts, the mouse dies. If she refuses, the mouse lives.
2   Bilateral market. The mouse is "entrusted to the seller's care". The 'buyer' is given a budget of €20 and negotiates the price with the seller. If a deal is struck, the mouse is killed. Both market parties have the right to refuse a transaction.
3   Multilateral market. There are seven buyers and nine sellers facing each other, current offers are displayed on a screen. Due to their superior number, the sellers run the risk of not being able to get rid of their 'goods'.

The results confirm the thesis. Just under 46% accepted the killing of the mouse for €10 in the individual scenario (the fact that not all subjects consented proves in particular that one is dealing with a morally relevant decision). On the bilateral market, the fate of the mouse was sealed in just over 72% of cases, on the multilateral market in just under 76% (Figure 2.6a). The development of the price is also significant (Figure 2.6b). While in the individual transaction the €10 was fixed, the price in the multilateral market fell over ten auction rounds from €6.40 to €4.50. There was no such development in a comparative experiment in which the sellers were provided with a coupon instead of a mouse, the sale of which was therefore associated not with moral 'costs' but with the so-called opportunity costs. Finally, it is worth noting that in a supplementary scenario using pricelists, €47.50 and over €50 had to be offered to the individuals in order to reproduce the acceptance rates from the bilateral and multilateral markets, respectively. If one takes the amount of money as a measure of moral inhibition, actors in the multilateral market display one tenth of the inhibition shown by actors deciding alone.

The authors attribute the observed effects to three characteristics of market-based interaction: First, since there are always two actors in a transaction, responsibility and guilt can be shared. Second, each actor reads the observed actions of the others as an indication of existing norms. When a good is traded, according to the social information, this is not associated with moral problems: the very existence of a market becomes a signal to the actors. Third, action and competition engage actors and divert their attention away from morally problematic externalities. To the objection that the killing of the mouse in an individual decision may be considered a direct consequence or even purpose of the transaction whereas in the market it is more of a side effect, the psychologists sought to produce a more

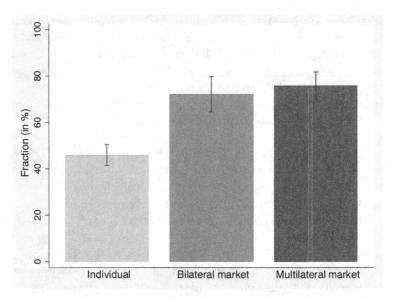

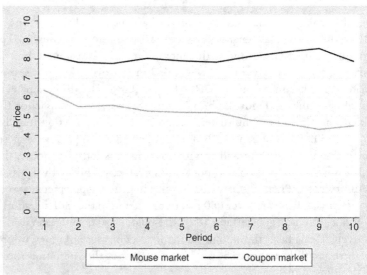

FIGURE 2.6 Markets erode moral values. (a) Proportion of test subjects, who accepted the killing of the mouse in the three scenarios. (b) Price development in the multilateral market over ten rounds for mice and in comparison to a morally neutral good but with opportunity costs.

Source: Falk and Szech (2013).

sophisticated experimental design in which the subjects could purchase a lottery ticket and had to accept the killing of the mouse as a side effect. The results were the same. The authors draw from their findings the particular lesson that in market situations appeals to morality can only ever be of limited effect.

We are certainly dealing with a robust experimental phenomenon here. Other experiments have produced similar results. For example, an experiment in Israeli day-care centres showed that the introduction of fines for parents who collected their children late almost doubled the number of late collections, forcing staff members to stay longer on site beyond opening hours (Gneezy and Rustichini 2000). One explanation for the unexpected result is that the introduction of the fine caused parents to perceive the situation as a market- rather than a moral one. While a favour offered altruistically entails obligations and may not, according to moral norms, be taken advantage of, this is no longer the case for help transformed by the fine into a paid service

Let us note two things before we take stock and discuss the methodological consequences. First, we can make a general statement that in such experiments individual motives clearly take a back seat to structural determinants. The rules of the game, in this case the rules of the market, prevail over the players if these rules are collectively anchored. Second, however, we can see in a more nuanced way that the individual findings do not necessarily harmonise with each other. The intercultural comparison had shown that norms of fairness correlate with market integration, which is not surprising, since in anonymous exchange relations one encounters the other quite differently than in the familiar network of relationships of the family or the clan. Now, however, we see that the market leads to an "erosion" of moral values, as the authors of the study put it. It is true that in the mouse market constructed in the laboratory, the behaviour between the market parties complies with social norms – in a deal it is the handshake that matters – and the moral consequences affect uninvolved third parties, who in this case are not even persons. Outside the laboratory, however, this constraint does not apply. The third parties affected by our daily decisions are very often people and, for example, as wage labourers, also market participants. The authors of the study have even used products from child labour as a case in point where our choices as consumers directly affect other people and even the most vulnerable among them. So everything points to the fact that one should be prepared for conflicting structural determinants in the study of real economic activity, e.g., the market, which drives us towards a general morality in dealing with the unknown other but at the same time prevents us from abiding by its commandments. We will return to this phenomenon of 'induced schizophrenia' in Chapter 3.

2.3 Free decisions or structural constraints?

All these empirical findings should, of course, be taken for what they are: laboratory results that cannot easily be transferred to the real economy. The fact that in the Ultimatum Game and its variants the players are freely provided with an initial budget may well influence their handling of the goods that have "fallen from the sky". The scientists certainly try to meet such objections. They set up preparatory experiments beforehand or try to move the experiment out of the laboratory – as, for example, in Werner Güth's Newspaper Experiment with readers of the weekly magazine *Die Zeit* (Güth, Schmidt and Sutter 2007). Such reservations notwithstanding, some general, methodologically relevant problems can nevertheless be read very precisely from these findings. Neoclassical economics follows a reductionist, individualist method. In such a framework, a person's behaviour is explained by a motive. Yet, it is clear that motives are epistemically complex. In the original neoclassical theory, which lacks any experimental foundation, they are linked analytically to the notion of preferences, as we emphasised from the beginning. Psychological research attempts to use motives as empirical explanations, but motives are not directly observable and can only be inferred indirectly. Thus in addition to studying behaviour itself, the so-called 'think-aloud' protocols can be used to try to determine motives. Moreover, theories of behavioural science can be taken as a warning that the connections between motive and behaviour may be highly complex. The attributes "egoistic", "fair", "altruistic", etc., refer in the first instance only to externally assessed behavioural patterns, and cannot legitimately be extrapolated into motives. It is even inscribed in the reductionist model of *homo œconomicus* that altruistic behaviour must have motives other than altruistic ones. These reflections, admittedly, do not constitute a refutation of the reductionist individual psychological approach. They only point to difficulties.

Moreover, these difficulties do not necessarily pertain to this approach alone, but also haunt alternative social-psychological approaches. This becomes apparent when a social-psychological disposition is itself to be explained in evolutionary terms. Because in the Darwinian evolutionary model the egoism problem reappears, but this time proves more intractable still. In evolutionary theory, egoism cannot be ascribed to the evolutionary subject on a motivational level but pertains, at most, to the mechanism of heredity: a phenotype can only cross the generational boundary if the evolutionary subject produces enough procreative offspring. Altruistic behaviour poses a serious problem for this model, since it seems to deprive itself of the opportunity for inheritance. Incidentally, this individualism enshrined in evolutionary theory is also the reason why game theory, which is shot through with individualistic rationality, continues to play a major role even in methodologically alternative approaches.

Beyond such difficulties, however, the neoclassical model of the rational actor is shaken more profoundly. It is now necessary to discuss what conclusions can and must be drawn from the discrepancy between prognosis and experimental data. What conclusions can be drawn from the fact that empirical people do not behave like *homo œconomicus*?

2.3.1 The wrong image of humanity?

The first and simplest inference would be to conclude that the image of humans in economics is inadequate and must be replaced by a more realistic one. This conclusion is indeed often drawn, and the new image usually shows us a friendlier face in the mirror: that of an altruistic and cooperative being. We have already seen, however, that this correction of the image of humanity is incomplete.

Homo œconomicus is not selfish in the true sense of the word, but represents a much more pared-down, purely self-referential being (↑ 1.2.2). The new conception of the human would therefore have to be expanded to include the entire range of character traits that are oriented to other humans, to which envy and resentment belong no less than benevolence and friendship.

Such an adjustment already demands a lot from neoclassical theory. Acknowledging the economic actor's orientation to others means admitting that the order of preference is not given for each individual in isolation. The marginal utility of a good is co-determined by the distribution of that good in society. A fair-minded person – or simply a shy person who wants to remain unobtrusive – will not derive any positive benefit from a good if he or she is distinguished from his or her fellow human beings by its acquisition. Conversely, an envious or less self-confident person will attribute a greater value to a good if his fellow human beings already possess it ("keeping up with the Joneses" – cf. Matt 2011). The explanans is thereby pushed back a step, to a human character whose reactions to given distributions of goods generate their respective preferences. But even if one takes into account the complexity of the 'complete' human being, one arrives at a model that does not yet do justice to experimental findings. Two important observations that emerge from experimental research are, first, the diversity of human behaviour in different cultural settings and, second, the influence upon behaviour of social mechanisms such as punishment. Both observations point to the same underlying phenomenon, namely the flexibility and malleability of behaviour, which goes beyond the spectrum of different reactions to different distributions of goods. Even a conception of the human being that is enriched by our orientation to others cannot do justice to these observations.

Put succinctly, the shortcoming can be stated thus: the problem in the theory is not what image of man one has, but that one has an image at all. A conception of the human being is always based on a static and unchangeable constitution of that being and thereby excludes a genuine social dynamic that intervenes not only in the distribution of goods but also in human character itself. This could be seen especially in the approach of bounded rationality, which adhered most firmly to the individualistic approach. But is it possible to dispense with an image of the human being in empirical social research, particularly in economics? What does an alternative to methodological individualism look like? Two answers are conceivable.

2.3.2 Preferences as endogenous variables

If one cannot explain the whole through the parts, then one must – so to say – proceed the other way round (remember Box 1.1, ↑ 1.2.1). To do this, of course, one must first be able to grasp the whole conceptually and to adequately characterise its being. What does it mean that society is 'more than the sum of its parts'? Whose good is the social good, if it is not ultimately that of individuals? Such questions – posed in this form – are anything but easy to answer. In

moral philosophy and political philosophy, the failure of the classical liberal programme has found an echo in, for example, a new Aristotelianism (Nussbaum
1990; O'Neill 1993). The concept of the common good was at the centre of
Aristotle's political philosophy: for many of his contemporary readers, the legacy
of Hobbesian anti-Aristotelianism is to be reversed and the common good again
become our orientation; even questions of global justice may be addressed with
the help of the ancient philosopher.

However, this 'communitarianism' is an *ethical doctrine* and does not offer a
social-scientific methodology. It is, in the words of Oscar Wilde, 'sentimentalist',
whereas the analysis of society requires a certain 'cynicism'. Any social-scientific
methodology must be able to give a *causal* explanation of the relation between
whole and parts (regardless of whether the causality flows from the parts to the
whole or vice versa). An action of the whole on its parts can, I suggest, be conceptualised in two steps. The first step is unquestionably to view preferences as
'endogenous' variables that do not co-determine the developmental dynamics of
the system in the form of external factors, but are instead co-determined by these
dynamics. This approach adopts the richer character traits of the new conception of
human beings, which encompass both other- and self-oriented impulses, but views
them as dependent variables, thus leaving more room for the formation of theories.

The second step, which strips the talk of a 'whole that is more than its parts'
of its mystical appearance, consists in translating the influence of the whole on
the parts into a developmental history. That the parts exist first and then come
together to form a system whose properties they determine is not difficult to
imagine. The fact that the whole is there first, that it produces its parts and determines their characteristics, certainly makes sense if one uses the concepts of
generation and reproduction. A society produces its offspring and determines
their characteristics through mechanisms of biological and cultural inheritance.
A theory of endogenous preferences turns out to be simply a theory of the distribution of cultural traits in a population, with the 'market' (in the sense of
the prevailing rules of allocation) and other economic institutions in particular
having a long-term influence on the frequency distributions. In other words, we
are dealing with a theory of the co-evolution of institutions and social norms
(Bowles 1998, p. 82 f.; Bowles and Gintis 1998, pp. 211 ff.).

Described thus, the approach may seem very abstract. In fact, however, it is
quite familiar. We know it, for example, from Erich Fromm, who in his early
studies on "characterology" sought to explain the character traits prevailing in
a culture in terms of cultural norms arising from the social structure (Fromm
1932). While Fromm used the then current theory of psychoanalysis as a heuristic, today a theory of cultural evolution is available to identify the underlying
mechanisms. Here, one can think of very concrete processes. The market and
other economic institutions have an influence on the social stratification of a
society and thus on rates of non-random pairing, on the frequency of interactions, on the cultural transmission process itself, on migration flows, etc. All
these factors influence the cultural characteristics and especially the preferences

of individuals. Unquestionably, such an approach still faces many challenges to-day. In particular, the evolution of cooperative behaviour is not yet understood. We have already seen the role of punitive measures (in the Ultimatum Game or in the TIT FOR TAT strategy in the prisoner's dilemma). But to the extent that these approaches rely on "altruistic punishment" (coming with costs), they fail to explain the emergence of altruism from non-altruistic behaviour (Bowles and Gintis 2002; Gintis et al. 2003). The developmental psychologist Michael Tomasello recently made an attempt to locate the origin of altruism in situations where cooperation becomes a necessity, such as sexual reproduction. In this case, the male and the female are dependent on each other for passing on their genes. "Now they are *inter*dependent and there is no prisoner's dilemma", Tomasello explains (2016, 15). In such situations where an individual's "self-interest" cannot be defined as opposed to the other's self-interest, the prisoner's dilemma starts to look less and less like a generally valid theorem. Nevertheless, we are talking here about an approach that is still being researched rather than a fully fledged theory.

2.3.3 Structural determinants

Perhaps one can even go a step further in turning away from the original individualistic-reductionist programme. Preferences are, as we recall, only rather precarious means of explaining behaviour. While in economic theorising, they are chained analytically to behaviour, in psychological theorising, they can only with difficulty be separated out as independent empirical entities. An evolutionary theory of preferences, such as the one just outlined, only has real explanatory value if these preferences can also explain something outside of the context which accounts for their adoption (Bowles 1998, p. 79). If preferences in such a theory are thus highly precarious links between external structural determinants and human behaviour, then the question arises whether they should not simply be dispensed with.

To this end, let us once again make clear the shift from individualistic to holistic or structural explanation of economic behaviour, i.e. from the explanation of behaviour by motives to the explanation by external constraints. Marx gives an instructive example from the history of child labour in England during the Industrial Revolution: at the beginning of 1863, 26 firms sought to persuade the state – today we would speak of lobbying – not to liberalise working hours for children, but on the contrary to impose a restriction on their working hours by means of a "compulsory law". Such a restriction, which they themselves apparently considered desirable in view of the suffering of the working children, was impossible for them to adopt voluntarily due to "competition with other capitalists". Marx elaborates in precise terms the methodological consequences of this episode for the analysis of economic processes:

> Capital is reckless of the health or length of life of the labourer, unless under compulsion from society. To the outcry as to the physical and mental

degradation, the premature death, the torture of overwork, it answers: ought these to trouble us since they increase our profits? But looking at things as a whole, all this does not, indeed, depend on the good or ill will of the individual capitalist. Free competition brings out the inherent laws of capitalist production, in the shape of external coercive laws having power over every individual capitalist.

(Marx [1887] 1990, p. 233)

Here, it is obviously the structural determinants, namely the institutionalised rules of the economic system, which override the motives of the actors (insofar as these cannot be institutionalised in the form of a law). This comes about through the mechanism of free competition. Those who, from human motives, do not abide by the rules of the game, e.g., by shortening working hours or paying higher wages, will soon have to close their factory.

Marx thus presents a thoroughly 'evolutionary' explanation of the behaviour homogenised by the laws of the market. As one can say with today's authors: while neoclassical theory claims that *homo œconomicus* gives rise to capitalism, one can just as well claim that capitalism gave birth to *homo œconomicus* (Bowles and Gintis 1993, p. 96 f.). But it is futile to say that this explains the preferences of the economic actor, since it remains and can only remain unclear whether, for example, the successful capitalists who abide by the rules of the game also internalise these rules and thus adopt them as preferences or whether they constantly act against their own moral values (as suggested by the results of the Ultimatum Game in international comparison). This raises the question of whether such a structural explanation of behaviour, regardless of the preferences underlying it, might already adequately capture the economic process – at least on *one* descriptive level. Of course in a second step, one could then descend the chain of determination further in the direction of individual behaviour. (We will see a concrete example in the following section via the concept of power relations).

Note that this turns the reductionist-individualist programme of neoclassicism on its head. No longer does one ascend from the individual to collective phenomena as in microfoundation, but instead one gradually descends in the opposite direction.

2.4 Power

2.4.1 Power in neoclassical economics

One of the key concepts in the previous section was that of cooperation, which denotes a phenomenon that cannot easily be reconciled with the model of *homo œconomicus*. The "evolution of cooperation" is a fashionable topic today, and if you look at the literature, you could almost believe that we live in a world in which everyone's most pressing desire is to do good for their neighbour. One can be grateful to economist Nancy Folbre for pointing out that intra-group altruism also favours docility, and thus hierarchically structured societies with a clearly distinguished top and bottom (Folbre 2012, p. 3). This brings us to the concept of power. In the following, we understand power as the ability to influence the behaviour of others in one's own favour through the threat of sanctions (Bowles and Gintis 1992, p. 325).

What role does power play in the economy, and what role does the concept of power play in economics? For neoclassical economics, the latter question is quickly answered: power plays no role, since the ideal market with perfect competition is fully self-regulating and leaves no room for power relations. Whether in the commodity-, labour- or credit market, supply and demand will always mechanically converge. This is ensured by the price mechanism: in the case of oversupply, the price falls, dampening supply but stimulating demand. If there is a shortage, the price rises, with inverse effects. In any case, the market will eventually clear, i.e. supply and demand will come to coincide exactly: in the world of the ideal market, every commodity finds a buyer once the price has adjusted accordingly; there is full employment once wages have settled into the interplay of supply and demand; and every loan is granted, at its correct interest rate (an interest rates is the 'price' of the loan). Such a situation leaves no room for power relations, because a surplus on one side would be the condition for the other side to exercise power. In the case of strict full employment, i.e. when there is neither overemployment nor underemployment, neither the employer nor the employee can threaten to quit. Their relationship thus becomes perfectly symmetrical, as Paul Samuelson shrewdly put it: "Remember that in a perfectly competitive market it really doesn't matter who hires whom: so have labour hire 'capital'" (Samuelson 1957, p. 894; cf. Perelman 2003b, p. 153).

The real power relations, which even the economist does not deny, must consequently be understood in this picture as a disturbance of the market. The disturbing factors are frequently identified with the spheres of the public and political, so that politics and the market, the public and the private are dichotomously opposed to each other: pure competition without power here, pure power without competition there. When the spheres mix, however, the market equilibrium is disturbed. If politicians impose a minimum wage, some workers will not find a buyer for their labour and unemployment will ensue, which also puts the employer in a position of power. But this is not an economic phenomenon. The study of power relations is the responsibility of political scientists and sociologists, not of economists.

2.4.2 Economy and power

However, things cannot be that simple. This can be seen, for example, in the phenomenon of profit (Häring and Douglas 2012, p. 141). In perfect competition there can be no profit, since the competing producers have to undercut each other – up to the point where they sell the good at the cost of production. If profit is made somewhere, it would actually be an indication of a monopoly structure.

But profit is not an occasional sputtering or clanking of the capitalist machine. Rather, this machine runs, one might say, for the sole purpose of making profit. Even the supporters of *laissez faire* capitalism do not claim that the purpose of capitalism is to satisfy the needs of humanity, but that the needs of all are most efficiently satisfied when everyone pursues their selfish motives in the most unregulated market possible. The efficient satisfaction of needs may be the main argument this school presents to justify capitalism to the general public, but in their economic picture it is really only a side effect. Actually, it is all about profit, and accordingly, economics should be primarily concerned with the phenomenon of power. "Money is power", as the saying goes (Ibid. p. 47).

Empirical examples can easily show that the idealised market conditions that would exclude the exercise of power are grossly violated everywhere and that power relations take on a very concrete form. Let us consider the financial market as a prominent example. To understand the financial market, especially in the run-up to the 2008 crisis, it is indispensable to consider the asymmetrical availability of information. In principle, financial institutions have an information advantage, which they also exploit: financial analysts tend to "strategically distort" the facts (Malmendier and Shanthikumar 2014) – simply put, they lie – and in the run-up to the crash, many clients of financial products, including local governments, were unaware of the risks of the increasingly complicated "securities" being sold to them (Sassen 2015, p. 144). The banking system, according to Norbert Häring and Niall Douglas, has been in a symbiotic relationship with political power since the days of the Fuggers, with governments often in the weaker position. Banks knew before the 2008 crisis that governments could not let them fail in an emergency, so they chose riskier business models. Ironically, by turning the financial crisis into a sovereign debt crisis through the so-called bank bailout, governments found themselves in a weaker position still. Häring and Douglas speak of a "takeover of government by Wall Street" (Häring and Douglas 2012, p. 70). A similar story could be told about the labour market with the expansion of the low-wage sector on the one hand and the explosion of high incomes on the other. In short, if we don't talk about power relations, we won't understand anything about today's economy.

2.4.3 Power in the market equilibrium?

What methodological implications are to be drawn from this? The first possibility is to stick to the idealised equilibrium model and to understand power relations as a consequence of a disturbance. From a purely logical point of view, this is possible. However, one then has to grapple with the fact that, first, the disturbance is not only occasional and negligible, but permanent and powerful. Power relations are the rule, not the exception. But there is no quantitative criterion for judging when a disturbing factor may be excluded as being foreign to the system. More serious, however, is the fact that without the factor which is regarded as a disturbance of an economic process, this very process would not exist. The ideal market knows no profit, but without profit there is no capitalist economy! "Profit is a dirty word for neoclassical economists", say Häring and Douglas (2012, p. 142), and this insight has deep methodological significance.

Interesting in this context are attempts to integrate power relations into the equilibrium approach, so that in this picture power is, as Bowles and Gintis aptly put it, neither simply exercised *outside* nor *in spite of* the market, but *in* the market and indeed *in the market equilibrium* (Bowles and Gintis 2008). Joseph Stiglitz and Andrew Weiss already took this approach in 1981 in examining the credit market and Bowles and Gintis in 1992 did the same for the labour market (Stiglitz and Weiss 1981; Bowles and Gintis 1992). The train of thought is the same in each case and the example of the labour market, which we will briefly discuss, can be transferred wholesale to the credit market: in the labour market there is no such thing as complete information and therefore any contracts signed are necessarily incomplete. The wage to be paid is contractually regulated, but the effort that the worker actually puts in during his or her specified working hours can neither be defined in the contract nor empirically verified in the employment relationship. In particular, the desired and appropriate performance cannot be legally enforced, which is why internal company measures must take effect ("endogenous enforcement"). The first measure is the threat of dismissal, but this is only credible and effective if the wage actually paid is *above* the so-called second-best alternative (i.e. a different job or unemployment benefits) – and thus above the traditional neoclassical equilibrium value for the wage. At this wage level, the threat of dismissal is serious for the worker and he or she will respond accordingly with increased effort. We are certainly dealing with an equilibrium, since the higher wage is paid in a competitive situation. At the same time, however, the market does not 'clear' because the worker is not indifferent to the prospect of changing or losing his or her job; he or she knows that there are other workers labouring under worse conditions or who may even be unemployed. Thus, in this case, power is indeed exercised on the part of the employer, who can threaten the worker with a credible sanction.

What we observe in this situation should not exist in the neoclassical world, since it is logically excluded from its conceptual system: the exercise of power leads to a Pareto improvement, since both parties are better off due to the higher wage and the higher output. The exercise of power, as an external disturbance, should actually always lead to a Pareto deterioration, since the free market alone produces the optimum in the form of equilibrium. The Pareto improvement shows in particular that power relations here actually take effect *in* the market equilibrium and are produced by the forces of competition and the price mechanism. Stiglitz and Weiss summarise this result in stark but perfectly correct terms: "The Law of Supply and Demand is not in fact a law" (Stiglitz and Weiss 1981, p. 409). The fact that the price mechanism leads to an adjustment of supply and demand is not a general market feature, nor are unemployment and credit constraints phantasms, but a historical reality in market economies (Stiglitz and Weiss 1981, p. 409).

In English, there is a linguistic distinction between the point zero of competitive forces (*equilibrium*) and the adjustment of supply and demand (*market clearing*), so that a question can at least be formulated whether the equilibrium actually leads to market clearing (what is doubtful, as we have just seen). Curiously, this conclusion cannot even be stated in the German technical language of economics. The notion of market clearing does not exist, and the market equilibrium is defined as the equality of supply and demand as established by the price mechanism. German economists are so sure that only fish live in the sea that they define "fish" as "sea dweller" and now have no word for the whale, which lives in the sea but is not a fish. This is all the more serious because we live in a world where the whale is in fact the largest sea creature: most economies today are dealing with significant unemployment.

2.4.4 Conclusion

After the critical remarks of the previous sections, one may have reservations about these ideas, since they nevertheless remain attached to the equilibrium approach and the model of *homo œconomicus*. At the same time, one should remember, contra Samuelson's symmetrical picture of the labour market, that this entire market exists only because of a deeper asymmetry: some have capital and others do not, and the latter must therefore sell their labour to the former.

But let us not confuse different levels: this asymmetry is located at the macro level of structural determinants, while the equilibrium models with their incomplete information discussed above operate at the micro level of market actors. But this micro level, as the critiques of neoclassical theory discussed in this chapter conclude, no longer serves as the starting level for explaining the entire economic process, but rather as the end point of research that begins with structural determinants and then descends towards the micro level. The equilibrium models with incomplete information should not be measured against the claim to offer a general theory of power or even comprehensive theories of the market (in the examples, the labour market and credit market). Rather, they merely deal with the behaviour of very specific actors in very specific constellations. Understood in this local sense, equilibrium models can certainly retain their relevance as an explanatory resource, and it is always surprising how flexible the conceptual framework of equilibrium theory proves to be.

Looking back at the chapter as a whole, we see that the proposal is not simply to add some sociological terms ("power relations", for example) to the vocabulary of economics. The change needed goes deeper and, following Samuel Bowles and Herbert Gintis, we can see that the even economics' basic abstractions are affected by the shift in methodology (Bowles and Gintis 2000). It has become apparent that economic actors with given preferences are not a suitable starting point for theory-building. Economic actors are born in society and are conditioned by it. The economic process therefore does not simply border upon other social processes. Rather, all these processes *intertwine* with each other.

Society provides the economy with the individuals who act. Conversely, the free market can also produce or prop up hierarchical relationships, which then structure the social realm, and so on. One senses the dramatic difference when one thinks back to the extremely individualising approach of behavioural economics, which was once polemically summarised as follows: "The world's poor are poor because they tend to make the wrong decisions" (Berndt and Boeckler 2016). No context, no culture, no structural determinants – just individuals and their (right or wrong) decisions.

The consequences for the underlying concept of the economy are considerable. Recall that neoclassical theory essentially conceives of the economy in terms of resource allocation, thus reducing the economic process to the mechanism of allocation. In the historical context of competing economic systems, the market and central control are the two relevant candidates that economists test for their efficiency on the basis of the Pareto criterion, with the vote clearly in favour of the market: there, and only there, is the ideal state mechanically established. Now we find this approach shaken in its foundations. Not only is it impossible to separate questions of efficiency from those of distributive justice, as neoclassicism assumes. We already saw this in Chapter 1 (↑ 1.2.7). Now it becomes apparent that with exogenous needs and orders of preference, the yardstick of efficiency is also lost. Preferences are no longer the externally determined variable by which economic processes can be explained and by which their efficiency can be measured. Rather, needs become an endogenous variable that is first determined in the economic process itself.

This overturns the neoclassical view of the economy: the economy no longer appears as a vast machine for the purpose of fulfilling needs. Indeed, we must be careful not to imply that this machine has a *purpose* at all. The market economy is simply the particular way in which a society tries to organise its life process. In doing so, it creates needs, some of which it will fulfil, even over-fulfil, others it will not fulfil at all. Instead of ascribing a purpose to it, the entirety of its causal consequences needs to be taken into account. Social inequality and ecological problems cannot simply be excluded as secondary consequences, but must be integrated into a picture of the whole. This allows one to then examine which of these consequences have a stabilising effect on the economic system in the form of positive feedback mechanisms and which ones tend to destabilise it. In the case of stabilising effects, one can, it is true, speak in a figurative sense of *purposes* or *functions*. It is in this sense that we have cautiously spoken above of *profit* as a purpose of the economy – this is legitimate insofar as it is an effect that contributes to the steady reproduction of the social fabric and its inequalities.

In the same cautious sense in which we speak of purposes and functions, we can also admit that functional explanations are an alternative to the individualistic-reductionist explanations of neoclassicism – that is, one can explain system properties by the fact that they are conducive to system purposes. If such explanations by expediency were weeded out of the canon of scientific tools by such past thinkers as Descartes, because the blind causal mechanism of nature knows no purpose, they are unproblematic in virtue of the weak concept of purpose proposed here. In fact, such an explanation simply consists in identifying the system-stabilising mechanisms and thus explaining the historical continuity of the system itself (cf. Cohen 1982). This talk of purposes will be relevant in Chapter 5, in which we look at *crises* in the economy as destabilising developments.

3

THE ECONOMY IN A COMMON WORLD

At the boundaries of the market and private property

Just as the individual, as the smallest-scale economic actor, does not stand in an empty space but in a society that shapes him or her, neither do goods and services circulate in a vacuum. They make up only a part of material abundance, the other part of which does not fall under the category of private property and is not accessed via a market. Here, we encounter a second 'interface' of the economic process. We will look at three examples: the commons, i.e. common property with common rights of use; knowledge, which is often compared to the commons and seems to resist the category of intellectual property; finally, unpaid work, which accounts for a large part of economic output but does not appear in economic accounting. In contrast to the previous chapter, we seem to be dealing here with purely practical or political problems. However, the theoretical significance will become clear. Our guiding question is: what is the relationship between the economic process and the extra-economic space and in what terms can this relationship be addressed? This becomes crucial when the relationship turns out to be one of dependence (just as, in the previous chapter, we came to understand the individual as dependent on society), because it forces us to thematise the external space when analysing the economic process.

3.1 The 'tragedy of the commons'

3.1.1 The historical commons

In economic history, the commons is a kind of anti-hero: its very disappearance opens an extremely important chapter in European economic history. Beginning in the 15th century, landowners in England increasingly withdrew land from common use through enclosure and used it for more profitable sheep farming. This prepared the ground for industrialisation in two ways. On the one hand, the

DOI: 10.4324/9781003204077-4

wool industry developed, and, on the other hand, farm workers were freed up to work as wage labourers. Wage labour only emerged at this time and its hardship gave no indication that it would one day form the most important integrating matrix of modern societies (cf. Castel 1995). The miseries caused by enclosures also left traces in the literature of European humanism, most prominently in Thomas More's famous *Utopia* of 1516. More describes the social ills of the time, such as the many thefts, which the state tried to curb through draconian punitive measures: "Thieves [...] were then hanged so fast, that there were sometimes 20 on one Gibbet". Interestingly, More blames the crimes not on immorality but on impoverishment. In a conversation with a cardinal, he bitingly names the "sheep" as the culprits – by which he means both the grazing animals and their "Christian" noble owners who are closely connected to the church:

> The increase of Pasture [...] by which your Sheep, that are naturally mild, and easily kept in order, may be said now to devour Men, and unpeople, not only Villages, but Towns: For where-ever it is found, that the Sheep of any Soil yield a softer and richer Wool than ordinary, there the Nobility and Gentry, and even those Holy Men the Abbots, not contented with the old Rents which their Farms yielded, nor thinking it enough that they living at their ease, do no good to the Publick, resolve to do it Hurt instead of Good. They stop the course of Agriculture, inclose Grounds, and destroy Houses and Towns, reserving only the Churches, that they may lodge their Sheep in them: And as if Forrests and Parks had swallowed up too little Soil, those worthy Country-Men turn the best inhabited Places into Solitudes [...].
>
> *(More [1516] 1684, S. 21)*

What type of process is More describing here? Let us be precise in anticipation of the discussion to come. The enclosed land was certainly already owned by noble families or the church, but it was occupied and worked by the so-called yeomen, who had already won this right a century earlier and now claimed a customary right as sub-tenants, their "copyhold" (Travis 2000, p. 786). We are therefore not dealing with expropriation. In so far as it disregarded customary rights, however, the enclosures were certainly illegal, even though they were carried out in accordance with the jurisdiction that lay in the hands of the upper classes, especially since the 18th century onwards. The consequences for the peasants were considerable, because since the individual peasant had on average only about four acres at his disposal, the commons was of substantial importance for him as a pasture land, but also as a source of peat, firewood, etc., as Marx already noted in a notable study of this chapter of economic history (Marx [1887] 1990, Part VIII: "The so-called primitive accumulation").

The enclosures mark the beginning of a chapter in the historical process of the "extensive and intensive occupation of land areas" (Wallerstein 2010a, p. 5) – i.e. the expansion of population and economy into undeveloped areas as well as their agglomeration in the growing urban centres – the arc of which seems to be completing itself in our present. "The degree of privatisation in the world", the sociologist Saskia Sassen points out,

> is higher than ever before. There is practically no longer any free land anywhere, no community that one could join without further ado. That is a categorical change. You can't just grow your vegetables anywhere today, to stay with the image of the soil. You probably also know how difficult it can be, even for the traditional inhabitants of a city, to find a shelter, an affordable flat. So even if they have crossed all kinds of national borders as a migrant, they no longer get 'in' so easily. The spaces are getting tighter everywhere. And the number of those who have to stay outside is increasing.
>
> *(Sassen 2015)*

We will return to this historical perspective in Chapter 5.

3.1.2 The gateway to the economic world: commodification

In the enclosures, we see a good passing through the gateway to the economic world. We are dealing, *grosso modo*, with a process through which a good that was previously equally accessible to all is transformed into a good that is only accessible through purchase (and thus dependent on purchasing power). The market thereby expands into areas not previously organised according to its rules. We now need the right vocabulary to describe this process. In the literature, which will occupy us in this and the next chapter, we find various terms that are used more or less coherently, but rarely explained properly, which is urgently needed, as the differences are sometimes subtle. Most often, this process, which Karl Polanyi already examined in 1944 (Polanyi [1944] 2001), is described as "commodification". However, this description is quite unnuanced. With the Canadian geographer Karen Bakker, we will make a finer distinction between privatisation, commercialisation and commodification proper, while taking into account two *prior* processes (Bakker 2005, p. 544, expanded on by Holland (1995) and Vatn (2000), as well as by Gómez-Baggethun and Ruiz-Pérez (2011)):

Aspects of commodification:

1 *Identification* (*itemising, framing*): Separating the good from its context and naming it by means of an (economic, possibly quantifying) term (e.g. "human capital");
2 *Enclosure*: (a) Initial occupation of the property with a title of ownership, irrespective of the owner; (b) exclusion of others from using it;
3 *Privatisation*: Transfer from public to private ownership;

4 *Commercialisation*: Establishment of the management of an asset according to commercial principles and methods and, if applicable, with commercial intentions (efficiency, cost minimisation, cost-benefit analysis, profit maximisation);

5 *Commodification* proper: Conversion of a good into a (possibly standardised) commodity with a market price.

Three points should be noted for a more precise understanding:

First, that all these terms can refer to types of goods as well as to individual examples of goods, a point which is not carefully distinguished in the literature.

Second, enclosure and commercialisation are changes occurring at an *institutional* level, i.e. they concern rules, norms and habits in a sociological sense. Privatisation, however, happens *within* the framework of existing institutions and can be seen more as a change at the *organisational* level. Further note that 'enclosure' is used here strictly metaphorically and in the absence of a proper term, since *historical* enclosures (legally problematic acts since they violated customary rights) consolidated existing property rather than creating property in the first place. Nevertheless, this usage corresponds to the established terminology.

Third, privatisation and commercialisation are necessary but not sufficient for commodification proper. Whether at the point of enclosure, i.e. the creation of a property title for a good (or a type of goods), commodification has already taken place, i.e. a tradable economic good has been created, is not as self-evident as many would like to believe. The American legal scholar Margaret Radin (Radin 1988, p. 1685, 1996b, p. 509 f.) draws attention to the fact that the liberal bourgeois tradition knows two distinct paradigms of property that cannot easily be reconciled and are still the source of tensions in the present-day property law – a Kantian and a utilitarian or Benthamite paradigm (Box 3.1).

The consequences for the relationship between enclosure and commodification differ in the two paradigms. In the Benthamite paradigm, every property title is per se a commodity that can be traded in the market and has an objective market value. We live in a commodity cosmos. In the Kantian paradigm, the processes diverge: there is inalienable property, and universal commodification must even appear as a threat to the person and to human flourishing. In debates over slavery, human trafficking, organ trafficking, prostitution and surrogacy, as well as patents on living beings, this paradigm is often at work (Radin 1987, 1996a).

In the discussion of the limits of market and property, one must be prepared to encounter both models of the concept of property. In the – clearly Benthamite – neoclassical orthodoxy, however, there is no place for either of the processes described, since it assumes that commodification is already complete. This orthodoxy only knows commodities and their laws of motion. But it is not in a position to determine its limits from within the commodity cosmos. Wherever it looks, it sees only commodities, and what is not a commodity, it cannot see. In this sense, we spoke following Luhmann of the closed system of the economy (↑ 1.3.4).

BOX 3.1 TWO CONFLICTING PARADIGMS OF PRIVATE PROPERTY ACCORDING TO M. J. RADIN (1996B, P. 509 F.)

The "Kantian" Paradigm

- "We reason about value based upon a commitment to an ideal of human flourishing."
- "We say that property is a natural right because it is necessary to the self-constitution of persons and to their freedom." (In particular, each woman and man has an unalienable property in his own person.)
- Ergo: "[T]here's a lot that loses its distinctive human value if conceived of and treated as a commodity."

The "Benthamite" Paradigm

- "We reason about value based upon market exchange and the reducibility of all values to a commensurable scale."
- "We say that property rights are created by the sovereign, by the legal authorities and not by the moral law. We say that their function is to maximize society's collective welfare (or happiness, preference satisfaction, or wealth)."
- Ergo: "We can conceive of the entire world of things people value as one giant market, and can evaluate every choice by cost-benefit analysis."

Here, we touch again on the question of *concepts* that is at stake in the philosophical analysis: What conceptual resources does economic theory have at its disposal to describe the interrelationship between the outside and the inside? We see that in the orthodox version, it is completely lacking. Orthodox economics must regard the processes of enclosure and commodification as sociological and thus extra-economic phenomena. In this context, the sociologist Immanuel Wallerstein recalls the old French expression *"mise en valeur"* for these processes – "valorisation" or, literally, "putting into value-form" (Wallerstein 2010a, p. 3). Only as a commodity does land have value, and only through commodification does land become visible and thematisable for neoclassical theory. Commodification is a real process that extends the economic process into its external space. In a sense, it represents the crudest, most tangible method of making the external space thematisable in economic terms, namely by physically appropriating it.

3.1.3 The tragedy of the commons: Hardin's diagnosis of 1968

The reappearance of the commons in modern social science and especially economic literature is ambivalent. The *locus classicus* is the essay "The Tragedy of the Commons" by the American ecologist Garrett Hardin (1915–2003) published in the journal *Science* in 1968 (Hardin 1968). Hardin's real concern is the rapid growth of the world's population. He compares what he sees as a looming overburdening of the global ecosystem by the growing number of people with the overgrazing of the commons, whose usage is unconstrained. The commons does not figure here as a model of success. His essay, which contains extremely controversial theses, such as the rejection of the protection of the family enshrined in the UN Declaration of Human Rights in 1948, certainly owes its fame to the game-theoretical analysis of its topic, which speaks the language of the self-confident social sciences of its time.

The structure of the "tragedy of the commons" resembles the prisoner's dilemma and, not incidentally, the Public Goods Game. The scenario is reduced to two cattle herdsmen who share the right to use a pasture (Figure 3.1). The piece of land can support a certain number of cattle, which the herdsmen share. If both respect this constraint, they will earn a certain profit X. However, there is a temptation to overgraze. If one of them increases the number of cattle, he harms the grazing land and reduces its productivity. However, both herdsmen have to share the costs Y, while one alone can make the extra profit Z. If both choose this option, however, cattle herding will eventually collapse.

Even if the commons may play only a marginal role in today's livestock farming, at least in Europe, there are nevertheless many other communally used goods which, despite their vital importance, were for a long time far too self-evident in many parts of the world to be perceived as such. Groundwater and the atmosphere are important examples, as is the environment in general in its function as a dumping ground for sometimes highly toxic waste. The tragedy of the commons can in this sense be transferred one-to-one to the problem of environmental pollution: if the manufacturer cleans his emissions of toxic substances, he alone bears the costs. If he releases the emissions unfiltered into the atmosphere, he shares the costs with the community (under a number of problematic assumptions that we will discuss in Chapter 4).

The well-known result arises once again and the tragedy takes its fateful course: individually rational actions (in the sense of the economist's concept of

		A	
		cooperates	defects
B	cooperates	every X	$X-Y/2+Z$ for A $X-Y/2$ for B
	defects	$X-Y/2$ for A $X-Y/2+Z$ for B	every 0

FIGURE 3.1 The tragedy of the commons as a prisoner's dilemma.

rationality) lead to a collectively irrational result, the invisible hand fails. For an understanding of Hardin's concern, it is important to know that he does not question the underlying model of rationality and thus considers the disastrous outcome of the game-theoretical analysis – the collapse of farming – to be a realistic prognosis.

Nevertheless, Hardin is far from anchoring the rationality model in the psyche of the actors. Instead, he speaks of actors being "locked into a system" and the "inherent logic of the commons remorselessly generating tragedy". But if the "logic" works with fateful necessity over the heads of the actors, then this obviously names a structural determinant as we have already come to recognise it (↑ 2.3.3).

This is an aspect of Hardin's thought that is hardly (perhaps never) taken into account, and which he continues in a remarkable discussion. In exploring possible solutions to the tragedy of the commons, Hardin consistently excludes one from the outset: the appeal to morality. If actions are determined by the rules of the game, there is little point in appealing to the individual players. Hardin thus anticipates the conclusion of the authors of the Morals and Markets Experiment (↑ 2.2.3). But he goes a step further and asks what effect a moral appeal to the 'prisoners' of the rules of the game would have. Since the appeal would come from fellow players, each must understand it in two ways: first, as the intended moral appeal, but second also as a strategic move by competitors who want to gain an advantage over the moral naïf.

This creates a *double bind*, a paradoxical situation in which the addressee will always violate one of the demands in whichever action he chooses: he will act either morally and stupidly or wisely and immorally. Hardin consciously bases this analysis on a contemporary theory of the development of schizophrenia, in which just such a situation is proposed as the cause of the mental disorder: a schizophrenic personality is one that fails to integrate a double bind (Bateson et al. 1956). While Hardin discusses the appeal to morality as an *option* that one can choose or not, we can ask ourselves whether moral demands are not in fact more firmly inscribed in our society, forming an established part of our self-understanding. As the research on the Ultimatum Game suggested, this morality may even come from the same source as the logic that compels us to act immorally. To speak of schizophrenia in an economic context may only be legitimate in a metaphorical sense, but it highlights the contradictory forces that members of a market society face and the efforts needed to develop and maintain a healthy personality in the face of them.

Once the 'moral' way out of the tragedy is rejected, there are only two other solutions for Hardin – the market and the state, or 'private enterprise' and 'socialism', as Hardin later put it (Hardin 1978, p. 314, cited in Ostrom 1990, p. 9). The first solution is to convert the commons into private property, which, the assumption goes, will be taken care of more responsibly by a private owner than would common property. Hardin obviously favoured this solution over state regulation. But he also recognises its practical limits, because water and air can hardly be enclosed. To the question of overpopulation (which is Hardin's real concern), these two solutions can be directly applied. The market solution would be to refrain from any regulatory family policy, but in return also to refuse any welfare state assistance, so that everyone is unconditionally entitled to have offspring but can only produce and keep alive as many offspring as their own economic means allow. Here, Hardin unmistakably tends towards the political solution, but without detailing it.

3.1.4 Governing the commons: beyond market and state

No less prominent than Hardin's analysis is the challenge posed to it by the American political scientist Elinor Ostrom (1933–2012), whose work was honoured with the Nobel Prize in Economics in 2009. In her book *Governing the Commons*, Ostrom devoted herself to analysing the rulebook of successful commons administrations at the local level (Ostrom 1990). She shows that the tragedy of the commons does not occur with the iron necessity that Hardin attributed to it. The empirical exceptions she points to, however, are not simply of a kind with the experimental refutations of the neoclassical model of economic rationality seen in Chapter 2. Hardin had understood the "logic of the commons" as the result of an external compulsion rather than of human psychological make-up. The basic assumption that Ostrom problematised was the exhaustive alternative of state or market. The functioning models of the commons at the local level which she examines have characteristics of self-organisation. In contrast to the market, one encounters other regulatory mechanisms than those of private property, and these all manage without the central authority of the state.

Ostrom considers both traditional alternatives – market and state – as unsuitable for overcoming the fatal logic of the commons. In the market solution, the common land would be divided into two halves and each of the two herdsmen would be given one of them to cultivate. Instead of playing against each other, the herdsmen would now play against nature (Ibid. p. 12). Efficiency would suffer from the investment now required: fences would have to be erected and, ironically, insurance would have to be taken out against risks that were previously shared. Immanuel Wallerstein also points out that this analysis does not even take inequalities of power into account. Historical processes of privatisation, for example, in the former Eastern Bloc or in the Global South teach us that small owners were often unable to withstand the power of capital and so had to sell their property to larger companies. They ended up worse off than in the days of collective ownership, Wallerstein concludes (Wallerstein 2010a, p. 7). Wallerstein sees this dynamic as a basic pattern which development has taken since the enclosures of 500 years ago. In this light, it may come as a surprise that privatisation and commodification could ever be seen as a way out of the logic of the commons, since they represent the historical royal road to the same ecological crisis that was Hardin's original focus.

However, Ostrom also criticises state solutions through a regulating central authority as inefficient. Such solutions consist, for example, in imposing severe penalties for the overexploitation of a resource, as is currently being attempted by the EU with fishing quotas. The penalty must be set so high that there is no longer the temptation to 'defect', since the extra gain over cooperation is eaten up by the penalty. However, Ostrom is able to show with a simple mathematical example that even low defection rates counteract these effects and the fatal structure of the prisoner's dilemma is re-established.

The solution beyond market and state, which Ostrom ultimately favours, is that of "self-financed contract enforcement". The prisoners are allowed to talk to each other and they negotiate rules among themselves that enable them optimally to exploit the resource, while neither the supervision of rule compliance nor the exercise of sanctions is handed over to an independent authority, but remains in the hands of the actors themselves.

This result is perhaps less startling today, since the dichotomy of market versus state has lost its ideological foundation and rhetorical force with the end of the Cold War. To be sure, neoliberal discourse still cultivates an anti-state rhetoric that warns against crippling overregulation and invokes the self-healing powers of the market, even in crises. But it can be considered an established thesis of political science that this rhetoric hardly does justice to the real circumstances, in which the role of the state is far less clear-cut (see e.g. Harvey 2005; chap. 3; Gray 2010; Mirowski 2013). The enormous state "bailout" programmes for individual financial institutions during the 2008 crisis have raised public awareness of this. Generalising from an analysis by a political scientist Miles Kahler, we can speak of the "paradox of neoliberalism", that the state is one of the most important tools for achieving neoliberal goals via reformist interventions, even if the invisible hand of the market is considered the only legitimate means (Kahler 1990, p. 55).

What is important for the philosophical analysis of economics is what Ostrom succeeds in doing methodologically. Functioning commons management, which is perhaps capable of providing a model for ecological economic management, must appear as an 'impure' case when viewed through the eyes of neoclassical theory, since the market is disturbed through the binding of the actors by a contract. Through a corresponding modification of the game-theoretical setting, namely by lifting the ban on communicating that had been imposed on the opponents in game theory with a view to analysing Cold War confrontations, this case, which lies in the forbidden territory beyond the market, now unexpectedly becomes approachable as a legitimate economic process.

3.2 Knowledge: private property or common good?

In retrospect, the enclosures that began in the 16th century appear as a turning point in modern economic history. It was only with them that Europe's economic development gained momentum. But this hindsight is not unclouded. Economic development has put humanity in ecological distress, and even material prosperity no longer glitters in many people's eyes as it once did. Respected journals openly state that income and gross national product do not provide reliable measures of a population's satisfaction (Kahneman and Deaton 2010 – more on this in Chapter 4). Conversely, the commons promises a counter-model to questionable aspects of contemporary economic activity.

If one follows some authors, however, our time is also witnessing new enclosures. According to the analogy used by Elinor Ostrom herself (Hess and Ostrom 2007), today's commons would be the public domain, the "commons of the mind", which includes intellectual creations in the broadest sense of the word (knowledge, artistic achievements, methods, inventions, etc.). People (ideally) enjoy unrestricted access to the commons of knowledge and can use the resources for their own purposes. But in recent decades, an "erosion" of this commons can be observed (Boyle 2002). The first granting of a patent for a living being, a genetically manipulated laboratory mouse, caused a stir as early as 1988 (Kevles 2002).

Knowledge, especially scientific knowledge and the knowledge of methods, has had a strange and ambiguous career in economic history, crossing the boundary between the inner and outer spaces of the economic process several times. Such knowledge sometimes challenged the capitalist form of economic activity, sometimes sprang to its aid, as the American economist Michael Perelman summarises (Perelman 2003a, pp. 305–309). By the 19th century, the natural sciences redeemed their old promise and became increasingly important at the onset of industrial production, i.e. in the advancement of machine technology as well as in the emerging chemical industry. At the same time, its ghostly substance eludes economic categories. Marx even thought that scientific knowledge was displacing the actual value-determining factor of labour, which would mean that the whole capitalist world would have to be discarded like an old cloak – it would no longer fit the coming age, of which it was the midwife (Marx [1858] 1987, p. 86). In any case, it is questionable how the doctrine of market rationality can be upheld when an important factor of production categorically evades marketisation. Conversely, knowledge in the form of intellectual property leaps to the aid of capitalism again in the "knowledge society", as a financial counterweight to the deindustrialisation of Western economies, as Perelman interprets the historical dynamic. However, this succour exacts a toll. The containment of knowledge, for example, in the form of patenting, threatens, in turn, to impede scientific progress. It is no coincidence that the *laissez faire* economists of the late 19th century were opponents of intellectual property, as Perelman notes, for they knew only too well the importance of freely circulating knowledge for scientific progress, which, in turn, fuelled economic development. Thus, intellectual property offers post-industrial society a way out, only to present it with new problems. In addressing the question of unpaid labour, it will become apparent that this ambiguous relationship is in fact a fundamental general pattern of the relationship between the market and its context (↓3.3).

3.2.1 The origins of intellectual property

Although today it is often the intellectual creators, scientists and artists themselves who warn of the consequences of restricting access to cultural heritage, historically speaking, intellectual property rights were fought for by their own peers. The establishment of intellectual property rights was a progressive innovation at the time, responding to a new social situation (for the following, see Hesse 2002).

Before the 18th century, writers would be highly unlikely to be paid for a manuscript; instead, they lived off grants from their patrons. The monarchs had reacted to the development of book printing in the mid-15th century by establishing the *privilèges:* they granted printing licences to publishers and in return retained control over the disseminated content. With the 17th century, however, a reading public emerged along with the bourgeoisie and a market in books gained momentum. Pirate editions flourished, and their authors were able to present themselves as defenders of the common good against the monopoly of the privileged publishers. The freelance writer was born and for the first time the question of his remuneration by the publisher and bookseller was seriously raised. A share of the profits was conceivable, or even ceding publication rights for a single edition in return for payment, instead of selling the manuscript once and for all. For this, however, the writer had to be able to see himself as the owner of his intellectual creation.

The French Enlightenment philosopher Denis Diderot was one of the first to emphatically advocate intellectual property. In 1767, in his *Letter on the Book Trade*, he compared intellectual creation to the land appropriated through its cultivation, which was unquestionably the most important form of property of his time, the feudal age:

> Indeed, what can a man possess, if a product of the mind, the unique fruit of his education, his study, his efforts, his time, his research, his observation; if the finest hours, the finest moments of his life; if his own thoughts, the feelings of his heart, the most precious part of himself, that part which does not perish, that which immortalises him, cannot be said to belong to him? What comparison can there be between a man, the very substance of a man, his soul, and a field, a meadow, a tree or a vine which, at the beginning of time, nature offered equally to all men, and which the individual claimed for himself only by cultivation, the first legitimate means of possession? Who has more right than the author to use his goods by giving or selling them? [...] Let me repeat, the author is the master of his work, or no one in society is the master of his possessions. (*Je le répète, l'auteur est maître de son ouvrage, ou personne dans la société n'est maître de son bien.*)
>
> (*Diderot 1767/1861, p. 29 f., translation from Rideau 2008,*
> *last sentence added from the original*)

It is worthwhile noting the circumstances of this work. One will already notice that Diderot, as a freelance writer, is himself an interested party in the question under discussion. But the situation is actually more complicated still (see Chartier 2002). Diderot wrote the letter on behalf of the booksellers' guild, which saw itself as under threat: contrary to custom, the royal council had recently refused to extend a *privilège* for La Fontaine's *Fables* to the publisher, but had instead assigned it to the author's descendants. Diderot now intervenes on behalf of the booksellers, with whom he himself was at war, and does so in the name of freedom of the press. His manoeuvre is one of his typically ambiguous masterstrokes: he defends the *privilège* of the booksellers against the policy of the royal council, but at the same time reinterprets it as a merely contractual sanction on the part of the king – and thus as a title of ownership, so that in reality he defends the author as the owner of his work against the booksellers. Diderot's is a brilliant and at the same time roguish example of commodification!

These questions will be on the minds of many in the coming decades. It is no coincidence that such prominent philosophers as Condorcet, Kant and Fichte also put their pens to work on this issue, because it touches on fundamental questions that affect our cultural self-understanding, such as the meaning of authorship, individuality and knowledge (Hesse 1990). Condorcet questioned the parallel drawn by Diderot between intellectual creation and land, and in doing so put forward arguments that still dominate the discussion today: a piece of land can only be cultivated by one person, just as a piece of furniture can only be useful to an individual; an intellectual creation, however, is a social good, private ownership of it is thus an obstacle to freedom and a restriction of civil rights (Condorcet 1776/1847, p. 309.). Fichte would introduce a further influential consideration, namely the distinction between expression and content, whereby an author may assert property rights for the former but the immaterial content will elude them (Fichte 1793).

3.2.2 Knowledge as an economic good?

The historical debate over an author's property rights suggests that intellectual creation resists its commodification. Complete commodification, however, is one of the assumptions of the ideal market. It is therefore worthwhile trying to clarify the reasons for this resistance. In doing so, two dimensions of commodification that are present in the discussion can provisionally be distinguished:

1 *Adequacy*: Does the good or resource fulfil the necessary conditions of commodification?
2 *Retroactivity*: Does the process of commodification change the good in a relevant way? What economic and what ethically relevant effects on producers does the process of commodification have overall?

The first aspect – adequacy – asks whether an element of the economic external space might not obstruct marketisation simply because its characteristics contradict the commodity form. In the example of intellectual creation, two features immediately stand out: scarcity and the monopoly question (see Radin 1996b; Boyle 2002; Perelman 2003a; Nuss 2012).

1   Knowledge and intellectual creations are not scarce commodities. Unlike physical goods, information is not lost when it is passed on: it can be *shared*. In this sense, one also speaks of 'non-rival' consumption, since the consumption of the good by one actor does not exclude or limit consumption by other actors. In particular, an intellectual good cannot be overused. Conversely, enclosure by property rights is often described as an artificial scarcity.

2   Intellectual property gives the owner a monopoly position. While monopolies are unpopular in economics because of their market-distorting effect, the monopoly position in the case of intellectual creation seems problematic for another reason. It presupposes an emphatic concept of individual creativity, which is the only way to clearly identify the intellectual owner. Since Condorcet, however, the 'social' nature of knowledge has been held up against this: knowledge arises from the acquisition and processing of knowledge. In this sense, commodification would already fail at the most basic step of 'identification' (↑ 3.1.2), since the individual's creative share cannot be determined (cf. Stehr und Adolf 2015, p. 187).

The second aspect – retroactivity – is crucial for any ethical evaluation, but also cannot be neglected for an empirical understanding of the economic process and its consequences. The question of the repercussions of commodification on the specific good arises, for example, in the case of services, such as care, which were previously based on personal relationships (Folbre 2008). We will return to this example in Chapter 4. The repercussions of commodification on producers have been analysed by Margaret Radin as a double bind, since economically profitable commodification is always associated with uncertain consequences for the person (Radin 1996a, p. 125). An example is provided by legal scholar Victoria Phillips in a study of the marketing of quilts traditionally handmade by African American women (Phillips 2007, pp. 374–376). The traditional patterns have been handed down for six generations and were never intended for sale. Phillips speaks here of an "anti-commodity". The trade in the quilts and the marketing of their patterns, over which they have not completely relinquished control, has brought the anonymous workers international appreciation for their artistry, provided them with an income and revived a dying craft. The effects on cultural identity are harder to specify. But it does seem certain that products change their cultural meaning in the process of commodification. For an Enlightenment-era intellectual like Diderot, these 'sentimentalist' concerns did not readily arise: he wanted his ideas to circulate, and he also wanted to make a living from them. The book market allowed him to achieve both goals at the same time, if only his negotiating position with the publisher was strong enough. Today, authors are divided: while supporters of intellectual property argue that without property rights there would be no (financial) incentive for intellectual creation, critics warn that the containment of knowledge threatens scientific progress, which would grind to a halt under the burden of the costs of user rights.

3.2.3 System costs. A dynamic notion of ownership

The development of information technology and the internet has made com-modification problematic in another sense. Knowledge, we have seen, is not in itself a scarce good. However, the thesis that it should be freely available pre-supposes that knowledge can be reproduced and passed on free of charge or at least at negligible cost. This assumption is not without its problems. Discussing it provides another interesting view of the realm of property.

The legal scholar (and co-founder of the Creative Commons organisation) James Boyle invites us to look at the question of intellectual property in terms of the question of long-term reproduction costs (Boyle 2002, p. 18). Before the invention of printing, i.e. until the 15th century, manuscripts had to be copied by hand at great expense. The costs were high and, accordingly, physical control over the manuscript was essentially enough to control the dissemination of its contents. With the invention of the Gutenberg press, reproduction costs fell, to which the first modern copyright protection – the so-called Statute of Anne of 1710 – responded. This development continued via copying machines to today's internet, so that the general thesis can be put forward that the development of copyrights responds to that of reproduction costs and is inversely proportional to them: the lower the reproduction costs, the stronger the legal protection of intellectual property must be in order to control dissemination.

Of course, as Margaret Radin points out in an early but strikingly far-sighted study of property rights in cyberspace, this protection is not itself free (Radin 1996b, pp. 516 ff.). If reproduction costs are high, they protect intellectual property by themselves. If the costs of copying fall, a system must be set up to control its distribution, e.g., in the form of copy protection of electronic media. The enclosure of the intellectual commons is not achieved with a one-off act of fence building, but requires constant and increasingly costly safeguarding. The costs of this system grow as the costs of reproduction fall. At some point, therefore, the point is reached where it is simply no longer worthwhile to raise the fences higher and higher, since the costs exceed the potential profit (Figure 3.2).

This model, though technically somewhat simplistic, is highly interesting for us for several reasons. First, in this analysis, issues of property and commodi-fication are not assumed to be resolved. Thus, unlike neoclassical theory, this model allows us to address the boundary between economic process and con-text. Unlike the theories of market expansion (imperialism), however, this model also allows for countervailing developments: we see goods crossing the border between market and context in both directions. In particular, this model offers a dynamic concept of property, since the scope of application of a property title

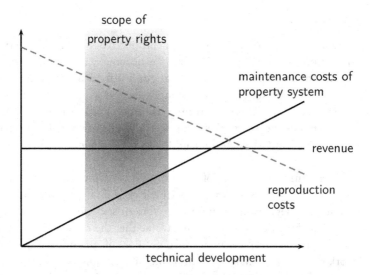

FIGURE 3.2 A dynamic model of intellectual property: in the case of high reproduction costs or high system costs, property titles are irrelevant.

changes over time depending on, for example, technical developments. Property is obviously no longer understood as an intrinsic quality of a good, but as a context-dependent, pragmatically justified attribution. Such a concept of property is highly interesting for an economic theory that also seeks to describe the dynamic relationship between market and context.

However, this dynamic model is also of philosophical or normative interest. The dynamic concept of property raises awareness that it is not a given of nature but a way of organising society. Early bourgeois thinkers such as John Locke, far from questioning private property, were nevertheless still aware of the fact that its establishment required a justification, or at least a theory of what property actually is. Since then, awareness of the problem seems to have been lost, and property became a kind of taboo. Marx already wrote, mockingly: "The English Established Church, e.g., will more readily pardon an attack on 38 of its 39 articles than on 1/39 of its income. Now-a-days atheism itself is *culpa levis*, as compared with criticism of existing property relations" (Marx [1887] 1990, p. 18).

In the application of the model, of course, care must be taken to ensure that all relevant factors are taken into account. The internet in particular offers an instructive example. In view of the development of information technology, the end of copyright was quickly proclaimed (Moglen 1999). And it is true that the internet today offers a wealth of free content. Nevertheless, the utopia of collective creativity envisaged in early cyberspace has not been realised. Today's reality looks more like a technocratic dystopia of intellectual control. The libertarian hacker culture of early cyberspace has ironically, as Radin notes, fostered an opaque and dangerous conflation of information and advertising.

3.3 Unpaid work

"Unpaid work" is a collective term for productive but unpaid activities. Following a proposal by Margaret Reid, it has become common to define it by the 'third-person criterion' in order to distinguish it from unproductive unpaid activities such as leisure activities. Accordingly, unpaid work is any activity that could be replaced by a paid service from a third party (Reid 1934, p. 11). This definition also points the way to the monetary valuation of unpaid work, namely via the wages that would have to be paid for its replacement (↓ 3.3.2 and 4.2.1, Box 4.2).

The most prominent example of unpaid work is domestic work in its various aspects – feeding, raising, caring – which is of direct importance for the reproduction of society. Even in modern, Western societies, this work is predominantly done by women, who often have neither their own (or comparable) income, nor equal say over the man's income. For this reason, the question of unpaid work was raised primarily in feminism. Nevertheless, this confinement of the issue to the female gender is by no means necessary. For one thing, domestic work can also be done by men, and there are other types of work that are also unpaid but do not show any marked gender inequality. Think of a large part of cultural work and voluntary work, for instance. But also in the debate on the new internet economy, the question arises as to whether users generate 'content' free of charge, which is then exploited by firms such as Facebook or Google (on the latter, see Cohen 2008; Hesmondhalgh 2010).

The orders of magnitude are impressive. According to data from the Federal Statistical Office for 2001, a total of 56 billion hours of gainful employment in Germany contrasts with 96 billion hours of unpaid work. Women perform the greater part of unpaid work, with just under 31 hours per week, compared to men with just over 19 hours work (Figure 3.3).

The translation of this number of hours into a value added expressed in a monetary figure is not unproblematic, and the same applies to the talk of unpaid "work", insofar as this applies an economic category to a phenomenon that does not directly belong to the economic sphere. We will return to these questions, which shape the methodological debate, after we have first discussed the question of the reciprocal relationship between the economic process and unpaid work.

3.3.1 Co-evolution of inside and outside

The thesis that economic activity in the narrower sense depends on communal, non-market reproductive work is widespread in feminist economics, but is rarely substantiated. A detailed case study can be found in the classic work *Femmes, greniers et capitaux* by Claude Meillassoux from 1975 (Engl. *Maidens, Meal and Money: Capitalism and the Domestic Community*, 1981; cf. also 1972, p. 101). In this book, the French anthropologist focuses on the typical parallel economy in developing countries, in which a capitalistically organised industrial sector and

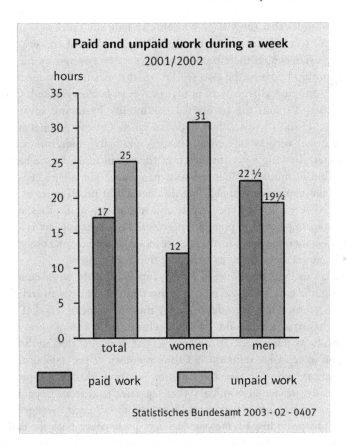

FIGURE 3.3 Paid and unpaid work in comparison.
Source: Statistisches Bundesamt (2003). In Germany, women perform the greater part of unpaid work. The figures for the USA are comparable (Krantz-Kent 2009, p. 49). In general, the
imbalance is more pronounced in poor countries than in rich ones, and within each country,
more pronounced in poor families than in rich ones (cf. Ferrant et al. 2014; Charmes 2019).

a village subsistence economy coexist. The contrast is striking: the latter ensures
the reproduction of the community and is characterised by low productivity.
Increases in production could only be achieved by extending working hours.
The former directs its material production towards the external market and is
characterised by high productivity, which can also be increased through technical innovation. Both sectors are linked by a steady stream of labour migration.

The existence of an underdeveloped sector with a high birth rate has usually
been explained in arrogant colonial terms – as due to the inertia of tradition,
mentality or customs that are resistant to the encroaching modernity and which
are no longer appropriate to the new era. Meillassoux offers an alternative
explanation that starts with the mutual relationship between the two sectors.
In particular, he does not attribute the low wages to an oversupply of labour.

Rather, he argues that the village community basically takes over provision of all the social services, from care for the elderly to care for the sick to feeding the unemployed, which therefore do not have to be covered by the employer. The relationship between the two sectors, market-oriented production and the subsistence-oriented village community, proves to be complicated. On the one hand, industry exploits the traditional community by taking advantage of its unpaid labour, and to this extent depends on it. On the other hand, the significantly better income offered by industry gradually undermines the village communities, drawing away too much of their workforce. In the end, we find a relationship of mutual influence and dependency. The alleged traditionalism of the village community appears in this new light much more as a result of migration between sectors, specifically as a reaction to it and thus as a modern phenomenon. In particular, population growth no longer appears as an outcome of a primitive mentality, but instead as a reaction to the colonial pressure exerted on the village community by its being deprived of labour.

This analysis casts the Western family and the unpaid work done in it in a different light. Again, at first glance, it seems that the family is an archaic institution that in a sense extends from prehistory into the modern world of capitalism. Its patriarchal structure should appear anachronistic in the modern world. But against this hasty judgement, it can be objected, first, that the family is not, like folklore, an expendable remnant, a fading memory of pre-capitalist times, but on the contrary fulfils an essential function in the workings of capitalism. It is no historically accidental boundary that separates paid from unpaid activities. Rather, those activities remain unpaid that are subordinated to wage labour and underpin it by providing for *the reproduction of labour power*, both the daily regeneration of the individual worker and the rearing of the next generation. The boundary between wage labour and unpaid labour is therefore that between production and reproduction.

Second, it is misleading to speak of 'the' family as a supra-historical constant. Modern capitalist societies have undergone profound demographic change: in birth rates, life expectancy, age structure and family size, each of which has changed dramatically since capitalism's origins (see Himmelweit and Mohun 1977, p. 23; Folbre and Nelson 2000). "[T]he reproduction of labour power is fundamentally altered by expansion of capitalism itself", as Nancy Folbre argues (1982, p. 328). This includes in particular an expansion into the traditional domain of the family, care and education. In particular, the housewife of the 19th and 20th centuries, the female reproductive worker, as Silvia Federici points out, is a twin of the modern male wage worker (Federici 2004, p. 75 and p. 98). Family and economy must be understood in their co-evolution.

On this reading, the history of enclosure is in a sense repeated in the 20th century. In the colonies on the periphery, but also in the family at the centre of capitalism, the history of the enclosures of the early modern period is replicated. The economic process feeds on the exploitation of a space of growth that renews itself, at least within certain limits. In fact, the concept of the commons is sometimes generalised in this sense and applied to unpaid labour. Silvia Federici speaks of an "enclosure of land, bodies or social relations" (Federici 2004, p. 220). And the double-edged relationship that we saw especially in the study of the intellectual commons is also present here. It turns out to be a fundamental pattern in the relationship between economic process and context: on the one hand, the economic process depends on its external space, as this plays an important role in social reproduction and provides it with resources. On the other hand, the external space also represents a sphere of expansion that the economic process threatens to colonise completely (De Angelis 2013, pp. 609 ff.). It will come as no surprise that we find the same relationship in Chapter 4, which is devoted to the external space of nature.

3.3.2 Work or care?

If one assumes the mutual influence and co-evolution of the market and the social outside space, the question arises as to which vocabulary can be used to describe this outside space in order to make it comparable to economic variables. How much value is added by unpaid labour? Are housewives exploited? Is there a net value flow from households into the market? Such questions cannot be asked unless economic categories are applied to the social outside. But the legitimacy of doing so is disputed among heterodox economists.

The shared motivation behind expanding the concept of work and speaking of "unpaid work" is obviously to make an 'invisible' service visible for the first time, to create an awareness of its value, and thus also to improve the status of the person who performs it, in most cases the housewife (James 1973; Federici 1975; Kaplan Daniels 1987). One pays the price of translating the value of these activities into economic value. Note, however, that the political demand "wages for housework" was not aimed at monetisation or even commodification, but was meant in the women's movement as a provocation and a call for social change, as e.g. Mariarosa Dalla Costa and Selma James clearly stated: "There has been some confusion over what we have said about [...] wages for housework. As we explained earlier, housework is as institutionalised as factory work and our ultimate goal is to destroy both institutions" (Dalla Costa and James 1972, cf. also James 1973; Federici 1975).

Recall that the distinction between 'ideal', 'emotional' or 'human' value on the one hand and economic value on the other is not possible in neoclassical theory, since its utilitarian concept of value combines all forms of value indiscriminately (↑ 1.2.3). What has an ideal value for someone contributes to his or her subjective utility, and this determines economic value. This is what we called the 'cynicism' of economists. We got to know a drastic example of it in the Introduction with the approach of Gary S. Becker, who analyses interpersonal relationships according to the model of a cost-benefit calculation. According to this model, which is clearly rooted in the Benthamite paradigm, people move through their environment like market actors, regardless of whether this environment is commodified or not. On this model, one's neighbours are transformed into "human capital", and caring for them becomes an investment (Becker 2008).

The 'sentimentalist' criticism of this endeavour feeds on doubts as to whether this transformation is legitimate. Can the human-affective value of caring for a loved one be expressed in money? Does this even involve work in the true sense of the word? Susan Himmelweit points out that the concept of work as a purposeful activity measured by its outcome rather than personal involvement, as adopted from the wage labour model, does not easily fit domestic work (Himmelweit 1995, pp. 3 ff.). And doesn't its application mean implicitly endorsing wage labour as the measure of all things?

The anthropologist Laura Agustín takes the opposite stance. Her example – sexuality as work – illustrates the tension between the 'sentimentalist' and the 'cynical' attitude particularly well, which is undoubtedly due to the contradictory cultural connotations associated with this example: on the one hand, we associate sexuality with intimacy to a certain degree; on the other hand, it is commodified with particular brutality. These contradictions also shape the way society deals with prostitution. Agustín, of course, is less concerned with (paid) sex work than with addressing sex as work in general.

She begins the article "Sex as Work & Sex Work" with a subtle joke which gives Reid's "third person criterion" a humorous twist (Agustín 2012). While a group of generals are waiting for the coffee prepared by a recruit before the morning briefing, they fall into discussing the question: How much of sex is 'work' and how much is 'pleasure'? Disagreeing, they turn to the recruit, who is sure of the answer: it must be 100% pleasure. Why? "Well, sir, if there was any work involved, the officers would have me doing it for them". With this punchline in mind, Agustín attempts to open our eyes precisely to the aspects of work in sexuality. Even in traditional relationships, sexuality is embedded in means-end contexts, in both biological reproduction and social reproduction, for instance, in the maintenance of the relationship. "The point is that reductions like lust and love don't go very far towards telling us what is going on when people have sex together", Agustín concludes.

Such reflections certainly indicate how much of the 'sentimentalist' reservations about monetisation and, *a fortiori*, commodification can be traced back to unreflective cultural determinations (would it not be conceivable to have a society quite similar to ours, except that brothels are accepted, whereas restaurants would have something disreputable about them?). What we can take from such reflections is that for an understanding of the co-evolution of the economic process and the social exterior, in which labour power in particular is reproduced, the concept of labour is indeed fundamental, but at the same time – as Susan Himmelweit and Simon Mohun point out – labour is not synonymous with wage labour (see Box 3.2). The labour character of domestic work is merely concealed by the fact that it is not remunerated. This expansion of the category of labour represents a fundamental deviation from neoclassical theory, which only recognises labour valued in monetary terms (Himmelweit and Mohun 1977). The expanded concept of labour, however, makes it possible to grasp important aspects of the social exterior in terms of its interaction with the interior. The family is

---

BOX 3.2 FOR LOVE OR FOR MONEY?

Or: Is the reproduction of the species – procreation, education, care – labour?

No wage labour:	*But labour:*
– No commodity production for the market, no wage	– Effort, expenditure of energy (opportunity costs)
– Emotional engagement	– Purposefulness
– Low standardisation of work processes, no internal division of labour	– External compulsion

---

not only a place of distribution of goods, but also of production proper (Gintis and Bowles 1981, pp. 9 ff.; Folbre 1982; Folbre 2012).

For building a new theory, the expansion of the category of labour represents an important step. However, the second step, the actual monetisation or valuation in monetary terms, represents a stage of its own, different from the first, which also brings its own problems, so that the meaning of monetisation in economic analyses must be examined precisely with regard to the actual purposes of the analysis (cf. Schäfer 2004). The pitfalls of giving a monetary value to unpaid work may be illustrated by two distinct methods. According to a first method, an unpaid service is valued according to a paid equivalent service. Nancy Folbre has shown that services are difficult to standardise and therefore resist commodification (Folbre 2008). She sees an indication of this in the fact that care costs rise faster than average consumer spending, which may have to do with the fact that it is more difficult to increase efficiency in this sector. Of course, if unpaid work is not easily commodified, this also means that measuring the value added through its commodified equivalent is problematic. There is no 'perfect substitutability' (Folbre and Nelson 2000, p. 129).

A second – and equally problematic – method is the attempt to calculate opportunity costs (BFS 2004, p. 24 f.). Opportunity costs refer to the revenues that the market actor has lost as a result of a certain choice. They thus represent a means of analysis at the microeconomic level. The opportunity cost of unpaid work is the income lost by foregoing waged work. The irony in applying this to the problem of domestic work is that women earn lower wages anyway. Their "foregoing" an occupation therefore appears rational, since the opportunity costs involved for women are correspondingly lower than for men. Conversely, if this method is applied to the valuation of domestic work, it is systematically valued lower because it is done by women.

Of course, we already have the conceptual tools to untie this knot. The analysis and argumentation using opportunity costs starts at the micro level, whereas gender inequality as a socio-historical boundary condition is to be located at the macro level. However, as long as the analysis of the individual actor is tied to the promise, referred to as 'microfoundation', of being able to decipher the entire economic process in this way, the theory must remain blind to these social realities (see Folbre 1982, p. 324 f.; Hirway 2015).

We have seen the consequences of this: at the macro level, one half of economic reality is simply ignored, namely 96 billion hours of unpaid work, which, remember, in Germany in 2001 contrasted with 56 billion hours of paid work. On the micro level, for its part, by ignoring structural conditions, actions must appear as "rational choices" that only perpetuate inequality. Paradigmatically, this can be seen in the debate on the legal status of prostitution, to take up this example again. Proponents of legalisation – for instance, Amnesty International in a recent controversial resolution – emphasise the difference between forced and voluntary prostitution, calling for the "decriminalising of all aspects of consensual sex work" (Amnesty International 2015), but without ever raising the question of the structural conditions under which the "voluntary" choice of such work occurs. In order to avoid the internal conflict of values (romantic love versus love work), a criterion of voluntariness is emphatically applied here at the individual level, while ironically it is taboo to say that – viewed at the societal level – wage labour is hardly ever voluntarily undertaken.

3.3.3 A commodity world?

The monetisation of unpaid work is sometimes viewed critically, even by heterodox economists, because it is suspected of encouraging its commodification and a neoliberal market ideology. Which leads us to the wider issue of the commodification of reproduction, which in a sense puts monetisation into practice. Let us keep in mind that this commodification in education, the household, childcare, care for the elderly, sexuality, etc., has been going on for a long time, the upper classes with their servants, private tutors and nannies playing a vanguard role. Two questions come to mind: is a universal commodification of reproduction conceivable, and would it be desirable?

In other words, is it conceivable – in purely theoretical terms – that reproductive labour takes place wholly in commodity form and that a society transforms all its relations into those between market actors? Can the market principle be generalised as the sole organising principle of a society?

Here, we touch again on the question of whether the market *depends* on its external space in an essential way. So far, we have only seen that the economic process in the narrow sense and the external space cannot *de facto* be considered or understood separately but are engaged in a mutual influence and co-evolution. Can it be argued further that there is a fundamental *interdependence*? That, for example, the economic process must collapse if it were ever to fully assimilate the external space?

The economist Marilyn Waring, for example, an influential writer from the founding generation of feminist economics and former MP for New Zealand's conservative National Party, claims: "Unpaid work makes all the rest of work. The market wouldn't survive if it wasn't able to survive on the backbone of unpaid work" (in Zerbisias 2010). It goes without saying that the market cannot exist without the reproduction of labour power (Figure 3.4). But is it really impossible that this reproduction be wholly assimilated by the market and take place according to market laws? Karl Polanyi certainly held this opinion in 1944:

> To allow the market mechanism to be sole director of the fate of human beings and their natural environment indeed, even of the amount and use of purchasing power, would result in the demolition of society.
>
> *(Polanyi [1944] 2001, p. 76)*

Polanyi, of course, based this diagnosis solely on the "essence" of the commodity, the idea that only things produced for the market could be traded in the market, and thus what he called the "fictitious commodities" of land, labour and money resisted commodification. The New York philosopher Nancy Fraser tries to adapt Polanyi's approach in such a way that its ahistorical definition of essence is replaced by a structural analysis of historical conditions. In doing so, she takes up an idea of Hegel's, according to which every contract also presupposes

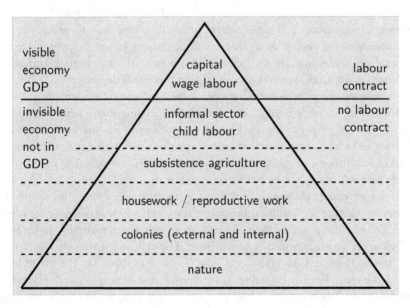

FIGURE 3.4 The iceberg model of paid and unpaid work, after Mies and Bennholdt-Thomsen (2000, p. 31).

social relations that cannot themselves be regulated contractually. She concludes that the market cannot subject the conditions of its possibility to its own law. Attempts to fully commodify labour, land and money are "conceptually incoherent and inherently self-undermining" (Fraser 2014, p. 548). "Society cannot be commodity all the way down", the philosopher concludes.

Conceptually incoherent, of course, is also the emergence of chickens from eggs that must themselves have been laid by chickens. What the philosopher rules out logically, the biologist must explain in evolutionary terms, because chickens exist despite all logic. Transcendental arguments on the part of philosophers should therefore be treated with caution. We will see in the final chapter that Polanyi's and Fraser's ideas, if embedded in a macroeconomic structural analysis, can certainly form the core of a theory of crisis (↓ 5.3). For the moment, however, we should look at things more matter-of-factly and assume, with the British economist John Harrison, that it could also be a *practical* question, one shaped by interests, which organisational form a society gives to its metabolism. Whether a society commits itself entirely to the market principle or, as is currently the case, allows two forms of production to coexist, can, for example, simply be a question of efficiency and depend on the respective productivity in the different sectors (Harrison 1973, p. 51). What is important for an understanding of the economic process is first of all that we are dealing with *two* (or more) coexisting and co-evolving forms of production, and that both are in fact forms of *production*, i.e. that work is done in both.

Harrison's analysis leads us to the second question, namely whether, assuming it is possible, commodification is actually *desirable*. As an ethical question, this may be less clear-cut than it first seems. After all, the external space beyond the market – institutions such as the family, political parties, the university, etc. – is no social paradise (either in its traditional or current forms) but obeys organisational principles that are no less morally problematic than market principles: hierarchies, patriarchal structures, feudal relationships of dependence. This is one of the reasons why the tension between 'cynicism' and 'sentimentalism' in the discussion of methods cannot easily be resolved: while many heterodox economists are again openly thinking about alternatives to the market economy in the face of today's multi-systemic crisis, capitalism can at least still offer to non-market institutions its old promise of emancipation: a wage that is measured solely by one's effort, not by one's origin or status.

If we ultimately do not understand it as an ethical question, but simply ask ourselves whether the commodification of the social sphere is desirable for someone, i.e. whether it serves their interest, then the answer naturally depends on which actor we are specifically considering. The principal actors are the capitalists, the workers and the consumers, and for none of them can the question be decided *a priori*. For the capitalist, as Harrison has shown, it depends essentially on the labour productivity in the two sectors whether, traditionally speaking, only the man is hired and receives a wage that feeds the whole family, or whether the market should also extend to domestic labour. For women – the majority of whom are affected – the result of the commodification that has already taken place is already a mixed one: the professions that have emerged in the tertiary sector are poorly paid, so that working there is less an emancipation from family duties than an additional burden. Where the additional income is enough to have household chores taken over by domestic servants, transnational chains of care services often emerge, with foreign domestic servants themselves leaving gaps in their home communities that are filled by a further set of migrant workers from yet poorer countries (Fraser 2014, p. 551). Finally, as far as the consumer is concerned, the question is to what extent the good is affected by its commodification. But of course, we must not simply contrast a cash-based and anonymous service with loving care, as both are misleading clichés. In fact, reproductive work, whether commodified or not, must always be considered in its social reality, where payment does not exclude genuine care any more than the family framework guarantees it, since there too it takes place in a structure of social norms, expectations and power relations. (See Folbre and Weisskopf (1998) on this. See also Zelizer (2005) on the ambiguities of monetary transactions, which in the empirical reality of people's lives cannot be limited to an economic sphere, but cross the border into the sphere of intimacy in complicated forms.)

If we think back to the original intentions of feminist economics, we find here again the structure of the double bind, which Radin has highlighted as a general feature of commodification (↑ 3.2.2): the theoretical translation of the value of unpaid work into economic value, like the practical process of commodification itself, may well lead to an improvement in the status of unpaid workers, since their performance is now economically visible. At the same time, however, it is not certain whether the actual value of their work is captured – and whether, in the case of actual commodification, it will be preserved.

4

THE ECONOMY IN A FINITE WORLD

Ecological economics

In this chapter, we turn to the 'natural' exterior of the economic process, in short, to nature or the environment. The scientific study of this aspect of the external space has already become quite well established under the title of ecological economics, perhaps also under pressure from the ecological crisis, which drastically demonstrates the dependency of the economic process. The original conundrum of ecological economics is that in economic analysis, reality is viewed solely through the lens of value. In this view, the economy presents itself as a cycle (Baumgärtner, Faber and Schiller 2006, p. 48): the producer supplies consumer goods and services and purchases labour, and since every movement of goods in the market is associated with a countervailing monetary payment, this cycle of goods corresponds to a countervailing monetary cycle. This picture ignores the fact that the supposed cycle of economic values involves a uni-directional throughput of material, energy and entropy: an inflow of resources into the economic process and an outflow of emissions and waste from the economic process.

Looking at the question of growth, we first consider the interdependence of the economy and the ecosystem (Section 4.1), and then discuss the two obvious ways of addressing the boundary between the economy and the ecosystem: from "inside to outside" through the monetary valuation of the ecosystem (Section 4.2), or from "outside to inside" through the description of economic production in natural-scientific terms (Section 4.3).

4.1 Growth

Discussion about the economy and nature is dominated by the concept of growth. We turn to this first, on the basis of the following four questions. What historical phenomenon are we really dealing with? What is actually growing in growth and how is it measured? What drives growth? Are there limits to growth?

DOI: 10.4324/9781003204077-5

It should be noted at the outset that growth *per se* is not an ecological problem, as can easily be shown. A sustainable society that ideally maintains its environmental integrity has a margin of growth (although sustainability will be more difficult to achieve as size increases). By contrast, a society that alters its environment unfavourably, typically by extracting finite raw materials, overexploiting renewable resources and emitting toxic waste, will deprive itself of its livelihood in the long run even if it does not grow. The decisive factor, therefore, is not growth itself, but rather the economy and the relative size of society in relation to the ecosystem, or more precisely to its regenerative capacities. Herman Daly uses the term *scale* to express this (Daly 1992).

This does not improve the situation for our society, however, which operates unsustainably *while* growing – the most unfavourable combination of both parameters.

4.1.1 Historical experiences of growth

Growth and the increase in material prosperity have been a defining experience for Europe since the Industrial Revolution (see Table 4.1). The average growth rate between 1700 and 2012, resulting from a growing population and increasing productivity of each individual, was 1.6%. This may seem low, but it means that total production may well double within a person's lifetime. European countries even saw much higher growth rates of 4% in the years after the Second World War. Thomas Piketty emphasises that this is a historical exception, explained by the regional catch-up process with the USA. Countries at the "technological frontier" can barely sustain growth above 1.5% over longer periods of time (Piketty 2014, p. 93). But this historical exception has also been formative for a generation and has strongly influenced expectations of what constitutes normal development.

One may speculate whether a generational break is currently taking place with regard to such formative experiences. If Piketty, born in 1971, never tires of emphasising the singular character of the so-called 'baby boomers' of post-war

TABLE 4.1 Global growth (average annual growth rate) before and since the Industrial Revolution

	Growth (%)		
	Global production	World population	Per capita production
0–1700	0.1	0.1	0.0
1700–2012	1.6	0.8	0.8
1700–1820	0.5	0.4	0.1
1820–1913	1.5	0.6	0.9
1913–2012	3.0	1.4	1.6

Source: Piketty (2014, p. 73).

cohorts, then it also reveals what is unique about today's younger generations, who feel that they are unlikely to repeat the success story of the older generation, and may even have to prepare themselves for enormous setbacks (Steuerle et al. 2013). This "Generation X" already seems to be less successful in accumulating wealth than their parents, which is also due to the growing social inequality that allows fewer and fewer people to participate in what little growth still exists. In addition, this generation is confronted with ever more noticeable "externalities", i.e. the negative (ecological) consequences of the patterns of consumption of previous generations. This shift in the formative basic experience of the generations now leads to the fact that the costs of this once steady and taken-for-granted flow of wealth are now being questioned (Figures 4.1 and 4.2).

4.1.2 What is growth?

So far, we have not said exactly what growth actually is. A number of misconceptions surround the concept. They can be summed up in the following equation:

Growth of the economy

  = Growth of GDP

    = Growth of material wealth

      = Growth of well-being

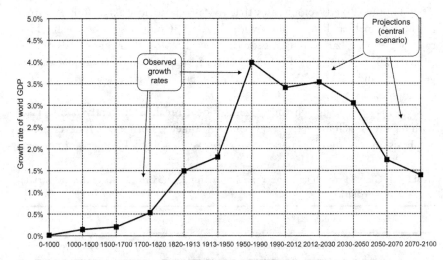

FIGURE 4.1   Growth rate of global output from ancient times to the year 2100. The future decline is mainly due to the slowdown in population growth projected by the UN (UN, *World Population Prospects: The 2010 Revision, 2011*). Growth is slowing, but remains. Piketty describes this as a return to historical normality, but he does not consider ecological limits to growth.

Source: Piketty (2014, p. 101).

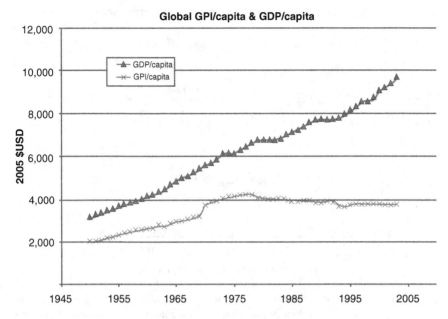

FIGURE 4.2 A different generational experience: while global production measured in gross domestic products is steadily increasing (light grey curve), the alternative *Genuine Progress Indicator* shows a different development (dark grey line). Taking into account damage to the biosphere (resource consumption, environmental damage) and to society (crime, disintegration of social structures), the result is a gradual decline in societal prosperity since around 1978.

Source: Kubiszewski et al. (2013, p. 63).

The first equation is meant as a measure: economic growth is measured or indicated by growth in gross domestic product (GDP). The second two equations are intended as logical or causal relationships: growth in GDP means increase in material wealth and this leads to higher levels of well-being. Each of these equations is problematic in its own right. We can see this by going through them in reverse order.

The fact that growth in material wealth is not synonymous with an increase in (subjectively estimated) contentment was first demonstrated empirically by Richard A. Easterlin in 1974. Recall that we saw in Chapter 2 that the structures of needs underlying these statements do not form unchanging benchmarks; strictly speaking, the expressions of contentment indicate the extent to which a society satisfies needs that it itself has helped to shape (Easterlin 1974, reiterated in Easterlin et al. 2010). Admittedly, Easterlin confirmed in an international study that within each of the countries studied, more individuals described themselves as content as their income rose. When he compared countries with each other, however, there was no correlation with per capita domestic product (Figure 4.3).

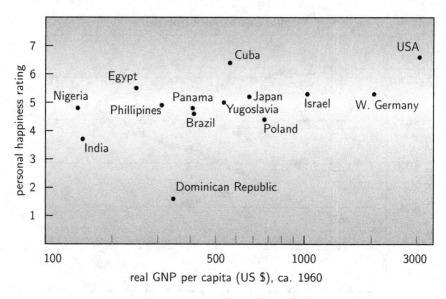

FIGURE 4.3   Is more really better? The average assessment of personal contentment in each country does not correlate with the level of per capita gross domestic product (after Easterlin 1974, p. 106).

This result suggests that *relative* income rather than absolute standard of living is decisive for contentment. Easterlin found a behaviour already described by Marx:

> A house may be large or small; as long as the neighboring houses are likewise small, it satisfies all social requirement for a residence. But let there arise next to the little house a palace, and the little house shrinks to a hut."
>
> *(Marx [1849] 1977, p. 219)*

Ironically, when everyone sets out to improve their situation, no one improves, because the ratios between top and bottom are maintained. In today's behavioural economics, one speaks of a "treadmill effect" (see Binswanger 2006). In a recent paper on the question of happiness, Kahneman and Angus Deaton point out that a certain level of income correlates with a positive attitude towards life, but not with emotional well-being (Kahneman and Deaton 2010).

It is interesting to note in this context that Easterlin's findings, which are in harmony with everyday psychology or folk wisdom, are referred to by economists as a paradox, the "Easterlin Paradox". The term "paradox", of course, does not simply denote an unexpected result, but is reserved for the case in which, at least *prima facie*, there is a logical contradiction. In fact, it is a basic assumption, an *axiom* in the model of *homo œconomicus*, that "more" is always "better". For a representative of neoclassical economics, the essentially banal finding must therefore really present itself as a paradox.

The error in the second equation – GDP = material wealth – lies in the very definition of GDP and related measures. These do not take into account the use-related depreciation of capital in the classical sense (roads, factories, etc.), nor the depletion of "natural capital", i.e. naturally renewable or finite resources. Moreover, legacy costs of environmental damage appear on the positive side of the balance sheet (Daly 2005). One thinks, for example, of the clean-up work at the devastated Japanese nuclear plant at Fukushima, which will continue for decades. These legacy costs of nuclear energy use are not seen as tying up funds (money, resources and manpower) that would otherwise have been socially available for other purposes, but as a positive factor in a country's economic activity and prosperity. The per capita wealth of a society can actually decrease while the per capita GDP increases (as happened in the Indian subcontinent and in Africa during the second half of the 20th century).

This leads us to the definition of GDP, the magic quantity of politics and economics, which today is increasingly competing with indicators that take into account factors such as unpaid work, the state of the ecosystem, or subjective well-being (e.g. *Ecological Footprint*, *Happy Planet Index* or *Genuine Progress Indicator*, ↑ 4.1.1, Figure 4.2). It is noteworthy in this context that the creator of Gross National Income, the Russian-born American economist Simon Kuznets (1901–1985), stated at the outset the limits of the productivity measure he proposed:

> [When income measurements are interpreted from the point of view of economic welfare,] additional difficulties will be suggested to anyone who wants to penetrate below the surface of total figures and market values. Economic welfare cannot be adequately measured unless the personal distribution of income is known. And no income measurement undertakes to estimate the reverse side of income, that is, the intensity and unpleasantness of effort going into the earning of income. The welfare of a nation can, therefore, scarcely be inferred from a measurement of national income as defined above.
>
> *(Kuznets 1934, p. 6 f.)*

Even Charles Dickens mocked the "addled heads", "who would take the average of cold in the Crimea during twelve months, as a reason for clothing a soldier in nankeen on a night when he would be frozen to death in fur" (in Knight 1865, p. 188). In his novel *Hard Times* – a reckoning with utilitarianism and economics – he aptly compares economic statistics to an "astronomical observatory [...] without any windows" (Dickens 1854, p. 120).

Dickens' comparison is no exaggeration. In fact, the definition of GDP has other problems, which mean that not even the first equation is correct: growth's impact on the environment, for example, is not measured by GDP. From an environmental standpoint, resource consumption and more generally the pressure on the ecosystem is of primary interest. GDP, as the sum of the market value of goods and services produced in a year, merely adds up prices. In particular, it does not distinguish between purely quantitative growth and qualitative technological development. The latter may improve the quality of goods and services without a corresponding increase in resource consumption. It is therefore seen by some as an alternative to the 'degrowth' strategy in the pursuit of sustainability. The concept of a 'Green New Deal' discussed by the United Nations Environment Programme (UNEP) is also based on the idea that growing economic activity can be combined with positive environmental effects. In summary, it can be stated that – at least theoretically – an increase in GDP can be accompanied by a loss of value but also does not have to result in increased ecological pressure, which severely limits the informative value of this indicator.

4.1.3 Conditions and causes of growth

The question of the causes of growth can have two meanings, and both are relevant. First, what are the enabling conditions of growth or what feeds growth? Second, is there a structural imperative for growth?

Both questions go beyond the scope of neoclassical growth theory. This is simply because these theories, contrary to their name, do not aim to explain growth but assume it as an exogenous given and then examine the effects on the variables relevant in production theory. Neoclassical growth theory is thus at root simply a dynamised theory of production, as we have already encountered (↑ 1.2.6), which itself was not a theory of production but an application of market theory to firms (Gowdy 2010, p. 38). Robert Solow, who developed the approach that is still authoritative today, takes the production function $Y = F(C, L)$ with capital C and labour L as the relevant factors of production as his starting point. Starting from an increase in labour power due to an exogenous population growth $L(t)$, he can then discuss the questions of how, for example, the savings rate should be chosen in order to avoid unemployment or labour shortages, or which market behaviour leads to a so-called growth equilibrium in which production and capital stock per capita remain constant (Solow 1956, p. 78). Solow seeks to account for the model's deviations from the empirical growth rate through another exogenous factor, technological progress, which is added to the production function as a scale factor $A(t)$:

$$Y = A(t) \cdot F(C, L(t))$$

When asked about the causes of population growth and technological progress, economists simply refer to the other social sciences that deal with cultural and institutional backgrounds (Acemoglu 2009, p. 20).

Of course, our aim cannot be to uncover the 'ultimate' causes of growth. Rather, the goal must be to go back far enough to address the dependence of the economic process on the natural external space. A step in the right direction towards a more comprehensive theory of growth would be to include technological progress, at least in part, as an endogenous factor in the theory and to understand it as the result of rational investment decisions (see Romer 1990; Solow 1994). But even if we take such an approach, the material basis of growth is omitted. Production is assumed to take place solely through capital and labour (which can to a certain extent replace each other), but without the resources of material and energy. The decisive step is only taken by Robert Ayres and Benjamin Warr, who name energy input as a factor of production (Ayres and Warr 2005). More precisely, they include a variable they call "exergy services". This term refers to the usable energy content of the resource input multiplied by a factor that takes into account the technically possible exploitation of this energy. While in the standard models falling energy prices appeared solely as a consequence of growth, in this model, they also play the role of a *cause* of growth. Rising energy consumption even turns out to be quantitatively the most important factor of growth compared to capital and labour.

This answers the first question about the enabling conditions of growth: the breathtaking growth of the capitalist economies since the Industrial Revolution owes much to the newly developed energy sources, above all fossil hydrocarbons (coal, oil, natural gas). But energy has proven to be a double-edged sword in human history: the technical development of energy has always expanded humankind's "ecological niche", which it could then fill with a process of economic growth, but which was always accompanied by a "redistribution" to the detriment of the ecosystem (Figure 4.4). At the same time, humanity is becoming increasingly dependent upon energy sources (Hall et al. 2003; Trauger et al. 2003; Czech et al. 2005). We will come back to this.

To the second question of whether there is a growth imperative, i.e. what makes a society, for example, choose a course of growth afforded by energy resources or actively seek it through research, three different types of answers are conceivable, which cannot always be sharply demarcated (Figure 4.5). Within the framework of *homo œconomicus*, an anthropological rationale is conceivable: the economy grows because people by their nature always strive for more. We saw in Chapter 1 that we should distrust such an explanation, since the model of *homo œconomicus* makes human nature out of what may in fact be historical systemic constraints. A second explanation could point to political or cultural factors and seek to understand growth as a kind of political agenda. The economy grows because society has chosen to do so (informally or formally, e.g., through political choice), and growth may be seen as valuable in itself or as a means to an end. Third, it could be argued that there is a structural compulsion for growth inherent in capitalism such that a lack of growth would lead to crisis. Hypotheses 1 and 3 have in common that they assume structural causes. In these cases, one can justifiably speak of a growth imperative. Hypotheses 2 and 3 share the assumption that the cause of growth can be permanently remedied (according to the first hypothesis, the human urge to grow would have to be permanently kept in check by social institutions). Hypotheses 1 and 2 agree that growth is at least independent of the capitalist organisation of the economy.

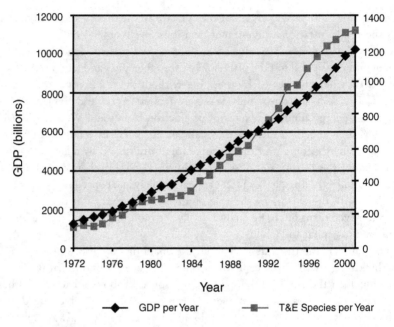

FIGURE 4.4 Redistribution of resources from nature to humans. The development of the USA's GDP correlates with the number of endangered species in the country.

Source: The Wildlife Society (2003, p. 13).

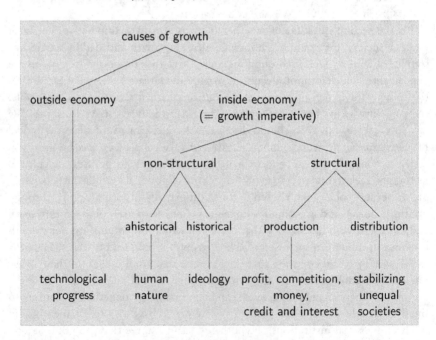

FIGURE 4.5 Potential causes of a growth imperative.

The question of what drives growth is of course a topic of discussion in ecological economics and in the degrowth movement, because of its practical implications. The answer one comes to will determine how great are the societal changes one deems necessary to achieve a sustainable economy. Is it possible to simply switch to renewable energies without making drastic changes in our way of life, or does the ecological crisis challenge our society at its organisational foundations?

Many authors from completely different camps assume that there is a real growth imperative in our society, which immediately gives the discussion a more dramatic colour. Classic candidates for structural growth imperatives are profit, on which our economic system is based, and interest, the mechanism of which underpins the credit system. If one wants to generate more and more, does the economy not in fact have to grow? And does this not apply all the more when companies operate on credit and the debt has to be repaid with interest? The former argument is often used by authors who follow Marxian analysis, but it can also be found far beyond these circles. A prominent example is the British economist Tim Jackson, who states in his well-known study for the *Sustainable Development Commission*: "Growth is necessary within this system just to prevent collapse" (Jackson 2009, p. 8). The interest rate argument is put forward, for example, by the Canadian political scientist Thomas Homer-Dixon, and in the German-speaking world is primarily associated with the Swiss economists Hans Christoph Binswanger and Mathias Binswanger (Binswanger 2009, 2013; Homer-Dixon 2011).

The thesis of a real (structural) growth imperative requires good arguments and is open to doubt. Profit does not imply growth if profit in rentier capitalism is simply eaten up by the capitalist. Under competitive pressure, there may be a compulsion to increase productivity, but only microeconomically, at the level of the individual firm (Gordon and Rosenthal 2003). This does not necessarily result in overall economic growth, since competition can also take the form of a distribution struggle over a constant sum. The interest rate argument is likewise the subject of controversy (Wenzlaff, Kimmich and Richters 2014; Strunz, Bartowski and Schindler 2015). However, the thesis of a growth imperative remains meaningful even in weaker form. Massimo De Angelis, for example, argues that the imperative does not arise directly from the conditions of stability of the economic process itself, but rather indirectly from the conditions of social acceptance of its social consequences, especially inequality: if things improve for everyone, inequality is more readily accepted (De Angelis 2013, p. 605).

4.1.4 Limits of growth

Growth in economic production is still a historical reality, as is the fact that this growth is *de facto* bound up with growing consumption of resources and emissions of pollutants, even though many economists expected a decoupling of these trends (Stern 2004; Jackson 2009, p. 52; Krausmann et al. 2015). As an expression of the finite nature of the resources humanity has to cope with, the American economist Kenneth Boulding coined the image of "Spaceship Earth" in a classic text of the American environmental movement, contrasting it with an older image of the "illimitable plains" of ever greater expansion (Boulding 1966, p. 9). The fact that the sheer scale of the economic process in relation to the capacities of the ecosystem has reached a critical point is something that various current theories are attempting to convey. The proposal to introduce the "Anthropocene" as a new geological epoch is well known (Crutzen 2002; Lewis and Maslin 2015), though the exact beginning point of this epoch is disputed (Ruddiman et al. 2015). The ecologist Robert O'Neill and the economist James Kahn speak in the same vein of humanity as a "keystone species" that controls its environment and determines which other species can survive in its presence (O'Neill and Kahn 2000). Against a background of worries about peak oil and a rapid decline in the rate of production, the American publicist Richard Heinberg has spoken of "peak everything" as an indication of what may be in store for humanity (Heinberg 2007).

If economists do not react to the alarming situation, this may simply be due to ignorance and ideological stubbornness. In a meta-study, economists Lewis Duane Chapman and Neha Khanna demonstrated that, in five relevant categories of economic climate models, their colleagues consistently chose those assumptions that would lead to the conclusion that climate change was no urgent cause for economic change (Chapman and Khanna 2000). In the face of climate change, Chapman and Khanna conclude, the economists' guild is unflinchingly betting on just one of 32 possible combinations of values that can be said to have a good 3% chance of being the right one. This tangible form of ignorance, however, is irrelevant to philosophical analysis. Our concern here is with the blind spots already inscribed in economists' conceptual systems. In fact, it is usually pre-programmed at the theoretical level that ecological concerns simply do not appear in economic models: as we have seen, environmental damage is excluded from theorising as a so-called "externality", i.e. as negative consequences for third parties (Kapp 2016, pp. 130 and 162); the question of resource scarcity is obscured by the basic assumptions of technological progress and the substitutability of goods. Should a good become scarce, it is assumed that market mechanisms will persuade the consumer to switch to an alternative. ("Then let them eat pastry", famously replied the princess in a truly neoclassical manner on being informed that the countryfolk had no bread – Rousseau [1789] 1897, p. 145.) We turn now to two strategies to remedy this theoretical deficiency.

4.2 How much is the World?

4.2.1 Nature as commodity

'Monetisation' (monetary valuation) is the valuation in terms of price of the 'natural capital' or 'services' provided by ecosystems and can be used as an instrument of economic theorising, policy-making and policy advice by economists (Box 4.1). The debate around this method is very similar to the debate around the economic valuation of unpaid labour which we saw in Chapter 3 (↑ esp. 3.3.2):

1   The practical aim of monetisation is to clarify our dependence on nature and to make its 'value' visible by translating it into monetary terms. This is the '*mise en valeur*', or valorisation, which Wallerstein referred to (↑ 3.1.2). To this end, nature is conceptualised as a tradable commodity.

2   The *critique* of this is not far behind. The extension of economic vocabulary to the extra-economic sphere (*economism, economic imperialism*), in this case nature, is illegitimate. It is wrong to speak of "natural capital" or "ecosystem services", just as it is questionable whether unpaid labour is labour at all in the precise sense (↑ 3.3.2). Various reasons are given for this: *principled* reasons, according to which monetisation contradicts the non-economic nature of the object in question; *ethical* reasons, according to which monetisation has ethically problematic consequences in dealing with nature; and *practical* reasons, according to which quantification or economic measurement of value cannot actually be implemented (these reasons may also be principled). Of course, the criticism of monetisation is also driven by the fear that the theoretical expansion of economics prepares the way for the practical expansion of the economy and the real subjugation of nature to the market. Market instruments of climate protection such as emissions trading can be seen as instances of this.

BOX 4.1 MONETISATION OF NON-MARKET GOODS

Step 1: Economic framing:

Sociosphere	Ecosphere
↓	↓
'unpaid work', 'social capital'	'ecosystem services', 'natural capital'
↓	↓
price	price

Step 2: Monetary evaluation:

wage based evaluation of time inputs: replacement costs, opportunity costs; value of outputs: market value of similar goods and services	cost based approaches: opportunity costs, replacement costs, replacement costs / clean-up costs; Valuation by consumers: directly, through ›stated preferences‹ in contingent valuation surveys, or indirectly, through ›revealed preferences‹: market prices, travel costs, etc.

(Statistics Canada 1995; Department for Environment, Food and Rural Affairs 2007)

3   These reservations are often answered with a dilemma: either one accepts the language of money in spite of all one's misgivings, or one refuses and remains unheard (as analysed by Harvey 1996, p. 156; prominent example: Costanza et al. 1997, p. 253).

4.2.2 Ecological factors in cost-benefit analyses

The monetary valuation of social services takes place, remember, through their hypothetical replacement by paid services: i.e. what would we have to pay if we were to transform all social relations into those between service providers and clients? The monetisation of ecosystem services proceeds in a similar way, as we will see in a moment. Problems still arise even when major concessions are made, however, which is why we may allow ourselves to consider them here without extensive discussion. Thus, in the following we always consider the 'value of nature' as a 'value for humans' and leave aside the 'sentimentalist' question of whether nature also has a value 'in itself' (for such a position see McCauley 2006 or Foster, Barrett and York 2009, p. 1091). Furthermore, we focus from the outset on economic value and leave aside questions of the cultural, aesthetic or spiritual value of nature for humans. And finally, we focus solely on the current balance sheet and so leave aside the question of the future and the value for future generations (the so-called 'discount rate problem').

We first consider in this section the more cautious attempts to include ecological factors in cost-benefit analyses, in order to turn in the following section to the more audacious attempt to quantify the value of the ecosystem. The starting point for monetisation comes from the orthodox arsenal of economic concepts:

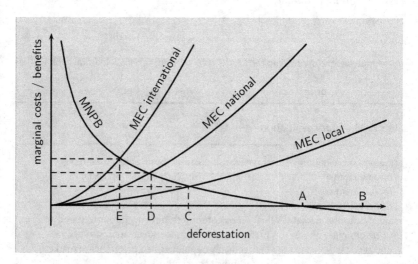

FIGURE 4.6 Cost-benefit analysis of deforestation for the creation of agricultural land: private net marginal benefit (PNMB) and external marginal costs (EMC) at local, national and international levels (after Daly and Farley 2011, p. 469).

marginal benefits and marginal costs (↑ 1.2.3). Figure 4.6 shows a simple example from the textbook of ecological economics by Herman Daly and Joshua Farley: an analysis of the clearing of tropical rainforest in Australia to create agricultural land. The marginal benefit of the initial clearances is 'infinite' (unquantifiable), since the farmer ensures his survival through them. Meanwhile, the (ecological) marginal costs of this minor intervention in the ecosystem are negligible. The marginal benefit of any further clearing then decreases, not least because the most suitable areas are cleared first. Ignorant of the ecological context, the farmer continues with forest clearance until the point where water and soil quality are affected and marginal utility even falls below zero, whereas the rational, utility-maximising farmer should have stopped at point A.

Next, we take the ecological costs into the picture. The ascending curves show these costs, including local, national and international consequences. While these consequences were left out of the neoclassical analysis as "externalities", they are now to be quantified and calculated. The consequences are manifold: the region's water supply, which is fed by the rainforests, suffers, the soil erodes, the rivers silt up, soil and nutrients are washed into the coral reefs off the coast, biodiversity decreases and the rainforest loses its climate-regulating function. In this case, the costs on which the economic analysis is based do not reflect the value of the ecosystem and its services, but only the economic losses resulting from its damage or – where possible – the expenditure necessary to repair the damage. Factoring in these costs (instead of covertly socialising them) shifts the amount of 'optimal' deforestation to the intersection of marginal benefits and marginal costs (C, D and E, respectively).

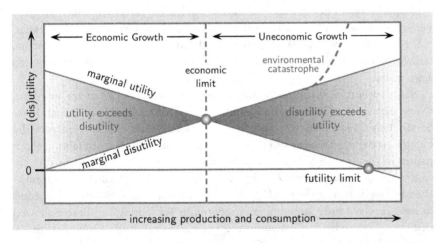

FIGURE 4.7 Bad growth: if the harm exceeds the benefit, growth is harmful. Marginal utility falls because elementary needs are satisfied first. Marginal damage increases because easy sacrifices are made first. At the point of intersection, total utility is at a maximum (after Daly 2005, p. 103).

The influential pioneer of ecological economics Herman Daly generalised this point in the concept of "uneconomic growth" (Figure 4.7). If disutility exceeds utility, any further increase in production will have a negative impact on the common good. (The harm is understood to be a subjective quantity that has not yet been translated into monetary terms.) In such a situation the economy produces not goods but more and more 'bads'.

The problem with these simple calculations, however, is that they obviously assume a uniform increase in the negative consequences of our interventions in the ecosystem. While this assumption is consistent with a good deal of our everyday experience, it cannot be generalised. Just think of the sudden collapse of a body of water, as has often been observed. This effect is the main concern of many ecologists, also with regard to the global ecosystem. There one has to be prepared for non-linear behaviour (Scheffer et al. 2001): an ecosystem's state may change gradually, but it may also change very dramatically after a long period of resistance, at a so-called 'tipping point'; finally, it may also shift suddenly to a completely different state of equilibrium. In the latter case, the consequences may be not only catastrophic but also irreversible. Such behaviour is inconceivable under the economic assumption of uniform marginal cost curves.

4.2.3 The value of the ecosystem

A group of scientists led by economist Robert Costanza went one step further. In a sensational article published in *Nature* in 1997, the researchers boldly estimated the "value of the ecosystem" at an average of 33 trillion US dollars, compared to a world GDP of 18 trillion at the time. For this purpose, Costanza's researchers identified 17 services ranging from climate regulation, water and food supply to "cultural" services (for aesthetic, spiritual or scientific purposes) which are provided by the various "biomes": open seas, coastal areas, forests, swamps, deserts, etc. For each individual service, they calculated a value per area of the biome, which then simply had to be extrapolated to the total areas of the biomes and aggregated.

Some authors have complained about the imprecision of Costanza's approach, whose method does indeed raise a number of difficulties (see Hueting et al. 1998; Serafy 1998). However, we can try to get to the heart of these problems by bluntly asking whether one can make rational decisions at all when talking about nature in the economic terms of value and price. This question stems directly from a critique of cost-benefit analysis as a guide to environmental policy formulated by the British economist David Pearce in 1976, which unfortunately seems to have received little attention (an exception is Richard 2012). Pearce showed that even if the individual economic actor (e.g. a manufacturing company) prices in the ecological consequences of its actions, the outcome will still be disastrous. The argument is very simple (Figure 4.8). If one formulates the problem in terms of cost-benefit analysis, it is 'rational' to increase production as long as the additional benefit is not outweighed by the additional harm. This means, however, that a certain amount of damage is accepted, i.e. the environment suffers. Even if the damage caused in each case is taken into account in the next round, a new 'optimum' is now calculated which again implies additional damage. The Pareto-optimal solution is "ecologically unstable", as Pearce soberly puts it (Pearce 1976, p. 106). Jacques Richard (Richard 2012, p. 75) speaks more dramatically (but not inappropriately) of an "infernal process" set in motion by the pursuit of the Pareto optimum: in the end, nature is ruined and production collapses.

Pearce's argument and the accompanying diagram seem technical. But they provide a lesson that is of philosophical significance. What does it mean to put a price tag on nature? The price is supposed to express the value of nature. But price is a double-edged sword. It expresses how much nature is worth to us – but also at what price we are willing to sell it. And this is exactly what happens in the determination of the Pareto optimum. A price is a selling price. Today, global wealth has grown to almost 400 trillion dollars. For the richest 1% of the world's population, which owns just under half of this wealth, the global ecosystem would be a real bargain (Credit Suisse Research Institute 2020, p. 23). Unfortunately for them – and this leads back to the theoretical core of the problem – ecosystems are not currently for sale (Box 4.2).

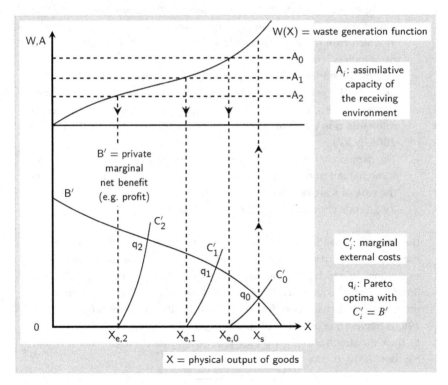

FIGURE 4.8 The metric of Pareto optimality gradually leads to environmental degradation and a decline in production (after Pearce 1976).

BOX 4.2 FUNDAMENTAL DIFFICULTIES IN THE MONETARY VALUATION OF NATURE

- *Complexity:* In a complex ecosystem that has evolved over long periods of time, individual elements (and thus their ecosystem services) may be impossible to fully identify and isolate from each other (Norgaard and Bode 1998; Vatn 2000, pp. 497 and 504).
- *Non-linearity:* The monetary metric is inherently linear (twice the quantity has twice the price), while ecosystems have tipping points and exhibit non-linear behaviour.
- *Non-substitutability:* Commodities, as economic values, are by definition exchangeable for equivalents. Monetary equivalents in ecosystems, however, are generally not functional equivalents. "In reality, natural wealth and human made capital are neither comparable nor interchangeable. If the soil is washed off the land, we cannot grow crops on a bed of derivatives" (Monbiot 2018).
- *Market-inalienability:* Prices are sale prices, and thus intrinsically refer to a market and the possibility of buying and selling. "[P]rice represents an expectation of payment, in accordance with market rates. In pricing a river, a landscape or an ecosystem, either you are lining it up for sale, in which case the exercise is sinister, or you are not, in which case it is meaningless" (Ibid.).
- *Holism:* Utilitarian valuation presupposes a means-ends relationship between the ecosphere as a provider of services and the human species as their consumer. "This reasoning ignores basic ecology: environments don't act for the benefit of any single species" (McCauley 2006, p. 27).
- *The human condition:* As a result of non-substitutability, we depend on some natural goods and these therefore have infinite marginal utility in the case of scarcity. Costanza's value is "a serious underestimate of infinity", as one critic mocked. (Toman 1998, p. 58).

Despite all these difficulties, economists continue to evaluate nature in monetary terms, for example, in the method of so-called 'contingent evaluation', in which prices are determined in public questionnaires (↑ 4.2.1, Box 4.1). The US courts have declared this method permissible, e.g., to measure ecological damage and determine compensation payments (Arrow et al. 1993). However, economists must be prepared for unsympathetic reactions to their questionnaires: "It's a totally disgusting idea!" (Clark, Burgess and Harrison 2000, p. 52).

4.3 Devil's dust

4.3.1 Economics as ecology

Let us turn to the second way of addressing the boundary between economy and nature, namely from the outside, in the vocabulary of physics, life sciences and ecology (in the sense of an empirical science of the interaction of organism and environment). From this perspective, the economic process appears as a (social) organism that exchanges material and energy with its environment. In this sense, Herman Daly suggested that we define economics as the sub-discipline of ecology that studies interactions *dominated by commodities* (Figure 4.9).

The ecologist Robert O'Neill and the economist James Kahn have attempted to work out what lies behind the traditional dichotomy between ecology and economics (O'Neill and Kahn 2000; in similar terms Moore 2015a, p. 47). According to the traditional paradigm of ecology, a pure ecosystem would be one *without* humans. The latter only ever enter the ecological model as an *external disturbance* (which is why traditional ecology actually only occupies the lower right-hand corner in the above table, but not the left-hand and upper adjacent fields). We have already had occasion to note how in the traditional, neoclassical paradigm of economics the economy is stylised into an autonomous process, its dependence on nature (resources) is forgotten and its influence on nature is sidelined as an *externality*. Economics is thus conceived as human action *without nature*.

O'Neill and Kahn, however, argue that such a separate investigation of two "pure" systems is only legitimate as an approach if the interactions *between* the two are orders of magnitude smaller than the respective processes *within* each – an assumption,

FIGURE 4.9 Input-output model of market and non-market interactions (after Daly 1968, p. 392).

however, that has arguably not been valid for centuries, as the discussion about the concept of the Anthropocene has strikingly demonstrated (one example: the genocide of indigenous populations perpetrated by Europeans arriving in the Americas and the resulting decline in agricultural activity already had an impact on atmospheric CO_2 levels that is still detectable today – cf. Lewis and Maslin 2015, p. 176).

O'Neill and Kahn's argument can be developed in an instructive way. The two authors discuss, in philosophical vocabulary, the identity conditions of "systems": when are we dealing with two interacting systems – and when with only one? The simplest case is when individuation is realised through spatial separation and geological barriers such as oceans or mountains. The ecosystems of North and South America or those north and south of the Alps can certainly be considered separately, at least as a first approximation. However, no such spatial separation exists between the economy and the ecosystem. The economic process takes place *in* nature. Nature and the economic process *interpenetrate* rather than simply *interact* with each other (Moore 2015a, p. 180). Talking about systems is therefore problematic from the outset and we would be better off talking about different *aspects* of *a single system*. This insight has a famous parallel in the history of philosophy. The British philosopher Gilbert Ryle, in his epoch-making book *The Concept of Mind* from 1949, pointed out that the mind and body, which ever since Descartes had been regarded as different substances, are actually two aspects of a single *person,* a personhood given to us in experience (Ryle 2009, p. 149).

So it may be a much more powerful intellectual framework from the European history of ideas that lay behind and supported the traditional separation of economy and ecology (on this dualism as a fundamental structural principle, see Sahlins 2008), namely the dualism of mind and body, which in its various manifestations structures our entire thinking: mind and body, culture and nature, divine spirit and animal flesh, content and form, truth and style – and finally money and matter, economy and ecology. The very term "ecological economics" must sound to the ears of orthodox economists like the "thinking matter" of the 18th-century materialists to the ears of the Cartesians!

The strand of ecological economics which seeks to view economics as a sub-area of ecology overcomes to some extent this dualism in a 'holistic' outlook. The depth of the break with tradition needed to achieve this perhaps explains why ecology's pioneers sometimes displayed a 'sentimentalist' tendency towards the esoteric and their holism was rhetorically exaggerated. In fact, however, ecological economics aims at an explanatory model that aims to let the interrelationships be truly, 'cynically' analysed. In particular, a holistic approach should not lead to a blurring of differences and relative autonomies. Above all, theories of cultural evolution, to which Daly referred as early as 1968 (although this field of research has only really been worked on recently – cf. e.g. Odling-Smee 2007), show that human culture provides independent mechanisms of transmission, which then interfere with the biological mechanisms of heredity. Human culture is thus grasped both in its connection with nature and in its specific difference and *relative autonomy.*

4.3.2 An anti-marginalist revolution?

Daly may have been aware that with his definition of the economy as a commodity-dominated part of the social metabolism he was basically proposing an anti-marginalist revolution that would abandon the subjective utility cornerstone of neoclassical theory and bring economics back close to the objective vocabulary of the classics Smith, Ricardo and Marx. In fact, ecological economics was presented as an alternative to orthodox economics in tandem with the critiques of neoclassicism (Chapter 2). John Gowdy and Jon Erickson offer a schematised overview that allows us to grasp the central differences (Box 4.3).

We already know almost all the elements of this overview. Only the question of how to deal with uncertainty about future developments in economic planning and decision-making has not yet been mentioned.

One speaks of "uncertainty" (following Knight 1921/1964, p. 19 f.; cf. Hodgson 2011) when not only the future course is unknown but also when no probabilities can be assigned to the scenarios to be decided upon. For a cost-benefit analysis, however, a *measurable* quantity is needed, which is why neoclassical analysis attempts to convert uncertainty into *risk*, where an underlying probability distribution is known or can be assumed. The concept of risk thus turns out to be a counterpart of the utilitarian concept of utility, through which neoclassical theory was able to control the moral diversity of a society by reducing value judgements to individual utility and translating this utility into commensurable amounts of money.

> By reducing threats to a common currency (usually mortality rates, dollars, or pounds) risk-benefit analysis permits actors with fundamentally incommensurable value commitments to make otherwise unfeasible trade-offs

BOX 4.3 A PARADIGM SHIFT IN ECONOMICS?

	Neoclassical Economics	Ecological Economics
Analytical framework:	Marginal utility, monetisation, cost-benefit analysis	e.g. complex adaptive system analysis
Systemic view:	Market & externalities	Dependency, co-evolution
Decision criteria:	efficiency	Equity, stability and resilience of environmental and social systems
Actor:	Homo economicus, consumers	Social actors, citizens
Uncertainty:	Reduction of uncertainty to risk	Precautionary principle
Production:	Allocation of resources	Production as a biophysical process

(with modifications from Gowdy and Erickson 2005, p. 213)

about priorities, goals, resources, and responsibilities. Thus, a discourse of
values is pushed aside by a discourse of valuation,

as the British social scientist Steve Rayner puts it. (Rayner 2007, p. 167, cf.
Rayner 2003, p. 166)

The proponents of ecological economics, of course, sense the hidden shift in
the underlying ethical premises from the *precautionary principle* to *risk management*:
while a risk (typically an investment) can actually be taken (after considering the
expected overall balance), this is illegitimate in the case of economic decisions
with uncertain ecological consequences.

At this point, we are no longer just discussing methods and empirical concepts, but are touching on an ethical question. An ethical-sentimentalist col-
ouring is sometimes given in ecological economics to the concept of the actor,
who is contrasted with the consumer, taken to be simply a *citoyen* (Gowdy and
Erickson 2005, p. 213). This is not without problems, though. While heterodox economists feel emboldened to make such ethical evaluations explicit on
the basis that neoclassical theory was itself implicitly evaluative (↑ 1.2.7), this
approach is not without a certain arbitrariness and, incidentally, also jeopardises
what is supposed to unite ecological economics and the critique of neoclassical
theory in a fundamentally different approach. Such a common critical approach
will be convincing only if it consists in a turn not at the level of values but at the
level of methods: the economic process is conceived as a biophysical process and
the actions of market actors are explained by structural determinants instead of
preferences (↑ 2.3).

4.3.3 Entropy

Attempts to describe economics in purely physical terms go back to the 19th
century (Martinez-Alier 1987) and we owe a number of interesting insights to
these endeavours (↓ Boxes 4.4 and 4.6). Perhaps the most momentous attempt
to make the objective vocabulary of the natural sciences fruitful for ecological
economics was the use of the thermodynamic concept of entropy as a general
framework for describing economic processes. This was undertaken in the 1970s
by the economist Nicholas Georgescu-Roegen, who came from Romania but
was mostly active in the USA.

The concept of entropy found its way into physics quite late, the word itself
being coined by Rudolf Clausius in the 1860s. Even for physicists, entropy as a
thermodynamic state variable remains something elusive. While it is no more
difficult to handle as a computational quantity than other quantities, it is rather
difficult to imagine exactly what kind of substance in nature it actually provides
information about. To understand Georgescu-Roegen's approach, one needs to
know a few elementary things about entropy and open systems (Box 4.5). The
tendency for entropy to increase, as demanded by the Second Law of Thermodynamics, contradicts the fact that we see nature creating order everywhere, from
star systems arranged into galaxies to organisms, and that we ourselves are also

BOX 4.4 INSIGHTS FROM THE ENERGETIC ANALYSIS OF ECONOMICS I: ENERGY RETURN ON INVESTMENT (EROI)

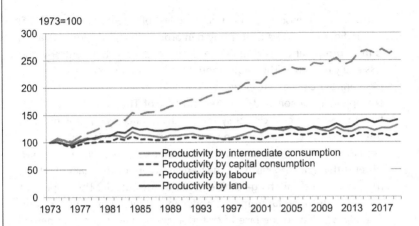

FIGURE 4.10   Productivity in agriculture over the 20th century.

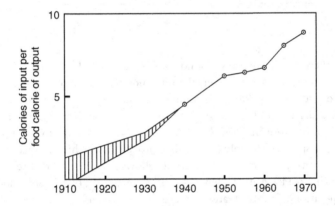

FIGURE 4.11   Energy-balance of agriculture over the 20th century.

In agriculture, productivity increased spectacularly over the 20th century – at least when measured in terms of yield per hectare or per worker (Figure 4.10, from Department for Environment, Food and Rural Affairs 2020). The EROI analysis (cf. Hall 2017) paints a very different picture: over the years, more and more calories have had to be invested – mainly in the form of petroleum products such as diesel, artificial fertilisers and pesticides – to produce one calorie of food (Figure 4.11, from Steinhart and Steinhart 1974). In its current report, the British government also considers energy merely as an economic factor – measured in money, not calories – and measures productivity only per hectare of land, per employee and capital input. Jason W. Moore (Moore 2015a, p. 86) sees this asymmetry of productivity measures as an indication of an ideology that only accepts humans as a source of value and systematically ignores nature.

BOX 4.5 FACT SHEET ENTROPY AND DISSIPATIVE STRUCTURES

- Entropy is a measure of the unavailability of energy (Kleidon 2016, p. 36). Energy must be concentrated in order to be used. Light radiation is low-entropy and easily utilisable, heat radiation is high-entropy and less easily utilisable. The huge amounts of heat in the oceans, for example, cannot be tapped to power a ship.
- Entropy is not a constant. The Second Law of Thermodynamics states that the entropy of a closed system is always increasing: It is heading towards a state of heat death in which no more energy is available.
- Structures (organisms, ecosystems, economies...) can only form as *open* systems that (like organisms in their environment or the planet Earth in the universe) can discharge their entropy to the outside. They represent *dissipative structures* far from thermodynamic equilibrium, which exhibit a *certain* stability in the face of disturbances in the system parameters. (Prigogine 1993).

---

constantly creating structures around us, from beautifully arranged bouquets of flowers to urban space. However, the tendency towards disorder asserts itself as soon as one considers the more comprehensive overall system: for every local order, disorder is paid for globally, at least to an equal degree (there is theoretically a limiting case in reversible processes, which are entropy-neutral) but in most cases disproportionately (irreversible processes, in which the accompanying increase in entropy precludes reversal). It follows in particular that technical devices in principle have an efficiency < 1. If, for example, one creates a local order in the operation of a refrigerator (by separating cold and heat against the natural tendency to mix and compensate each other), one will never use the electricity supplied completely efficiently, but will always create additional waste heat. This has enormous consequences for the ecological consideration of the economy.

In the work of Nicholas Georgescu-Roegen, one encounters an extremely bleak picture that conjures up the heat death of human life. According to him, even a steady-state economy without growth cannot exist indefinitely in a finite environment, but must inevitably bury itself in its entropy production, i.e. reach the limits of its environment in irreversible changes (Georgescu-Roegen 1975 p. 367). A differentiation can be indicated here. Georgescu-Roegen treats planet Earth as a *closed* system that exchanges neither energy nor matter with its environment, the universe. For matter, this may be approximately true. The situation is different for energy because the atmosphere allows a constant influx of sunlight to pass through. It is true that the Earth is in a radiation equilibrium and so gives back to the universe what energy it receives from the sun. But this exchange is linked to a negative net flow of entropy: the Earth receives the high-quality, low-entropy energy of sunlight, but gives off higher-entropy, non-usable thermal radiation, which constantly removes entropy from the ecosystem. This is the only way that a complex ecosystem has been able to develop on Earth. Georgescu-Roegen's judgement is therefore correct only for material resources. Even a steady-state economy cannot rely on finite resources, as these will eventually be used up. If, however, it is supplied by renewable sources, it may well generate entropy without having to fear heat death, since it can discard its entropy into space.

Applying the concept of entropy to the economic process is tempting but deceptive. Remember, the goal is to capture the dependence of societal metabolism on the surrounding ecosystem. The first approach to this was to monetise it, i.e. to describe the dependency 'from the inside out', namely in the original economic vocabulary of the interior. Of course, hardly anyone would fall for the idea of wanting to capture the entire external space in this vocabulary as well, i.e. to deliver a theory of nature in economic terms. This is not altered by the fact that the natural sciences and economics have often influenced each other and that economic analogies in the natural sciences have proved fruitful. But even if physics strives for an 'economy of nature' (as in the extremal principles), this remains an economy of physical quantities, but not of human wealth.

In the complementary 'outside to inside' approach, which describes the relationship of dependency in the vocabulary of the outside space, the situation is different. Every economic process is simultaneously a physical process in the literal sense. Could this insight provide the basis for a physical economic theory? The early applications of the concept of entropy in ecological economics sometimes aimed high, such as an entropic theory of value or at least an entropic measure of pollution as a term of the production function. But these ambitions visibly failed (for rather technical reasons, for which the reader is referred to the literature). What remained was again a purely qualitative and often even merely metaphorical framework to circumscribe dependence on the environment (Binswanger 1993, p. 227; Baumgärtner 1996, p. 134).

The most important merit of this framework is unquestionably the recognition of certain issues that had been excluded from neoclassical theory: (1) irreversible changes in the environment; (2) finite resources and limited substitutability of resources; and (3) limited efficiency in all activities and thus ubiquitous waste heat. Indeed, it is with entropy that the concept of *time* first enters economic theory, from which it had hitherto been completely absent. (We will take up this point in Chapter 5.)

An attempt to unite these aspects in a theory of production can be found in the approach of 'joint production' by Stefan Baumgärtner, Malte Faber and Johannes Schiller. While this term was originally applied to work processes that produced two goods – such as meat and leather in hunting – these authors reinterpret it to refer to the unavoidable co-production of (structured and therefore low-entropic) goods and high-entropic waste, such as waste heat, exhaust gases and dust (Figure 4.12). The theory of joint production does not bracket these out as externalities. It also admits that the co-production of "devil's dust" (after an expression from cotton processing, which Marx occasionally used for the "refuse of the labour process", Marx [1887] 1990, p. 178) is unavoidable according to the laws of thermodynamics.

Discussion of this model can be taken further, in an instructive way. One might ask whether the image of the co-production of goods and dust is not itself too optimistic. First, many products are only used for a short time and, measured against the rhythms of the ecosystem, quickly end up on the scrap heap. In effect, we are dealing with the co-production not of goods and unwanted by-products but *solely* of 'devil's dust', because the short time that the goods remain in human use before they are discarded as waste is insignificant from an ecological point of view. This diagnosis can even be generalised and extended to those goods that are not discarded but are preserved from wear and tear or decay for various – practical or cultural – reasons, such as infrastructure (transport routes, sewage systems, systems of units of measurement, etc.) or cultural heritage (paintings, buildings, etc.). Their preservation requires a permanent effort in the form of maintenance and protection, which, in turn, entails a permanent emission of unwanted by-products, as if the good were constantly being produced anew.

A second necessary correction to the image of joint production would be that the raw materials used are not necessarily present in high concentrations in the goods produced. Especially in modern electronic production, valuable raw materials are used only in extremely small quantities or in highly dispersed form or in alloys and composite materials. A laptop contains 30 different metals, 10 types of alloyed steel are used in cars and a superalloy used in aviation technology is made up of up to 15 different metals (Figure 4.13).

This statement brings the question of recycling into focus. Georgescu-Roegen transferred the Second Law of Thermodynamics to matter without further ado: like energy, matter is also subject to a constant process of depreciation, which is also irreversible. Georgescu-Roegen thus considered the complete recycling of materials or energy impossible for physical reasons. This "fourth law of thermodynamics" (Georgescu-Roegen 1986, p. 6) has been rejected as untenable in such a strict form (Bianciardi, Tiezzi and Ulgiati 1993). It is certainly true that recycling will in principle also produce undesirable by-products. But the problem with recycling is not of a fundamentally physical nature but has contingent practical roots: many rare raw materials are processed today in such a way – namely in very low concentrations or in the form of alloys and composite materials – that recycling is technically impossible without considerable further expenditure of energy. In addition to many products of the new technologies such as laptops and mobile phones, this applies to technologies for the generation of renewable energy themselves, such as the use of rare elements in wind turbines. The recycling problem may thus threaten to thwart the ecological energy transition, which is why some authors even see the future in a new "low-tech" (Bihouix 2011, 2013).

Both reservations about the theory of joint production, although not easily dismissed, have a catch, of course. If one consistently follows to its conclusion the intellectual path of 'radical ecology' to which these objections are committed, one arrives at the result that humans must ultimately refrain from all action in nature, indeed should actually abolish themselves in favour of nature. A depressing result, but one that has a weak point. It still rests on a 'Cartesian' conception of nature, as we saw it at work in traditional ecology at the beginning of this section (↑ 4.3.1). But the idea of a pure nature without humans fails to realise that humans are themselves natural beings.

What alternative do we have to this concept of nature? The alternative is to abandon the fiction of a 'pure' nature and to take into account the empirical fact that ecosystems and organisms, nature and humans have always been engaged in a co-evolution in which they mutually shape and produce each other (see Moore 2015a). If one wants to measure the influence of humans on 'nature', one cannot assume a pure nature, something that will only lead to catastrophic scenarios that overlook the historical reality (its adversities as well as its possibilities). Rather,

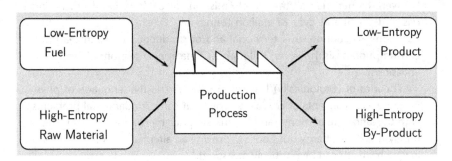

FIGURE 4.12 Joint production of the desired product and the undesired highly entropic by-product: waste heat, exhaust gases, dust (after Baumgärtner, Faber and Schiller 2006, p. 4).

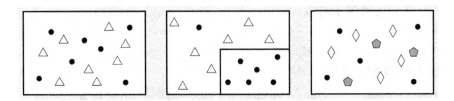

FIGURE 4.13 Production from a thermodynamic point of view: (1) natural occurrence of the raw material with a certain initial concentration (e.g. as ore); (2) enrichment of the raw material using a low-entropy energy source (e.g. in a blast furnace); (3) use of the raw material in the manufactured good – sometimes in extremely low concentrations or in alloys and composite materials.

BOX 4.6 INSIGHTS FROM THE ENERGETIC ANALYSIS OF ECONOMICS II: ECOLOGICALLY UNEQUAL EXCHANGE

In the 1960s, the economist Arghiri Emmanuel posited that the symmetrical flows of value on the world market mask asymmetrical flows of labour, energy and resources between the Global South and the Global North (Emmanuel 1972). It is no longer through colonial violence but through "fair exchange" that the South is plundered. The mechanism is based on the difference in labour productivity and production costs. On the world market, a dollar is a dollar, but in a poor country, a dollar can mobilise more labour and resources.

In recent years, this theory has experienced a revival and has been expanded into a theory of Ecologically Unequal Exchange. The North not only appropriates labour and raw materials, but also externalises its ecological costs, which are shifted to the South. Lucy Baker notes: "In 2004 the emissions generated in China for the production of goods consumed in the UK were higher than all the direct emissions of UK households, including gas and car fuel at over 81 million tonnes of CO_2e" (Baker 2018, p. 56). Emissions accounting on a territorial and/or production basis, instead of a consumption basis, however, still makes China appear responsible for these emissions.

Theories of (Ecologically) Unequal Exchange use the language of physics, especially concepts of energy, to point out some fundamental problems with the language of money and the market price mechanism. But this use is purely negative. Energy does not yet provide an alternative metric of wealth in which wealth can be positively measured.

---

we should start from the assumption of a man-made nature and then examine in what condition it can be preserved and what kind of life it enables its inhabitants to lead. One thing is certain: humanity's home will never be an untouched nature.

4.3.4 Conclusion

Finite resources, recycling, pollutant emissions – all these problem areas must be considered essential aspects of the production process in the "full world" (Daly 2005) in which we live today, and must not be conceptually separated from its economic core. In neoclassical theory, however, this is precisely what happens, as they are incompatible with the (subjective) concept of value based on individual preferences and utility maximisation that defines the scope of economics. Ecological economics strives to integrate both perspectives. The first strategy of monetisation rests on shaky ground, as we have seen, even if one is prepared to make a whole series of 'cynical' concessions. But even the second strategy has not yet led to success. In particular, the concept of entropy eventually dwindled into a rather metaphorical framework, a kind of *memento mori* that reminds us of our finitude but has not generated any new economic theorising. Nevertheless, the theory of joint production points a way forward by formulating the goal of *fully* mapping production, and that must mean showing how a particular production technique not only influences the price of the finished good, but also co-produces a social and 'natural' environment with the good.

In the following chapter, we will turn to the question of what methodological lessons can be drawn from these insights.

5

THE ECONOMY IN A
HISTORICAL WORLD

Global and historical perspectives

5.1 Metaphors or theories?

In the panorama of the previous three chapters, we have formed a picture of the embeddedness of the ostensibly autonomous economic process that runs solely according to internal laws: the individual actor is not a given of nature, but is embedded in a society that affects and shapes him or her; the enormous turnover of commodities on the market is embedded in a human-made world, which, however, does not consist of commodities, and is finally embedded in a nature that, for its part, does not submit to the laws of the market. In particular, we have looked over the shoulders of economists (and other social scientists, legal scholars, natural scientists and especially ecologists) in the conceptual work that is required in order to be able to address these interfaces in the social life process. What general lessons can be drawn from our findings for the methods of economics?

Quite a number of researchers clearly see in the same possibility of viewing the different boundaries in parallel – an approach that has been substantiated in the present book – the opening up of a new theoretical perspective. These researchers thereby aim at a theoretical *unification* of disparate phenomena (see, for example, Hornborg 1998; Mahnkopf 2013; Fraser 2014; Moore 2015a). For example, as we have seen, the term *commons* has lent itself to a more general or figurative use by many authors. While it originally referred to communally used land, it was then applied to the totality of common goods – i.e. goods that are neither non-excludable nor can be consumed by only one person at a time (non-rivalrous) – and from there to knowledge understood as the "commons of the mind". Finally, it has been applied to everything that existed outside the economic sphere. Silvia Federici explicitly mentions in this context the land, the body and social relations (↑ 3.3.1). "Commons" thus became a general term

DOI: 10.4324/9781003204077-6

for the space exterior to the economy in its ambiguous quality of being both a non-economic realm of freedom and a realm of expansion for capitalism. Conversely, the result of its enclosure was described by treating in parallel the concepts of productive capital, human capital and natural capital.

The examples could be continued. Are we now dealing with mere metaphor or with the beginnings of new theoretical approaches? It may come as a surprise that this question – from a philosophy of science perspective – is hasty in its critical zeal. The boundary between theory and mere metaphor cannot easily be drawn, which becomes clear when one considers that scientific theorising and explanation consist essentially in metaphorical redescriptions (Barnes 1974, p. 53). In metaphorical redescription, one manages to connect a new and unknown phenomenon to the known world and to describe it in familiar terms, that is, to *understand* it. Think, for example, of the wave and corpuscular theories of light, which try to capture light either in the manner of water or small material spheres, or of the electrical "charge" that produces a "field". Taken literally, this may be nonsensical in each case. But a metaphor as such is not a scientific *faux pas*. Admittedly, in the case of economics, the necessary metaphors are only germinal. They will prove theoretically fruitful when they not only describe structural similarities, but also reveal structurally similar processes behind them and perhaps even a common root.

This can be seen particularly clearly in the recent work of the prominent New York sociologist Saskia Sassen, who generalises the term 'expulsion' and related concepts in precisely this sense, widening it to include socially induced damage to the ecosystem. With considerable empirical skill, she draws parallels between the social and ecological consequences of economic activity: for example, that as a result of poisoning by industrial waste, "plants cease to grow and even people become sterile". Or she speaks of the "eviction of [...] flora, fauna, villages, smallholders, and the traditional rules that organised land ownership or use". Expulsion thus affects culture and nature at the same time. Not only are people expelled from their society, but there is also an "expulsion of bits of life itself from the biosphere". As an example, she mentions dead land and dead bodies of water, which can be imagined as 'holes' in the environment's fabric: "I conceive of these holes as sites marked by the expulsion of biosphere elements from their life space" (Sassen 2014, pp. 2, 115, 150 and 175). The well-known Indian scientist and activist Vandana Shiva makes similar parallels between "the rape of the earth, of local self-reliant economies, the rape of women" as consequences of modern economic policies in India (Shiva 2012).

Sassen never tires of emphasising that there is a "global system" behind each of these processes. Exclusion is "the concrete process behind which there is a complex dynamic that is more difficult to grasp". She speaks of "conceptually invisible, subterranean trends that go beyond the familiar meanings and concepts with which we explain our economy and society" and which can simply no longer be grasped by "old familiar categories" (Sassen 2014, p. 253 f.). But this is precisely where the limitations of such a theoretical approach become clear, because Sassen does not provide the necessary new categories. In view of the extinction of a species, to speak of "exclusion" from the biosphere is prima facie only a metaphorical description, which quite rightly points to the necessity of mutually integrating social and environmental history and, in particular, of researching the connections between social and ecological crises. But the metaphorical use of terms such as 'commons' or 'exclusion' *alone* does not achieve this; in particular, it does not expose the respective mechanisms at work. This is not to say that such a unifying approach is misguided, but it is clearly only in its infancy and is still struggling to find its categories.

Later, we will get to know a more developed and perhaps more promising attempt in Jason W. Moore's approach (↓ 5.2.3). If we want to make progress in our conceptual and methodological investigation, however, we must first take a step back. We will then notice another feature that characterises the approaches discussed in the preceding chapters even if it was not specifically addressed: that which such an economics investigates, no matter which categories it eventually develops, are obviously *processes*, often *irreversible* processes: evolutionary processes of the formation of structures, especially of the co-evolution of structures, but also processes of destruction and eradication of structures and elements. Such an economic science has thus again become a *historical* science.

With this, we have indeed found the lowest common denominator of the approaches we have studied: they all admit a historical dimension. Only ecological economics, based on thermodynamics, introduced a real concept of time into economics, i.e. a time that runs in one direction and recognises irreversible processes. But the other heterodox approaches also had to take the historical dimension into account. The shaping of the individual by society, the evolution of cooperation, the enclosure of the commons – each of these are historical processes, and in the interweaving of economics with the other social sciences on the one hand and the evolutionary life sciences and ecology on the other, economics inherits the historical approach to its object of research. So we turn to such a historical economics, which will prove to be a post-neoclassical economics.

5.2 World history

Economics is indeed gradually rediscovering history. Sometimes, calls are made to integrate economic history into curricular teaching. However, the coexistence of neoclassical economics and economic history does not mean that a historical economic science has finally been established. In this section, we will take a few examples to illustrate the concrete problems that such a discipline faces.

5.2.1 Piketty's historical macroeconomics

The rehabilitation of history in economics has been taken up by the French economist Thomas Piketty, who became known to a large audience in 2013 with the ambitious and comprehensive book *Capital in the 21st Century*. This book is generally associated with the thesis that inequalities within society are again growing after the more balanced post-war decades and have already almost reached the level of the rentier society in the Belle Époque. Globally, Piketty identifies the ratio of return on capital r to economic growth g as the decisive variable for inequality. In times of low economic growth ($g < r$), which has historically been the norm (↑ 4.1.1, Table 4.1), wealth that was accumulated in the past and passed down the generations grows faster than the overall economy, which is why its owners keep bettering their position. Inherited wealth determines the social hierarchy in such a society and casts it in a rigid mould. When there is strong growth, the situation changes. Consider, for example, the Chinese economy, in which disproportionately larger fortunes can be accumulated today than one or two generations ago and inheritance consequently plays no major role.

Piketty's empirical findings on the inequality of wealth distribution, which in fact could only be obtained with enormous effort (large fortunes are often hidden from view), have raised considerable controversy – presumably because the oligarchic dominance of inherited wealth contradicts the capitalist legitimising narrative of equality of opportunity. Of course, we are not interested in Piketty's data but in the fact, already clear after this short summary, that with this author's work and its wide reception, history is experiencing a renaissance. His book pulsates with a grand historical narrative and numerous impressive historical diagrams, often covering a period of two millennia. So how do neoclassical theory and history relate to each other in Piketty's work?

We will be primarily interested here in Piketty's "Second Fundamental Law of Capitalism", which is a historical law. Before that, however, we will take a look at his theory of wages, from which the author's strangely ambiguous and hesitant attitude to neoclassical theory quickly becomes evident. According to neoclassical theory, the wage level reflects the marginal productivity of the worker (↑ 1.2.6), i.e. he or she is paid what he or she adds to the company. Piketty positions himself at the outset in fundamental opposition to this assumption. The neoclassical thesis is "rather naïve"; the marginal productivity of the individual worker cannot be easily determined, especially for highly paid managers, whose salaries must instead be explained by power relations and social norms, for which sociology, psychology and cultural history are no less relevant than economics (Piketty 2014, pp. 330 ff.). These criticisms are not new and have been voiced before in a more fundamental way (Sen 1982). Now, on the same page of his book, Piketty surprisingly turns around and declares that the theory of marginal productivity nevertheless provides a "plausible explanation of the long-term development of wage distribution, at least up to a certain upper limit of wages and with a certain degree of accuracy" (Piketty 2014, p. 333; see also Syll 2014). The key concept in the model that Piketty has in mind is that of long-run evolution, which is apparently intended to reconcile sociology and neoclassical theory by linking them to different time scales: sociology for short-term fluctuations, neoclassical models for the long run.

This impression is confirmed by Piketty's "Second Fundamental Law of Capitalism" on the capital/income ratio β (i.e. total wealth measured as a multiple of GDP), which is determined – again: *in the long run* – by the quotient of the savings and growth rates s/g:

$$\beta = s/g$$

This law describes a state of equilibrium in which disturbances immediately cause counteracting forces that push the system back into its initial state. If wealth β is below the value of s/g, the savings s from income ensure that wealth grows faster than the economy, so that β rises. Should wealth β exceed the value of s/g, the fixed savings rate s is no longer sufficient for wealth growth to keep up with that of the economy, and β gradually falls back to the equilibrium value (Piketty 2014, p. 170). This applies at least to the state of balanced growth, in which all variables, including total income, increase at the same rate. We recognise in the assumptions behind this law nothing other than the conventional growth model of neoclassical theory with all its weaknesses (↑ 4.1.3), which has consequently brought Piketty considerable criticism from heterodox economists. Yannis Varoufakis openly accused him of "[employing] the logically incoherent tricks that have allowed mainstream economic theory to disguise grand theoretical failure as relevant, scientific modelling" (Varoufakis 2014, p. 19, cf. also Foster and Yates 2014).

If we are now interested in the relationship between this law and history, we encounter the same idea as in Piketty's theory of wages. The Second Law is an asymptotic law that prevails only in the long run, the time scale being defined by the mechanisms underlying the gradual accumulation of capital. In the short term, however, β may well deviate from the value s/g due to contingent influences (Ibid., p. 168 f.). This is the framework within which Piketty explains the trend he has uncovered in the size of total wealth, which in the 20th century follows a U-curve with a scandalous rise in recent decades (Figure 5.1); at the beginning of the 20th century, by contrast, there was a dramatic drop, due not only to the physical destruction of wealth in the world wars but far more to the collapse of foreign portfolios, low savings rates and low asset prices. Piketty speaks in this context of "Europe's suicide" and the "euthanasia of European capitalists" (Piketty 2014, pp. 147 ff.). All this can be explained by the external impact, he suggests, of a "political shock" which throws the economic process out of its equilibrium trajectory. When the external disturbance disappears, he suggests, the macroeconomic indicators gradually return to their target values.

Piketty thus reconciles historical observation and the neoclassical model by splitting history into two parts: short-term variations (fluctuations) due to shocks emerging from the darkness of world political history, and long-term trends interpreted as a gradual return to the equilibrium state defined by the model.

This model of Piketty's has also received much criticism from the heterodox camp. From the various objections, we select one that is relevant to our

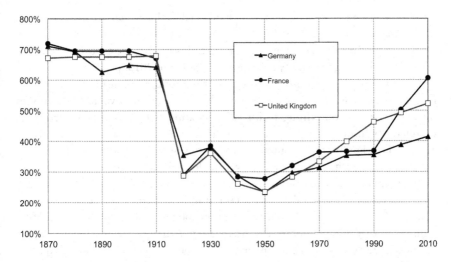

FIGURE 5.1 Piketty's U-curve: total wealth (public and private, measured as a multiple of total annual income) in the old world between 1870 and 2010.
Source: Piketty (2014, p. 147).

methodological question of the relationship between economics and history. On the face of it, this is a rather technical objection, but on closer inspection, it reveals in a striking way how much room for interpretation Piketty's empirical data leave.

Many commentators have taken exception to Piketty's use of the concept of capital because he defines it too broadly. Capital in the strict sense is fixed capital, namely the resources required in production, such as tools, machines, buildings, etc. When he speaks of capital, Piketty actually means wealth, because he includes securities, cash assets, land ownership, etc., in the term. As with any quantity, this wealth must also be expressed in a unit. Piketty, remember, chooses the annual total output of the national economy, which results in a manageable quantity that, in contrast to the usual monetary expression, does not depend on fluctuations in the value of the currency. However, as Piketty's compatriots Gérard Duménil and Dominique Lévy astutely point out, the annual output of the national economy is by no means an innocent and neutral reference value in relation to capital in the true sense, as one demands of a unit of measurement. The two are functionally linked and their relationship itself provides information about a third quantity: production per capital invested is of course nothing other than the so-called apparent capital productivity, which indicates how much capital is needed to produce a certain quantity of goods. For the interpretation of the historical course of β, the social wealth expressed in multiples of total production, this has perplexing consequences. The sharp drop in β, which Piketty plausibly interpreted as impoverishment, even as the "suicide" of the capitalists, can just as well express an increase in capital productivity due to technical developments, and thus a development beneficial to the propertied classes, which compensated for the impoverishment that actually took place (Duménil and Lévy 2015, p. 233). In a similar analysis, Mary O'Sullivan also attests to a "substantial ambiguity" lurking in Piketty's narrative (O'Sullivan 2015, p. 565).

This insight throws Piketty's story and the causal relationships he identifies into disarray. The long-term trend towards the equilibrium value of β vanishes into thin air. For one thing, technical innovation, which is crucial for capital productivity, influences the development that Piketty interpreted as a return to equilibrium. For another, political history takes on a different role than the one Piketty assigns to it, that of the dark storm cloud from which sudden shocks are unleashed. First, causality is not just one-way, as in Piketty's shocks. Rather, economic development has political effects, as it influences the balance of power and alliances between economic parties. And second, the role of politics cannot be reduced to that of a temporary disturbance – it actually has considerable impact on what Piketty would like to understand as a purely economic state of equilibrium. In a word: the economic process constantly takes place in the surrounding medium of politics, with which it causally interacts. Curiously, shortly after the publication of *Capital in the 21st Century*, Piketty unceremoniously admitted this in an article: the political shocks are of course *endogenous* variables of economic development (Piketty 2015, p. 48). As we saw at the beginning of the book, his new book *Capital and Ideology* appears with the claim to actually tell the real, much more radical historical story (↑ 1.4.2).

5.2.2 World-systems analysis

The challenge is thus to understand the economic process itself as a historical event instead of merely admitting that history sometimes has a disruptive effect. There is at least one level on which this is quite easily possible, once one has learned the lesson from ecological economics that our economic activity, as it has organised itself over the past 500 years, is embedded in an environment and is accompanied by irreversible changes in this environment, changes which it both causes and is affected by. Tracing these changes in the framework variables already reveals the economic process as an essentially historical event.

This change in approach can be readily illustrated by the example of urbanisation. Of course, traditional economists are also familiar with this process, which they try to grasp with their conceptual tools in urbanisation economics. For example, they ask whether the degree of urbanisation, i.e. the percentage of a country's population living in urban centres, is related to the level of GDP in order to be able to make a policy recommendation on this basis (see e.g. Bloom, Canning and Fink 2008). The advantages and disadvantages of location are weighed against each other (e.g. more effective infrastructure versus higher land prices). This approach is based on an assumption: the degree of urbanisation is seen as an exogenous variable whose regulation can and should be freely adjusted by policy-makers so that society enjoys the desired economic benefits.

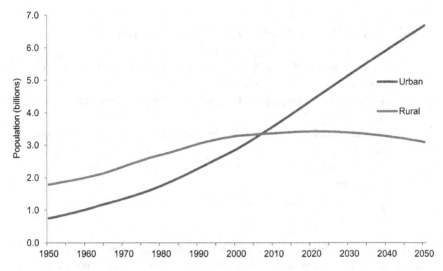

FIGURE 5.2   Number of people living in cities and rural areas (in millions) from 1950 to 2014 and the projected development until 2050.
Source: United Nations (2019, p. 5).

The historical reality, however, is different: the urbanisation process is a long-term global trend. Urbanisation is not a slider that can be pushed up or down, but is in its historical reality a *unilinear* process. Second, it seems to be subject to a global dynamic, since it begins in the Old World and then spills over to the periphery. Clearly, there is an external dynamic behind urbanisation that can only be grasped in global terms. The analyses undertaken by urbanisation economics, however, proceed strictly within the categories of the national economy and do not step outside the national framework. Third, the degree of urbanisation is obviously finite, so that urbanisation must come to a standstill at some point. In Europe today, 73% of the population lives in cities, in the USA as much as 82%. In 2007, for the first time in human history, the majority of humans lived in cities (Figure 5.2). It is striking that the economic development of the past century is closely related to this trend, but that this trend must necessarily come to a gradual halt, which, in turn, will have an impact on economic development. Even before clarifying the relevant causal relationships, it is already clear that in this approach a fundamental change of perspective has taken place compared to urbanisation economics.

This change of perspective can be generalised and systematised, and this is carried out in the so-called world-systems analysis, which was developed primarily by the American sociologist and social historian Immanuel Wallerstein (Box 5.1; for an introduction with a glossary, see Wallerstein 2004).

The most fundamental elements of world-systems analysis are long-term trends. With urbanisation, we have already become acquainted with a typical long-term trend. Globalisation, with its typical pattern of interaction between

---

BOX 5.1 OVERVIEW WORLD-SYSTEMS ANALYSIS

- A theory of development that examines both cyclical phases (e.g. Kondratiev waves) and secular trends;
- the focus is on long-term developments (*longue durée*) of historical capitalism;
- political, social and economic development are examined in their interaction;
- in a global perspective, the interaction of economic *centres* and *peripheries* is examined.

'centres' and 'periphery', is another such trend, except that in world-systems analysis the development of historical capitalism from its beginnings in the 15th century onwards is conceived as a history of globalisation, so that the common conception of 'globalisation' as a trend beginning only in the second half of the 20th century is misleading (Wallerstein 2000).

Compared to neoclassical theory's image of the economy as an autonomous, reversible, self-stabilising and potentially infinite system, this already marks a categorical, conceptual-methodological turn, since the development of historical capitalism is grasped from the outset as one that is accompanied by *unilinear* changes in the world, such as urbanisation. The economic process is thus understood as an intrinsically historical event. Political, social and economic aspects in particular are on an equal footing, because it is clear that urbanisation as a historical development is at the same time a political, social and economic phenomenon. In this way, the endogenisation of "political shocks" suggested by Piketty is put into practice in concrete terms.

5.2.3 From world system to world ecology

Wallerstein traces the development of historical capitalism primarily along the axis of centre and periphery. He thus interprets the concept of the boundary, as we understand it in this book, geographically. A generalisation of world-systems analysis that explicitly integrates developments at the boundaries of the undeveloped socio- and biosphere has been advanced in recent years by the social scientist Jason W. Moore under the title "Capitalism as World Ecology" (Box 5.2). The 'horizontal' axis of geographical expansion that Wallerstein focuses on is widened by Moore to include the 'vertical' axis of expansion into the social and natural space of reproduction – i.e. the unpaid labour and ecosystem services that still allow expansion in the centres (Moore 2014, p. 304). This makes it possible to integrate the concerns and insights of feminist and ecological economics into the developmental framework of world-systems analysis.

It is characteristic of this approach that it does not merely examine the *effects* of the economic process on its social and natural environment. Rather, it seeks to understand historical capitalism as a comprehensive "civilizatory project": the economic process unfolds *in and through* these spaces, opening them up and structuring them. In this perspective, society is no longer conceived as the antithesis of nature. Against such Cartesian dualism, Moore gives us a relational analysis that looks at society as part of nature and, conversely, at nature in its respective historical form as 'part' of society, that is, as socially shaped.

The distinctive and now visibly problematic success story of historical capitalism over the past 500 years has consisted in tapping into sources of unpaid labour and energy in its exterior spaces. With relatively little investment, enormous energies could be unleashed: colonial plunder, the extraction of coal and then oil, the revolutionising of agriculture. Moore calls the specific magnitude of these conquests the *ecological surplus*, which he defines as the ratio of mobilised 'unpaid labour' to total capital (Moore 2015a, p. 102):

ecological surplus = mass of capital/unpaid work and energy.

Moore thus applies the concept of exploitation to the entire environment, i.e. the biosphere and the sociosphere. The concept of 'unpaid work' is accordingly generalised to mean all the free services that our economic system has managed to mobilise in its five centuries of 'free ride', be it the unpaid labour of women, of the colonies or of the ecosystem. Incidentally, 'labour' in this application to nature is clearly – and in principle legitimately (↑ 5.1), in line with the concept of labour in physics – being used metaphorically (and for this reason, Moore puts it in inverted commas; cf. Moore 2015a, pp. 85, 134, 225 and 299).

The aim and consequence of this conceptual manoeuvre is obvious. We have already seen that with the factor of production *land*, nature disappeared from the neoclassical theory of production and only capital and labour remained as sources of wealth (↑ 1.2.6). As long as the dispute was fought between the poles of capital and labour, the ecological deficit of neoclassicism was thus bound to linger on. The concept of ecological surplus value is supposed to remedy this deficit by viewing labour as the only source of wealth but at the same time granting the status of labour to unpaid human labour and processes in non-human nature too.

BOX 5.2 CORE THESES OF "CAPITALISM AS WORLD-ECOLOGY"

- Historical capitalism is a project of civilisation in the sense of a particular way of organising nature;
- its historical development consists in a series of crisis responses through the opening up of new ecological, social and geographical spaces;
- its boundaries are not "external" but "internal", where a certain technology meets a historically shaped nature.

Since the ecological surplus is a relational measure – i.e. it relates a flow of matter and energy (on the nature side) to a quantity of capital (on the society side) – it certainly meets the holistic demand of the analysis. The historical demand is also met, since the theory is only ever applied in concrete historical constellations. Strictly speaking, coal, for example, is not a 'natural' resource. It only becomes one at the moment when the technology for its utilisation is available. Coal then emerges from the geological background to become a historical actor. Conversely, it is also not simply 'nature' that imposes limits on society's growth. The limits are *internal* rather than *external*. Of course, the quantities of available petroleum, for example, are limited. But whether this physical limit becomes relevant to society depends on the concrete technical shape society gives to its metabolism.

Moore fills this abstract framework with concrete historical case studies that reveal how "commodity frontiers" were pushed across the globe in historical capitalism in order to maintain ecological surplus value. For example, the "sugar frontier" which, feeding on available land and available slaves, moves from Madeira (1452–1520s) to the island of São Tomé in the Gulf of Guinea (1540s–1590s) to northeast Brazil (from the 1570s onwards), each leaving behind deforestation on a previously unknown scale. Or silver production, which likewise thrives on cheap labour and forests as fuel, and which shifts its frontier from the central European mining boom after 1450 to Bolivia's Potosí (1540–1640) and finally to Mexico in the 18th century. Each step involves considerable investment, which however – and this is crucial – allows disproportionately unpaid work to be exploited until the respective sources – soils, communities, ore deposits – dry up, at least for the respective project in its technically specific form. A chapter of this story that is particularly relevant for our discussion tells how it is during this period that the notion of an *external* nature first emerges, which, as some anthropologists remind us, is quite unique in human history (see Descola 2005; Sahlins 2008). Paradigmatically, this notion is expressed in the work of René Descartes. There, subject and external object confront each other as ontologically independent substances. It is this image of an external and invisible nature, which allows the necessary material to flow steadily into the economy and which boundlessly reabsorbs its waste, that we also found assumed in neoclassical economics.

These striking insights notwithstanding, the notion of ecological surplus value raises questions that are directly relevant to our study. Note that, unlike the related EROI (↑ 4.3.3, Box 4.4), it is a monetary quantity, which has provoked criticism from other proponents of eco-Marxism that Moore thus remains wedded to the categories of market and money (Foster and Burkett 2018; Hornborg 2020). Moore seems to have been aware of this problem, though, and added a qualifying note to the definition of ecological surplus value: "This is an imperfect formulation, precisely because the condition for quantification within the commodity system (units of labor-time) is a world of unpaid work that cannot be quantified" (Moore 2015a, p. 102). This formulation may be unsatisfactory for the reader – but it is so for a methodologically meaningful reason: at the limits of economics, one is thrown back on the transcendental conditions of economic categories.

5.3 Crisis

The conceptual framework of world-systems analysis and its generalisation by Moore virtually poke us on the nose with a term that will now be our final focus of attention: crisis. Wallerstein and Moore tell a story of historical capitalism in which unilinear but in principle limited changes play an essential role. What happens when the limits are reached? The example of urbanisation is telling. The history of capitalism is also one of urbanisation. If the economic process depends on a constant supply of cheap labour from the *outside*, namely from the countryside, but this supply is finite, with a decisive milestone having already been passed, is crisis not inevitable?

5.3.1 Structural crisis

But what exactly is a crisis? Since 2008, we have once again been living through a crisis that seems to be dragging on and is occupying public attention accordingly. But what the crisis actually means remains unclear. Something is not going as it should; yet, we are not even able to rule out that the crisis may have actually brought about a potential Pareto improvement. Because in a crisis there are not only losers but also profiteers, and who knows whether the profiteers have not gained more than the losers have lost?

   Let us first try to clarify the concept of crisis. Of course, there are different types of crises. But the example of urbanisation or even that of the 'limits to growth' invoked in the ecological debate draws our attention to a specific type of crisis. When the economic model induces a certain unilinear change in the biosphere or the sociosphere, typically over a longer period of time, and this development reaches its limit, a critical situation arises – and this is inevitable, i.e. it is due not to an unfavourable constellation of external factors but to the internal conditions of the economic process. One can speak here of a *structural* crisis.

   Thanks to the knowledge we have acquired so far, we are in a good position to anchor the concept of structural crisis theoretically. We have described societies with their characteristic ways of organising the economic process in the words of the Russian-Belgian chemist Ilya Prigogine as "dissipative structures" that can keep themselves stable far from thermodynamic equilibrium by constantly releasing entropy into their environment (↑ 4.3.3, Box 4.5). We thus considered them in direct analogy to organisms and ecosystems. Wallerstein makes this analogy explicit: "All systems have lives", he says (cf. Daly 1968, p. 396; Wallerstein 2011b, p. 76), and this analogy is also true of a structural crisis, which we know well from organisms – especially the organisms that we ourselves are. Ageing and death occur not only as a result of wear and tear or damaging external influences, both of which could in principle be avoided, but are also structurally – in this case genetically – inherent in many organisms.

   We can therefore speak of a structural crisis when a structure is configured in such a way that it produces effects that inevitably undermine its own ability to function over time. This is the case when, in the overall causal balance, desta-bilising feedback effects gain the upper hand over stabilising feedback effects, i.e. when, to use the vocabulary introduced above (↑ 2.4.4), the system fails to achieve its purpose. A candidate for a purpose that plays a distinctive role in capitalism is profit. Accordingly, crisis here would mean a situation where the opportunities to make profit are dwindling.

The experience of historical capitalism teaches us that crises are not the excep-tion but the rule. It is well known that Marx learned this lesson in the first global economic crisis of 1857/58. When the crisis broke out, he was worried about fin-ishing his own book on economics and "[finding] the world no longer attentive to such subjects" (Marx and Engels 1983, p. 271). But he was wrong about the na-ture of that crisis. It did not lead to collapse, and as early as the summer of 1858, capitalism even emerged from it stronger (Heinrich 2008). Jason Moore's studies, briefly touched on above, vividly illustrate how, over the past 500 years, ever new resources and external spaces have been mobilised to overcome historical limits. The Western world, one can say, developed in the very medium of crises.

But what happens when there are no more new external spaces, no more barriers to open? The outer space has now disappeared. After the territories that the collapsed Soviet Union opened up to capitalism, there are no more continents left to discover, and the remaining territories are becoming increasingly difficult to exploit. The race to the North Pole, which is gradually being released from the 'eternal ice', has already begun (Beary 2008), and even the deep sea bed and asteroids are arousing speculators' interest (Martens 2003). So what happens when the 'small' crises can no longer be overcome for lack of new territory and lead to a 'big', structural crisis?

Again, Prigogine's theory of "dissipative structures" can be invoked here (Prigogine 1993): if such a structure is subjected to too great a stress, it begins to "fluctuate", the system becomes unstable and reaches a "bifurcation", at which point a small, random shock can finally tip the structure over into a new local equilibrium (Figure 5.3).

Such a process cannot be predicted, but can at most be tentatively recon-structed in retrospect. Wallerstein is nevertheless bold enough to interpret today's crises as chaotic fluctuations that indicate an impending bifurcation (Wallerstein 2011a). Only time will tell whether his diagnosis is correct. Other authors still see enormous capacities for new profit in the new, multipolar world, since indus-trialisation in India, China and Africa is only at its beginnings (Heinrich 2007). However, this question is inconsequential for our investigation. The important thing for us is that Wallerstein's conceptual framework allows economic analysis to be based on real, *historical time*, i.e. time in which fundamentally new and un-predictable things happen.

5.3.2 Crisis theory: nomothetic or idiographic?

This leads directly to a question that first appears as a practical and almost urgent question, but at the same time raises an interesting epistemological issue: is it

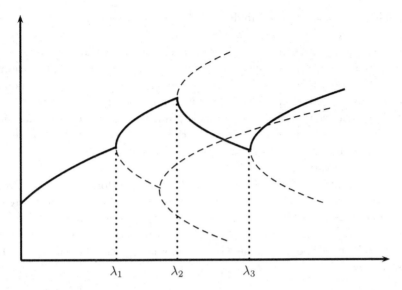

FIGURE 5.3 Trajectory of a dissipative structure in historical time, with several bifurcations, i.e. upheavals in which the form of societal organisation changes abruptly. The upheavals do not have to be revolutions, and the system trajectory is not predictable, but is at best reconstructable.

necessarily the case that capitalism needs an "external space" upon which it feeds and into which it simultaneously expands further and further?

We have already encountered this question several times in the preceding chapters. In the ecological discussion of the 'limits to growth' we encountered it as a question about a structural *imperative* of growth (↑ 4.1.3). This question is of political-practical importance because it determines whether capitalism can be ecologically restructured (key words: steady-state economy, degrowth and also Green New Deal). Earlier, we encountered it as the problem of whether there is a contradiction in commodifying all unpaid work (↑ 3.3.3) and whether market transactions are actually based on social norms that have an extra-economic origin (↑ 2.2.2 and 2.2.3).

This question gains philosophical significance through the modality of *necessity* involved. In the three earlier cases, the question is indeed about the necessity of an external space. But in each case we have seen how difficult it is to substantiate the assertion of such a necessity argumentatively. And it is no different in the case of crisis theory, which takes up these examples, summarises and unifies them.

The epistemological background to this difficulty is as follows: no matter how convincing we find Wallerstein's and Moore's stories about how historical capitalism constantly opened up new external spaces over the centuries, they remain 'stories', i.e. statements about how the historical course *de facto* happened. If, however, one posits the thesis of the *necessity* of external space, one detaches oneself from these empirical findings and asserts that history *had to* proceed in this way and could not have proceeded differently.

The experimental natural sciences can, to a certain extent, arrive at such statements by repeatedly producing the phenomenon in question in the laboratory, even when conditions are varied. If the phenomenon only occurs when another factor is also present, it can be assumed that this factor is necessary for its occurrence. Such a determination is thus made possible by negative cross-checking. History, however, only occurs once. We cannot say, for example, how things would have turned out if, in 1812, the winter had not taken Napoleon's Russian campaign by surprise.

This peculiarity of historiography has been known for a long time. Some philosophers went so far as to assume that it meant a fundamental difference from experimental natural science: while the latter describes classes of phenomena in general terms, history deals solely with unique and one-off instances. Wilhelm Windelband coined the terms "nomothetic" and "idiographic" for this distinction:

> [T]he empirical sciences seek in the knowledge of reality either the general in the form of the natural law or the particular in the historically determined form. They consider in one part the ever-enduring form, in the other part the unique content, determined within itself, of an actual happening. The one comprises sciences of law, the other sciences of events; the former teaches what always is, the latter what once was.
>
> *(Windelband [1894] 1998, p. 13)*

The true situation, however, is more complicated. If historiography is really about the individual in strict contrast to the general, one should not stop at general terms in one's description. If, however, one refers to an event as "war", "crisis", "campaign" or "natural disaster", one has subsumed it under a general term and thus assumed comparability with similar events. Since the historian can in fact never exhaust the individuality of events in his or her descriptions, this alleged essential difference between historiography and natural science breaks down (Hempel 1942, p. 37). Windelband himself emphasised that the contrast between "what always is" and "what once was", between what is always the same and what is unique, is a relative one and simply depends on the periods of time one is considering: everything is in motion, just at different speeds.

Admittedly, a difference remains in the fact that the historian is largely dependent on passive observation and cannot assure him- or herself of a causal connection by replicating his or her phenomenon in the laboratory. But he or she can attempt to formulate a hypothesis about which *mechanism* is at work in the background and which may be driving the presumed necessary connection. And this is precisely what applies to our case about the connection between historical capitalism and its external space.

The template for the assertion of a necessary outside was arguably provided by Rosa Luxemburg in her book *The Accumulation of Capital*, first published in 1913, in which she asserted the necessity of "non-capitalist *milieus*" for the smooth functioning of capitalism: "the accumulation of capital, as an historical process, depends in every respect upon non-capitalist social strata and forms of social organisation [existing side by side with it]" (Luxemburg 1951, p. 365 f.). Today, Moore speaks in apparently similar terms of a "constitutive outside" (Moore 2015a, p. 191). "[N]ot only does capitalism have frontiers; it is a frontier civilisation" (Moore 2015b, p. 4). Frontiers are *necessary* for capital accumulation.

At second glance, however, the two quotations reveal quite different ideas about why the outside space is necessary: while Moore, as we have seen, sees the outside space as a source of unpaid work (of humans and nature) which is *imported* into the inside space, Rosa Luxemburg assumed an overproduction of goods which must then be *exported* to newly (and, if necessary, forcibly) opened-up markets.

Indeed, quite different candidates, some compatible, some incompatible, emerge in the literature as explanations for the mechanism that is supposed to be behind the need for an external space or space of expansion. The core idea each has in common is that a competition-based and profit-oriented economic structure cannot form a stable system. In a competitive economy, profit-making opportunities inevitably dwindle. The reason for this, however, is disputed. Marx referred to an empirically demonstrable "tendency of the rate of profit to fall" in the late 18th and 19th centuries: under the compulsion of competition, he assumed, pressure was exerted on labour as a factor of production, but production thereby became more and more capital-intensive and therefore the opportunities to make profits inevitably declined. We would be dealing with an over-accumulation crisis, since existing capital can no longer be invested profitably. Other thinkers also refer to the competitive pressure on the factor labour, but now see a deficit in expenditure on the part of the wage-dependent but increasingly less well-paid population. The crisis was therefore one of overproduction or underconsumption. (According to Luxemburg, the external space – in the colonies – is needed precisely as a market to absorb such overproduction.) Wallerstein assumes – contrary to this – that behind the fall in the rate of profit, there is an increase in the price of labour with rising real wages and demands for education, health care and old-age pensions (Wallerstein 2010b). For him, the external space therefore guarantees an influx of cheap labour that can counteract this development. However, this view, on the one hand, seems beholden to the empirical conditions of the 1970s and, on the other, stands on a shaky economic ground, as it does not take into account the growing productivity of labour. Moore reverts to the Marxian idea of increasingly capital-intensive production, but emphasises that this tendency can be compensated for by the 'ecological surplus value' from newly developed external spaces.

It is therefore clear that we are dealing with a controversial and, for the time being, unresolved question (see Duménil and Lévy 2014). Perhaps there is no general explanation of every crisis that would immediately propel us into the realm of nomothetic science and general statements of law. Not that this means that one has to be content with idiographic descriptions of individual events. Rather, the proper place of a historical economy seems to lie in the field between these two poles, in which a historical economy oscillates between an empirically appropriate recording of individual events and the formation of hypotheses about general mechanisms.

5.3.3 Multi-systemic crises

Such attempts at unification in crisis theory aim to uncover the common root of the current crisis phenomena in structural features of our economic process. However, empirical theorising does not have to put all its eggs in this basket. Even without such a theoretical framework, it can contribute greatly to understanding the present if it examines today's crisis phenomena in their causal interaction. The World Economic Forum's latest *Global Risks Report* once again gives an impressive list of crisis threats in the five categories of economy, environment, geopolitics, society and technology (World Economic Forum 2020). The list of environmental crises is not even complete. While the public usually reduces the ecological crisis to climate change, it is precisely the other aspects of this multiple crisis that scientists consider more alarming still: the loss of biodiversity (the "sixth mass extinction"), the disruption of global nitrogen and phosphorus cycles, and the degradation of soils, combined with desertification and loss of arable land (Steffen et al. 2015).

A group led by Canadian political scientist Thomas Homer-Dixon has developed a conceptual framework for understanding the interactions between such crises. The empirical starting point is the fact that the financial crisis of 2008 coincided with an energy crisis and a food crisis, each of which manifested itself in enormous price increases that plunged millions of people into destitution and triggered revolts in many countries (Homer-Dixon et al. 2015). Instead of accepting this concurrence with the financial crisis as a coincidence, the authors explore possible links and attempt to understand the dynamics of future global and *inter-systemic* crises. As a general conclusion, Homer-Dixon et al. state that all of today's "socio-ecological" systems now tend to be more susceptible to crises. This is because, first, they have reached an enormous scale in relation to the ecosystem, second, they spread matter, energy and information more quickly due to their degree of density and interconnectedness, and third, they are becoming increasingly homogeneous globally (in the case of ecosystems, the connection between biodiversity and stability or, conversely, loss of diversity and vulnerability is well known, cf. Cleland 2011). Overall, the resilience of socio-ecological systems suffers. They are susceptible to stress, more difficult to control due to their complexity, prone to non-linear behaviour (as we have already learned in the discussion of monetisation, ↑ 4.2.3, Box 4.2), and harmful inputs, be it a pathogen dangerous for livestock or information that causes stock market panic, spread rapidly within them, encountering the same structures everywhere, with exactly the same vulnerabilities.

In light of this approach, two moments are thus crucial for understanding large-scale, inter-systemic crises. First, it is necessary to understand how each individual system came under pressure over a longer period of time and how this paved the way for the system's non-linear behaviour, taking into account too the interactions between the systems; second, it is necessary to identify the local, short-term factors which then triggered the non-linear reaction of the system.

Consider the example of the multiple crises of 2008, which affected the financial, energy and food systems simultaneously.

1   The transformation of the financial system, which took place in the context of a general shift away from demand-oriented Keynesianism since the 1980s, is well known: the world saw a certain liquidity glut, which already contributed to the formation of economic bubbles in Asia. Deregulation of financial markets and a practice of easy credit allowed for the trading of credit claims in the form of complex and opaque securities. According to estimates, this derivatives market meanwhile grew to 20 times the global gross domestic product, i.e. to more than one quadrillion dollars. The financial system thereby became considerably larger and even more inscrutable than it had been. At the same time, its architecture changed, a large part of trading was concentrated in a few financial institutions and these were more interconnected than ever before.

2   Energy, especially from fossil fuels, was very cheap in the final decades of the 20th century, but from the 1990s onwards the energy system came under increasing pressure. Global energy demand grew, driven too by the emerging economies of China and India. At the same time, conventional oil fields reached peak production, while unconventional fossil fuel reserves came within technical reach, making extraction much more capital- and energy-intensive. While in Texas in the 1930s, 100 energy units were extracted for every unit of energy invested, this value has fallen to 4 energy units in today's Canadian exploitation of oil sand deposits.

3   The food system came under stress due to three factors: with a growing and more affluent world population with changing eating habits, the demand for food increased. At the same time, agricultural production is becoming increasingly difficult to expand because, on the one hand, less and less new fertile land is available and, on the other, the intensification of cultivation of already developed land is reaching its limits. In industrialised countries, the use of more fertiliser or more machinery can barely increase production. Third, weather extremes and water scarcity as a result of climate change are affecting agriculture worldwide.

All three systems are thus exposed to a stress that brings with it the danger of non-linear or even catastrophic reactions. The systems are not isolated.

Homer-Dixon et al. identify at least one interaction of the energy and food systems with the financial system: the high liquidity of the pre-crisis decades also increased the demand for oil, while cheap oil, in turn, both drove globalisation and influenced the food system, namely advancing the mechanisation and chemicalisation of agriculture. As energy prices rose, the cultivation of so-called energy crops for bio-fuels, in addition to rising production costs, put double pressure on the food system.

In such a situation, all that is needed is a factor that is not dramatic in itself and the system crosses the threshold into a violent, non-linear reaction that spreads rapidly, potentially affecting other systems as well. Homer-Dixon et al. speculate that it was the high price of oil that eventually acted as a trigger for the subprime crisis, as households taking out such "second-rate" mortgages felt the impact of rising petrol prices particularly acutely due to their tight budgets. As a result, many of them defaulted on their payments, triggering the shockwave in the banking system now known as the 2008 financial crisis.

The reaction of the financial sector itself deepened the multiple crisis. As a result of the bursting of the real estate bubble, investors were desperate for new investment opportunities and increasingly turned to commodity markets, primarily crude oil but also agricultural product markets, which drove up the prices of energy sources and food (Wahl 2009, p. 12). Homer-Dixon et al. suspect that this, along with other factors such as the ongoing drought in Australia, triggered the food crisis.

The merit of this theoretical approach is that the factors that are often named as the causes of the crisis appear to be merely proximate triggers, while the deeper causes are also identified which over the long-term led to the systems coming under pressure and reacting to the triggering factors in a dramatic, non-linear way. The shock wave then continued in cascade. Rising food prices affected tens of millions of people, leading to malnutrition and social unrest in several countries. In the USA, in the wake of the subprime crisis, the number of annual foreclosure notices rose to almost four million, and between 2005 and 2010, there were over nine million evictions (Sassen 2014, p. 150).

5.4 The future

This analysis opens up a somewhat depressing outlook on a future that will undoubtedly have to struggle with further multi-systemic crises. However, we are not concerned here with the question of how we will live tomorrow, but with the question of how and with what concepts we think about essential aspects of our lives today and, in particular, how we theorise scientifically. Our future fate will also depend on which concepts we use in the here and now to reach which conclusions.

What will happen next? Economics is a discipline in transition. At the same time, it is dealing with a world in transition, which makes the situation more complicated still. Philosophers today, however, are modest enough to refrain from dictating the future development of a science, and it would be presumptuous to make a statement about 'the' economic science that will follow the neoclassical paradigm. But some trends can certainly be discerned. Let's take a look at the whole picture once more!

Life means metabolism with surrounding nature. Over the millennia, human beings have given this metabolism a complicated form of organisation, one based on a division of labour which spans the globe and which is the subject of economics. The last two millennia have seen the emergence of a remarkable doubling in economic practice: alongside acts of producing, distributing and consuming the means of subsistence, another practice has emerged, linked in particular to a new *symbolic* practice and way of speaking. People began to use money and to talk about the things of the economy as values that can be expressed and accounted for quantitatively as prices in amounts of money. This is indeed a real doubling: we suddenly have two levels, that of matter and that of values. Both constitute flows which, although not completely independent of each other, seem to obey different laws.

Neoclassical economics views the economy solely through this symbolic practice: it reduces the economy to the market (in particular, its theory of development is a dynamised theory of production and this, in turn, is a market theory of resource allocation applied to production). The neoclassical paradigm sees only what has value in the market. It is not unreasonable, of course, to use market valuation as a criterion for determining whether an event that takes place in our world is economic and falls under economic laws, or whether it was just a shooting star or an indignant slap in the face (i.e. subject to physical or moral laws, respectively). What in particular is correct about the neoclassical approach is its aspiration to analyse and explain. This is the 'cynical' concession that even heterodox approaches must be willing to make. But the view of King Midas, for whom everything becomes gold (↑ 1.2.3), has blind spots when it comes to the interconnection between the economic and the social and the natural. With today's crises, however, this interconnection becomes dramatically apparent to us. Some authors, as we have seen, go so far as to regard this interconnection as a necessary one: the sphere of circulating values can only exist if it is embedded in a context that eludes its laws, but which is nevertheless economically relevant and must be addressed by economic theory. Monetisation is certainly one approach to this issue. But through its lens, the world appears upside down:

> Instead of a concentric view in which the economy is within the social, itself framed by a thousand feedback loops within the biosphere and the Earth system, the environment became a new column in the bookkeeping of big corporations [...]: the biosphere, the hydrosphere and the atmosphere appear as mere subsystems of the financial and commodity sphere.
>
> *(Bonneuil and Fressoz 2016, p. 23)*

In stark contrast to this view, it will be necessary, as we have argued throughout, to understand the economy in its *context*, in its social and ecological constitution. This requires new, additional concepts. We encountered, for example, the concepts of power relations, structural determinants, societal influence, historical time, secular trends, and structural and inter-systemic crises. We got to know these concepts mainly via the empirical theories in which they are embedded, and this is of course the place where they will have to prove their usefulness and fruitfulness. Nevertheless, they are (for better or worse) not limited to these specific theories. Research is progressing, and in ten years' time we will undoubtedly have a completely different picture of the most recent crises and their causes. Even if the detail of this picture is still unknown to us, we can still speculate about the colours in which it will be drawn, and certainly a whole range of the concepts we have just mentioned will in future be found on the economists' palette.

At the same time, however, things will not stop at the simple addition and expansion of concepts. Rather, as we have seen, the new concepts induce a decisive turnaround in the method. It can plausibly be stated that the reductionist programme will dissolve along with the model of *homo œconomicus*, in particular the 'microfoundation' of macroeconomic phenomena in microeconomic models. Perhaps the entire method of economics will itself 'tip over', like an iceberg whose centre of gravity has shifted and which suddenly swings its lowest point upwards. One would then start with macroeconomic variables and slowly work one's way down to the individual economic actor. This is not so improbable, since macroeconomic variables provide the framework in which our actions begin, even if they then have their effects on the framework.

What is perceptible in current economics is at least the attempt, which can be perceived in many places, to endogenise exogenous variables, i.e. to include them as dependent variables within economic theory. We saw this in the case of the preferences and actions of individuals, which are clearly shaped by their social environment, but also in the case of "political shocks", which Piketty, surprisingly, quite openly considered as dependent variables. The welcome tendency to include in economic theories factors that were previously seen as external should not be confused with the "economic imperialism" mentioned in the Introduction, for which basically every action counts as economic. Instead, it reflects the real significance that economic actions have in our lives. After all, economic activity is not limited to the actions of businessmen, but encompasses our very metabolism with our environment insofar as it is socially organised. In this respect, one can give voice to the hope that not only economic science will integrate itself more willingly into the totality of empirical social sciences, but conversely that social scientists, cultural scientists and humanities scholars will overcome their 'economophobia' and recognise the importance of economics in the (intellectual) history of humankind.

BIBLIOGRAPHY

Acemoglu, Daron (2009). *Introduction to Modern Economic Growth*. Princeton (NJ): Princeton University Press.

Agustín, Laura (2012). "Sex as Work & Sex Work". In: *The Commoner* 15:262–277.

Albert, Hans (1998). *Marktsoziologie und Entscheidungslogik. Zur Kritik der reinen Ökonomik*. Tübingen: Mohr Siebeck.

———— (2012). "Model Platonism: Neoclassical Economic thought in Critical Light". In: *Journal of Institutional Economics* 8(3):295–323.

Amadae, S. M. (2003). *Rationalizing Capitalist Democracy. The Cold War Origins of Rational Choice Liberalism*. Chicago (IL): University of Chicago Press.

Amnesty International (2015). *Global movement votes to adopt policy to protect human right of sex workers*. Press Release. url: https://www.amnesty.ie/news/ global-movement-votes-adopt-policy-protect-human-rightssex-workers.

Arrow, Kenneth J. (1950). "A Difficulty in the Concept of Social Welfare". In: *Journal of Political Economy* 58(4):328–346.

Arrow, Kenneth J. and Gerard Debreu (1954). "Existence of an Equilibrium for a Competitive Economy". In: *Econometrica* 22(3):265–290.

Arrow, Kenneth J. et al. (1993). "Report of the NOAA Panel on Contingent Valuation". In: *Federal Register* 58:4601–4614.

Axelrod, Robert (1980). "More Effective Choice in the Prisoner's Dilemma". In: *The Journal of Conflict Resolution* 24(3):379–403.

———— (1981). "The Emergence of Cooperation among Egoists". In: *The American Political Science Review* 75(2):306–318.

Axelrod, Robert and William D. Hamilton (1981). "The Evolution of Cooperation". In: *Sciences* 211(4489):1390–1396.

Ayres, Robert U. and Benjamin Warr (2005). "Accounting for Growth: The Role of Physical Work". In: *Structural Change and Economic Dynamics* 16:181–209.

Backhouse, Roger E. (1985). *A History of Modern Economic Analysis*. Oxford: Blackwell.

Baker, Lucy (2018). "Of Embodied Emissions and Inequality: Rethinking Energy Consumption". In: *Energy Research & Social Science* 36:52–60.

Bakker, Karen (2005). "Neoliberalizing Nature? Market Environmentalism in Water Supply in England and Wales". In: *Annals of the Association of American Geographers* 95(3):542–565.

Barnes, Barry (1974). *Scientific Knowledge and Sociological Theory*. London: Routledge & Kegan Paul.

Bateson, Gregory et al. (1956). "Toward a Theory of Schizophrenia". In: *Behavioral Science* 1(4): 251–264.

Baumgärtner, Stefan (1996). "The Use of the Entropy Concept in Ecological Economics". In: *Ecological Economics. Concepts and Methods*. Ed. by M. Faber, R. Manstetten, and J. Proops. Cheltenham: E. Elgar. Pp. 115–135.

Baumgärtner, Stefan, Malte Faber, and Johannes Schiller (2006). *Joint Production and Responsibility in Ecological Economics*. Cheltenham: Edward Elgar.

Beary, Brian (2008). "Race for the Arctic". In: *CQ Global Researcher* 2(8):213–242.

Becker, Gary S. (1997). "The Economic Way of Looking at Life. Lecture to the Memory of Alfred Nobel, December 9, 1992". In: *Nobel Lectures. Economics 1991–1995*. Singapore: World Scientific Publishing. Pp. 38–58.

——— (2008). "Human Capital". In: *The Concise Encyclopedia of Economics*. Ed. by David R. Henerson. url: http://www.econlib.org/library/Enc/HumanCapital.html.

Bergh, Jeroen C. J. M. van den and John M. Gowdy (2003). "The Microfoundations of Macroeconomics: An Evolutionary Perspective". In: *Cambridge Journal of Economics* 27:65–84.

Berndt, Christian and Marc Boeckler (2016). "Behave, Global South! Economics, Experiments, Evidence: Editorial". In: *Geoforum* 70:22–24.

Besley, Tim and Peter Hennessy (2009). "The Global Financial Crisis – Why Didn't Anybody Notice?" In: *British Academy Review* 14:8–10.

BFS, ed. (2004). *Satellitenkonto Haushaltsproduktion. Pilotversuch für die Schweiz*. Neuchâtel: Schweizer Bundesamt für Statistik.

Bianciardi, C., E. Tiezzi, and S. Ulgiati (1993). "Complete Recycling of Matter in the Framework of Physics, Biology and Ecological Economics". In: *Ecological Economics* 8:1–5.

Bihouix, Philippe (2011). *Des limites de l'économie circulaire: la question des métaux*. Working Paper. http://www.institutmomentum.org: Momentum Institut.

——— (2013). *L'Âge des low tech. Vers une civilisation techniquement soutenable*. Paris: Seuil.

Binswanger, Hans Christoph (2013). *Die Wachstumsspirale. Geld, Energie und Imagination in der Dynamik des Marktprozesses*. Fourth Edition. Marburg: Metropolis.

Binswanger, Mathias (1993). "From Microscopic to Macroscopic Theories: Entropic Aspects of Ecological and Economic Porcesses". In: *Ecological Economics* 8(3):209–234.

——— (2006). "Why Does Income Growth Fail to Make Us Happier? Searching for the Treadmills behind the Paradox of Happiness". In: *The Journal of Socio-Economics* 35:366–381.

——— (2009). "Is There a Growth Imperative in Capitalist Economies? A Circular Flow Perspective". In: *Journal of Post Keynesian Economics* 31(4):707–727.

Bloom, David E., David Canning, and Günther Fink (2008). "Urbanization and the Wealth of Nations". In: *Science* 319(5864):772–775.

Bonneuil, Christophe and Jean-Baptiste Fressoz (2016). *The Shock of the Anthropocene*. London: Verso Books.

Boulding, Kenneth E. (1966). "The Economics of the Coming Spaceship Earth". In: *Environmental Quality in a Growing Economy*. Ed. by Henry Jarrett. Baltimore (MD): Johns Hopkins Press.

—— (1969). "Economics as a Moral Science". In: *American Economic Review* 59(1):1–12.

——, MDBourdieu, Pierre (1975). "The Specificity of the Scientific Field and the Social Conditions of the Progress of Reason". In: *Social Science Information* 14(6):19–47.

Bowles, Samuel (1998). "Endogenous Preferences: The Cultural Consequences of Markets and Other Economic Institutions". In: *Journal of Economic Literature* 36(1):75–111.

—— (2004). *Microeconomics. Behavior, Institutions, and Evolution.* New York: Russell Sage Foundation.

—— (2011). "Is Liberal Society a Parasite on Tradition?" In: *Philosophy & Public Affairs* 39(1):46–81.

Bowles, Samuel and Herbert Gintis (1992). "Power and Wealth in a Competitive Capitalist Economy". In: *Philosophy and Public Affairs* 21(4):324–353.

—— (1993). "The Revenge of Homo Economicus: Contested Exchange and the Revival of Political Economy". In: *Journal of Economic Perspectives* 7(1):83–102.

—— (1998). "How Communities Govern: The Structural Basis of Prosocial Norms". In: *Economics, Values, and Organization.* Ed. by Avner Ben-Ner and Louis Putterman. Cambridge: Cambridge University Press. Pp. 206–230.

—— (2000). "Walrasian Economics in Retrospect". In: *The Quarterly Journal of Economics* 115(4):1411–1439.

—— (2002). "Homo reciprocans". In: *Nature* 415(6868):125–127.

—— (2008). "Power". In: *The New Palgrave Dictionary of Economics.* Ed. by S. N. Durlauf and L. E. Blume. New York: Palgrave Macmillan.

Boyle, James (2002). "Fencing Off Ideas: Enclosure and the Disappearance of the Public Domain". In: *Daedalus* 131(2):13–25.

Brandstätter, Herrmann, Werner Güth, and Hartmut Kliemt (2003). "The Bounds of Rationality: Philosophical, Psychological and Economic Aspects of Choice Making". In: *Homo Oeconomicus* XX(2/3):303–356.

Bromley, Daniel W. (1990). "The Ideology of Efficiency: Searching for a Theory of Policy Analysis". In: *Journal of Environmental Economics and Management* 19:86–107.

Buchanan, James M. and Gordon Tullock (1962). *The Calculus of Consent: Logical Foundations of Constitutional Democracy.* Ann Arbor: University of Michigan Press.

Castel, Robert (1995). *Les Métamorphoses de la question sociale. Une chronique du salariat.* Paris: Fayard.

Chamayou, Grégoire (2018). *La société ingouvernable. Une généalogie du libéralisme autoritaire.* Paris: La fabrique.

Chapman, Lewis, Duane and Neha Khanna (2000). "Crying No Wolf: Why Economists Don't Worry About Climate Change, and Should. An Editorial Comment". In: *Climatic Change* 47:225–232.

Charmes, Jacques (2019). *The Unpaid Care Work and the Labour Market. An Analysis of Time Use Data based on the Latest World Compilation of Time-Use Surveys.* Geneva: International Labour Office.

Chartier, Roger (2002). "Property & Privilege in the Republic of Letters". In: *Daedalus* 131(2):60–66.

Clark, Judy, Jacquelin Burgess, and Carolyn M. Harrison (2000). "'I Struggled with This Money Business': Respondent's Perspectves on Contingent Valuation". In: *Ecological Economics* 33:45–62.

Cleland, Elsa E. (2011). "Biodiversity and Ecosystem Stability". In: *Nature Education Knowledge* 3(10):14.

Cohen, Gerald Allan (1982). "Reply to Elster on 'Marxism, Functionalism, and Game Theory'". In: *Theory and Society* 11(4):483–495.

Cohen, Nicole S. (2008). "The Valorization of Surveillance: Towards a Political Economy of Facebook". In: *Democratic Communiqué* 22(1):6–22.

Condorcet, Nicolas de (1776/1847). "Fragments sur la liberté de la presse (1776)". In: *Œuvres complètes XI*. Paris: Firmin Didot Frères. Pp. 255–314.

Costanza, Robert et al. (1997). "The Value of the World's Ecosystem Services and Natural Capital". In: *Nature* 387:253–260.

Credit Suisse Research Institute (2020). *Global Wealth Report 2020*. Credit Suisse. url: https://www.credit-suisse.com/about-us/en/reportsresearch/global-wealth-report.html.

Crutzen, Paul J. (2002). "Geology of Mankind". In: *Nature* 415:23.

Czech, Brian et al. (2005). "Establishing Indicators for Biodiversity". In: *Science* 308:791–792.

Dalla Costa, Mariarosa and Selma James (1972). *The Power of Women and the Subversion of the Community*. Bristol: Falling Walls Press.

Daly, Herman E. (1968). "On Economics as a Life Science". In: *Journal of Political Economy* 76(3):392–406.

––––––– (1992). "Allocation, Distribution, and Sacle: Towards an Economics That Is Efficient, Just, and Sustainable". In: *Ecological Economics* 6(3):185–193.

––––––– (2005). "Economics in a Full World". In: *Scientific American* 293:100–107.

Daly, Herman E. and Joshua Farley (2011). *Ecological Economics. Principles and Applications*. Second Edition. Washington (DC): Island Press.

De Angelis, Massimo (2013). "Does Capital Need a Commons Fix?" In: *Ephemera: Theory & Politics in Organization* 13(3):603–615.

Deaton, Angus (2010). "Instruments, Randomization, and Learning about Development". In: *Journal of Economic Literature* 48:424–455.

Department for Environment, Food and Rural Affairs (2007). *An introductory guide to valuing ecosystem services*. url: www.defra.gov.uk.

––––––– (2020). *Agriculture in the United Kingdom 2019*. url: https://www.gov. uk/government/statistics/agriculture-in-the-united-kingdom-2019.

Descola, Philippe (2005). *Pa-delà nature et culture*. Paris: Gallimard.

Dickens, Charles (1854). *Hard Times. For These Times*. Copyright edition. Leipzig: Tauchnitz.

Diderot, Denis ([1767] 1861). *Lettre sur le commerce de la librairie (1767)*. Paris: L. Hachette.

Duflo, Esther (2017). "The Economist as Plumber". In: *American Economic Review* 107(5):1–26.

Duménil, Gérard and Dominique Lévy (2014). "The Crisis of the Early 21st Century: Marxian Perspectives". In: *The Great Recession and the Contradictions of Contemporary Capitalism*. Ed. by Riccardo Bellofiore and Giovanna Vertova. Cheltenham: Edward Elgar. Pp. 26–49.

––––––– (2015). "Welche Geschichte erzählen Pikettys Daten? Zwei Lesarten". In: *Zeitschrift für kritische Sozialtheorie und Philosophie* 2(2):219–254.

Easterlin, Richard A. (1974). "Does Economic Growth Improve the Human Lot?" In: *Nations and Households in Economic Growth: Essays in Honor of Moses Abramovitz*. Ed. by Paul A. David and Melvin W. Reder. New York: Academic Press. Pp. 89–125.

Easterlin, Richard A. et al. (2010). "The Happiness-Income Paradox Revisited". In: *Proceedings of the National Academy of Sciences* 107(52):22463–22468.

Emmanuel, Arghiri (1972). *Unequal Exchange. A Study of the Imperialism of Trade*. London: Monthly Review Press.

Falk, Armin and Nora Szech (2013). "Morals and Markets". In: *Science* 340:707–711.

Federici, Silvia (1975). *Wages against Housework*. Power of Women Collective and the Falling Wall Press.

——— (2004). *Caliban and the Witch*. Brooklyn (NY): Autonomedia.

Fehr, Ernst and Simon Gächter (2002). "Altruistic Punishment in Humans". In: *Nature* 415(6868):137–140.

Ferrant, Gaëlle, Luca Maria Pesando and Keiko Nowacka (2014). *Unpaid Care Work: The Missing Link in the Analysis of Gender Gaps in Payment Outcomes*. Paris: OECD Development Centre.

Fichte, Johann Gottlieb (1793). "Beweis der Unrechtmässigkeit des Büchernachdrucks. Ein Räsonnement und eine Parabel". In: *Berliner Monatsschrift* 21:443–483.

Field, Alexander J. (2001). *Altruistically Inclined? Behavioral Sciences, Evolutionary Theory, and the Origins of Reciprocity*. Ann Arbor: University of Michigan Press.

Fischer-Kowalski, Marina (1998). "Society's Metabolism. The Intellectual History of Materials Flow Analysis, Part I, 1860–1970". In: *Journal of Industrial Ecology* 2(1):61–78.

Fischer-Kowalski, Marina and Walter Hüttler (1998). "Society's Metabolism. The Intellectual History of Materials Flow Analysis, Part II, 1970–1998". In: *Journal of Industrial Ecology* 2(4):107–136.

Fitzsimons, Patrick (2000). *»Neoliberalism and ›Social Capital‹: Reinventing Community«*. url: http://www.amat.org.nz/neoliber.htm.

Flood, Merrill M. (1952). *Some Experimental Games*. Research Memorandum 789-1. U.S. Air Force Project RAND.

Folbre, Nancy (1982). "Exploitation Comes Home: A Critique of the Marxian Theory of Family Labour". In: *Cambridge Journal of Economics* 6(4):317–329.

——— (2008). "When a Commodity Is Not Exactly a Commodity". In: *Science* 319:1769–1771.

——— (2012). *The Rise and Decline of Patriarchal Capitalism*. Working Paper 298. Political Economy Research Institute, University of Massachusetts.

Folbre, Nancy and Julie A. Nelson (2000). "For Love or Money – Or Both?" In: *The Journal of Economic Perspectives* 14(4):123–140.

Folbre, Nancy and Thomas E. Weisskopf (1998). "Did Father know Best? Families, Markets, and the Supply of Caring Labor". In: *Economics, Values, and Organization*. Ed. by Avner Ben-Ner and Louis Putterman. Cambridge: Cambridge University Press. Pp. 171–205.

Foster, John Bellamy, Brett Clark Barrett, and Richard York (2009). "The Midas Effect: A Critique of Climate Change Economics". In: *Development and Change* 40(6):1085–1097.

Foster, John Bellamy and Michael D. Yates (2014). "Piketty and the Crisis of Neoclassical Economics". In: *Monthly Review* 66(6).

Foster, John Bellamy and Paul Burkett (2018). "Value Isn't Everything". In: *Monthly Review* 70(6).

Frank, Philipp (1957). *Philosophy of Science. The Link between Science and Philosophy*. Englewood Cliffs (NJ): Prentice-Hall.

Fraser, Nancy (2014). "Can Society be Commodities All the Way Down? Post-Polanyian Reflections on Capitalist Crisis". In: *Economy and Society* 43(4):541–558.

Freudenthal, Gideon (1986). *Atom and Individual in the Age of Newton: On the Genesis of the Mechanic World View*. Dordrecht: Reidel.

Fromm, Erich (1932). "Die psychoanalytische Charakterologie und ihre Bedeutung für die Sozialpsychologie". In: *Zeitschrift für Sozialforschung* 1:253–277.

Georgescu-Roegen, Nicholas (1975). "Energy and Economic Myth". In: *Southern Economic Journal* 41(3):347–381.

——— (1986). "The Entropy Law and the Economic Process in Retrospect". In: *Eastern Journal of Economics* XII(1):3–25.

Gigerenzer, Gerd and Henry Brighton (2009). "Homo Heuristicus: Why Biased Minds Make Better Inferences". In: *Topics in Cognitive Science* 1:107–143.

Gintis, Herbert and Samuel Bowles (1981). "Structure and Practice in the Labor Theory of Value". In: *The Review of Radical Political Economics* 12(4):1–24.

Gintis, Herbert et al. (2003). "Explaining Altruistic Behavior in Humans". In: *Evolution and Human Behavior* 24:153–172.

Gneezy, Uri and Aldo Rustichini (2000). "A Fine is a Price". In: *The Journal of Legal Studies* 29(1):1–17.

Gómez-Baggethun, Erik and Manuel Ruiz-Pérez (2011). "Economic Valuation and the Commodification of Ecosystem Services". In: *Ecological Economics* 35(5):613–628.

Goodwin, Neva et al. (2014). *Microeconomics in Context. Third Edition.* Armonk (NY): M. E. Sharpe.

Gordon, Myron J. and Jeffrey S. Rosenthal (2003). "Capitalism's Growth Imperative". In: *Cambridge Journal of Economics* 27:25–48.

Gowdy, John M. (2010). *Microeconomic Theory, Old and New. A Student's Guide.* Stanford (CA): Stanford University Press.

Gowdy, John and Jon D. Erickson (2005). "The Approach of Ecological Economics". In: *Cambridge Journal of Economics* 29(2):207–222.

Graeber, David (2011). *Debt: The First 5000 Years.* London: Penguin.

Gray, John (2010). "The Nanny Diaries. Neoliberalism has Delivered not a Small State, but a Bloated Market State in which Government Interference Is Omnipresent". In: *New Statesman* 139(4983):52–53.

Güth, Werner, Carsten Schmidt, and Matthias Sutter (2007). "Bargaining Outside the Lab: A Newspaper Experiment of a Three-Person Ultimatum Game". In: *The Economic Journal* 117(518):449–469.

Güth, Werner and Hartmut Kliemt (2003). "Experimentelle Ökonomik, Modell-Platonismus in neuem Gewande?" In: *Experimente in der Ökonomik.* Ed. by Martin Held, Gisela Kubon-Gilke, and Richard Sturn. Vol. 2. Jahrbuch Normative und institutionelle Grundfragen der Ökonomik. Marburg: Metropolis.

Güth, Werner, Rolf Schmittberger, and Bernd Schwarze (1982). "An Experimental Analysis of Ultimatum Bargaining". In: *Journal of Economic Behavior and Organization* 3:367–388.

Hall, Charles A. S. (2017). *Energy Return on Investment. A Unifying Principle for Biology, Economics, and Sustainability.* Cham: Springer.

Hall, Charles A. S. et al. (2001). "The Need to Reintegrate the Natural Sciences with Economics". In: *BioScience* 51(8):663–673.

——— (2003). "Hydrocarbons and the Evolution of Human Culture". In: *Nature* 426(6964):318–322.

Hardin, Garret J. (1968). "The Tragedy of the Commons". In: *Science* 162(3859):1243–1248.

——— (1978). "Political Requirements for Preserving our Common Heritage". In: *Wildlife and America.* Ed. by H. P. Bokaw. Washington (DC): Council on Environmental Quality. Pp. 310–317.

Häring, Norbert and Niall Douglas (2012). *Economists and the Powerful.* London: Anthem Press.

Harrison, John (1973). "The Political Economy of Housework". In: *Bulletin of the Conference of Socialist Economists* III(3):35–52.

Harvey, David (1996). *Justice, Nature & the Geography of Difference.* Cambridge: Blackwell.

—— (2005). *A Brief History of Neoliberalism*. Oxford: Oxford University Press.

Heinberg, Richard (2007). *Peak Everything. Waking Up to the Century of Declines*. Gabriola Island: New Society Publishers.

Heinrich, Michael (2007). "Profit without End: Capitalism Is Just Getting Started". In: *MRZine (Monthly Review)* 28/07/07. url: http://mrzine.monthlyreview.org/2007/heinrich280707.html.

—— (2008). "The Current Financial Crisis and the Future of Global Capitalism". In: *MRZine (Monthly Review)* 09/06/2008. url: http://mrzine.monthlyreview.org/2008/heinrich090608.html.

Hempel, Carl Gustav (1942). "The Function of General Laws in History". In: *The Journal of Philosophy* 39(2):35–48.

Henrich, Joseph, Steven J. Heine, and Ara Norenzayan (2010). "The Weirdest People in the World?" In: *Behavioral and Brain Sciences* 33:61–135.

Henrich, Joseph et al. (2001). "In Search of Homo Economicus: Behavioral Experiments in 15 Small-Scale Societies". In: *American Economic Association Papers and Proceedings* 91(2):73–78.

—— (2005). "›Economic Man‹ in Cross-Cultural Perspective: Behavioral Experiments in 15 Small-Scale Societies". In: *Behavioral and Brain Sciences* 28:795–855.

—— (2010). "Markets, Religion, Community Size, and the Evolution of Fairness and Punishment". In: *Science* 327:1480–1484.

Hesmondhalgh, David (2010). "User-Generated Content, Free Labour and the Cultural Industries". In: *Ephemera: Theory & Politics in Organization* 10(3/4):267–284.

Hess, Charlotte and Elinor Ostrom, eds. (2007). *Understanding Knowledge as a Commons: From Theory to Practice*. Cambridge (MA): MIT Press.

Hesse, Carla (1990). "Enlightenment Epistemology and the Laws of Authorship in Revolutionary France 1777–1793". In: *Representations* 30:109–137.

—— (2002). "The Rise of Intellectual Property, 700 B.C.–A.D. 2000: An Idea in the Balance". In: *Daedalus* 131(2):26–45.

Hicks, John R. (1939). "The Foundations of Welfare Economics". In: *The Economic Journal* 49(196):696–712.

Himmelweit, Susan (1995). "The Discovery of ›Unpaid Work‹: The Social Consequences of the Expansion of 'Work'". In: *Feminist Economics* 1(2):1–19.

Himmelweit, Susan and Simon Mohun (1977). "Domestic Labour and Capital". In: *Cambridge Journal of Economics* 1:15–31.

Hirway, Indira (2015). *Unpaid Work and the Economy: Linkages and Their Implications*. Working Paper 838. Levy Economics Institute.

Hodgson, Geoffrey M. (2011). "The Eclipse of the Uncertainty Concept in Mainstream Economics". In: *Journal of Economic Issues* XLV(1):159–175.

Holland, Alan (1995). "The Assumptions of Cost-Benefit Analysis: A Philosopher's View". In: *Environmental Valuation: New Perspectives*. Ed. by K. W. Willis and J. T. Corkindale. Wallingford: CAB International.

Homer-Dixon, Thomas (2011). "Growth Won't Last Forever". In: *Foreign Policy* 184:56.

Homer-Dixon, Thomas et al. (2015). "Synchronous Failure: The Emerging Causal Architecture of Global Crisis". In: *Ecology and Society* 20(3):6.

Hornborg, Alf (1998). "Towards an Ecological Theory of Unequal Exchange: Articulating World System Theory and Ecological Economics". In: *Ecological Economics* 25:127–136.

—— (2020). *Dialectical Confusion: On Jason Moore's Posthumanist Marxism*. Historical Materialism Blog. url: http://www.historicalmaterialism.org/blog/dialectical-confusion-jason-moores-posthumanist-marxism.

Hueting, Roefie et al. (1998). "The Concept of Environmental Function and Its Valuation". In: *Ecological Economics* 25:31–35.

Jackson, Tim (2009). *Prosperity without Growth? The Transition to a Sustainable Economy.* Sustainable Development Commission.

James, Selma (1973). "Women, the Unions and Work, or... What Is Not To Be Done". In: *Radical America* 7(4 & 5):51–72.

Kagel, John H. (1997). "Economics According to the Rats (and Pigeons Too): What Have We Learned and What Can We Hope to Learn?" In: *Laboratory Experimentation in Economics. Six Points of View.* Ed. by Alvin E. Roth. Cambridge (MA): Cambridge University Press. Pp. 155–192.

Kahler, Miles (1990). "Orthodoxy and Its Alternatives: Explaining Approaches to Stabilization and Adjustment". In: *Economic Crisis and Policy Choice: The Politics of Economic Adjustment in the Third World.* Ed. by Joan M. Nelson. Princeton (NJ): Princeton University Press. Pp. 33–61.

Kahneman, Daniel (2003). "Maps of Bounded Rationality: Psychology for Behavioral Economics". In: *The American Economic Review* 93(5):1449–1475.

Kahneman, Daniel and Amos Tversky (1979). "Prospect Theory: An Analysis of Decision under Risk". In: *Econometrica* 47(2):263–292.

Kahneman, Daniel and Angus Deaton (2010). "High Income Improves Evaluation of Life But Not Emotional Well-Being". In: *Proceedings of the National Academy of Sciences of the United States of America* 107(38):16489–16493.

Kaldor, Nicholas (1939). "Welfare Propositions of Economics and Interpersonal Comparisons of Utility". In: *The Economic Journal* 49(195):549–552.

Kant, Immanuel (1998). *Critique of Pure Reason.* Cambridge Edition of the Works of Immanuel Kant. Cambridge: Cambridge University Press.

——— (2007). *Anthropology, History, and Education.* Cambridge Edition of the Works of Immanuel Kant. Cambridge: Cambridge University Press.

Kaplan Daniels, Arlene (1987). "Invisible Work". In: *Social Problems* 34(5):403–415.

Kapp, K. William (1961). *Towards a Science of Man in Society.* The Hague: Nijhoff.

——— (2016). *The Heterodox Theory of Social Costs.* Ed. by Sebastian Berger. London: Routledge.

Kevles, Daniel J. (2002). "Of Mice & Money: The Story of the World's First Animal Patent". In: *Daedalus* 131(2):78–88.

Kleidon, Axel (2016). *Thermodynamic Foundations of the Earth System.* Cambridge: Cambridge University Press.

Knight, Charles (1865). *Passages of a Working Life during Half a Century: With a Prelude of Early Reminiscences.* Vol. III. London: Bradburry and Evans.

Knight, Frank H. (1921/1964). *Risk, Uncertainty and Profit.* New York: Augustus M. Kelley.

Krantz-Kent, Rachel (2009). "Measuring Time Spent in Unpaid Household Work: Results from the American Time Use Survey". In: *Monthly Labor Review* July 1:46–59.

Krausmann, Fridolin et al. (2015). "La société industrielle mondiale ne connaît aucune dématérialisation depuis le XIXe siècle". In: *La revue durable* 53:22–24.

Kubiszewski, Ida et al. (2013). "Beyond GDP: Measuring and Achieving Global Genuine Progress". In: *Ecological Economics* 93:57–68.

Kuhn, Thomas S. (1962/1996). *The Structure of Scientific Revolutions.* Vol. 3. Chicago (IL): University of Chicago Press.

Kuznets, Simon (1934). *National Income, 1929–32. Letter from the Acting Secretary of Commerce. Senate Document No. 124.* Washington (DC): United States Government Printing Office.

Lange, Oskar (1936/1937). "On the Economic Theory of Socialism. Part One and Two". In: *Review of Economic Studies* 4(1–2):53–71, 123–142.

Latour, Bruno and Steve Woolgar (1986). *Laboratory Life. The Construction of Scientific Facts*. Princeton (NJ): Princeton University Press.

Lave, Lester B. (1962). "An Empirical Approach to the Prisoners' Dilemma Game". In: *The Quarterly Journal of Economics* 76(3):424–436.

Leontief, Wassily (1982). "Academic Economics". In: *Science* 217(4555), pp. 104–105.

Lerner, Abba (1972). "The Economics and Politics of Consumer Sovereignty". In: *American Economic Review* 62(1/2):258–266.

Lewis, Simon L. and Mark A. Maslin (2015). "Defining the Anthropocene". In: *Nature* 519(7542):171–180.

Lindenberger, Dietmar and Reiner Kümmel (2002). "Thermodynamics and Economics". In: *Post-Autistic Economics Review* no. 14.

Luhmann, Niklas (1989). *Ecological Communication*. Cambridge (MA): Polity Press.

Luxemburg, Rosa (1951). *The Accumulation of Capital (1913)*. London: Routledge and Kegan Paul.

Mahnkopf, Birgit (2013). *Peak Everything – Peak Capitalism. Folgen der sozialökologischen Krise für die Dynamik des historischen Kapitalismus*. Working Paper 02. DFG-KollegforscherInnengruppe Postwachstumsgesellschaften.

Malmendier, Ulrike and Devin Shanthikumar (2014). "Do Security Analysts Speak in Two Tongues?" In: *The Review of Financial Studies* 27(5):1287–1322.

Marginson, Simon (1993). *Education and Public Policy in Australia*. Cambridge: Cambridge University Press.

Martens, Per Nicolai (2003). "Extraterrestrial Mining and Deep Sea Mining – Trends and Forecasts". In: *Mining in the 21st Century – Quo Vadis? 19th World Mining Congress New Dehli. Vol. 1*. Ed. by A. K. Gose and L. K Bose. Lisse: A. A. Balkema Publishers. Pp. 75–97.

Martinez-Alier, Juan (1987). *Ecological Economics. Energy, Environment and Society*. Oxford: Blackwell.

Marx, Karl ([1849] 1977). "Wage Labour and Capital". In: *Marx Engels Collected Works*, Vol. 9. London: Lawrence & Wishart. Pp. 197–228.

———— ([1858] 1987). *Grundrisse, Part 2*. In: *Marx Engels Collected Works*, Vol 29: *Economic Manuscripts of 1857–58*. London: Lawrence & Wishart.

———— ([1887] 1990). *Capital. A Critical Analysis of Capitalist Production (1887)*. Marx Engels Gesamtausgabe (MEGA), Vol. II.9. Berlin: Dietz.

Marx, Karl and Friedrich Engels (1983). *Letters 1856–59*. Vol. 40. Marx Engels Collected Works. London: Lawrence & Wishart.

Matt, Susan J. (2011). *Keeping Up with the Joneses: Envy in American Consumer Society, 1890–1930*. Philadelphia: University of Pennsylvania Press.

McCauley, Douglas J. (2006). "Selling Out on Nature". In: *Nature* 443(7107):27–28.

McKinnon, Susan (2005). *Neo-liberal Genetics. The Myths and Moral Tales of Evolutionary Psychology*. Chicago (IL): Prickly Paradigm Press.

McLaughlin, Peter (1990). *Kant's Critique of Teleology in Biological Explanation. Antinomy and Teleology*. Lewiston: Edwin Mellen Press.

Mearman, Andrew, Sebastian Berger, and Danielle Guizzo (2019). *What Is Heterodox Economics?* London: Routledge.

Meillassoux, Claude (1972). "From Reproduction to Production. A Marxist Approach to Economic Anthropoloy". In: *Economy and Society* 1(1):93–105.

———— (1981). *Maidens, Meal and Money. Capitalism and the Domestic Community*. Cambridge: Cambridge University Press.

Merton, Robert K. (1939). "Science and the Economy of Seventeenth Century England". In: *Science & Society* 3(1):3–27.

Mies, Maria and Veronika Bennholdt-Thomsen (2000). *The Subsistence Perspective. Beyond the Globalised Economy.* London: Zed Books.

Mirowski, Philip (1984). "Physics and the 'Marginalist Revolution'". In: *Cambridge Journal of Economics* 8:361–379.

———— (1989). *More Heat than Light. Economics as Social Physics, Physics as Nature's Economics.* Cambridge: Cambridge University Press.

———— (1990). "Learning the Meaning of a Dollar: Conservation Principles and the Social Theory of Value in Economic Theory". In: *Social Research* 57(3):689–717,

———— (2009). "Postface: Defining Neoliberalism". In: *The Road from Mont Pèlerin. The Making of the Neoliberal Thought Collective.* Ed. by Philip Mirowski and Dieter Plehwe. Cambridge (MA): Harvard University Press.

———— (2013). *Never Let a Serious Crises Go to Waste. How Neoliberalism Survived the Financial Meltdown.* London: Verso.

Moglen, Eben (1999). "Anarchism Triumphant: Free Software and the Death of Copyright". In: *First Monday* 4(8). https://firstmonday.org/ojs/index.php/fm/article/view/684/594.

Monbiot, George (2018). *The UK government wants to put a price on nature – but that will destroy it.* url: https://www.theguardian.com/commentisfree/ 2018/may/15/price-natural-world-destruction-natural-capital.

Moore, Jason W. (2014). "The End of Cheap Nature. Or How I Learned to Stop Worrying about ›the‹ Environment and Love the Crisis of Capitalism". In: *Structures of the World Political Economy and the Future of Global Conflict and Cooperation.* Ed. by C. Suter and C. Chase-Dunn. Berlin: LIT.

———— (2015a). *Capitalism in the Web of Life. Ecology and the Accumulation of Capital.* London: Verso Books.

———— (2015b). "Endless Accumulation, Endless (Unpaid) Work?" In: *The Occupied Times.* url: http://theoccupiedtimes.org/?p=13766.

More, Thomas ([1516] 1684). *Utopia.* Trans. by Gilbert Brunet. London: Richard Chiswell.

Nace, Ted (2003). *Gangs of America. The Rise of Corporate Power and the Disabling of Democracy.* San Francisco (CA): Berrett-Koehler.

Nash, John (1951). "Non-Cooperative Games". In: *Annals of Mathematics. Second Series* 54(2):286–295.

Neumann, John von (1928). "Zur Theorie der Gesellschaftsspiele". In: *Mathematische Annalen* 100:295–320.

Neumann, John von and Oskar Morgenstern (1948). *Theory of Games and Economic Behavior.* Third Edition. Princeton (NJ): Princeton University Press.

Newton, Isaac (1729). *The Mathematical Principles of Natural Philosophy.* London: Benjamin Motte.

Norgaard, Richard B. and Collin Bode (1998). "Nect, the Value of God, and Other Reactions". In: *Ecological Economics* 25:37–39.

Nowak, Martin A., Karen M. Page, and Karl Sigmund (2000). "Fairness versus Reason in the Ultimatum Game". In: *Science* 289:1773–1775.

Nuss, Sabine (2012). "Umkämpftes Copyright. Der Streit um das geistige Eigentum". In: *Blätter für deutsche und internationale Politik* 12:85–94.

Nussbaum, Martha (1990). "Aristotelian Social Democracy". In: *Liberalism and the Good.* Ed. by Henry S. Richardson R. Bruce Douglass Gerald M. Mara. London: Routledge. Pp. 203–252.

Odling-Smee, F. John (2007). "Niche Inheritance: A Possible Basis for Classifying Multiple Inheritance Systems in Evolution". In: *Biological Theory* 2(3):276–289.

O'Neill, John (1993). *Ecology, Policy, and Politics. Human Well-Being and the Natural World.* London: Routledge.

O'Neill, Robert V. and James R. Kahn (2000). "Homo Economus as a Keystone Species". In: *BioScience* 50(4):333–337.

Ostrom, Elinor (1990). *Governing the Commons. The Evolution of Institutions for Collective Action.* Cambridge (MA): Cambridge University Press.

O'Sullivan, Mary (2015). "Review of Thomas Piketty, Capital in the 21st Century". In: *American Historical Review* 120(2):564–566.

Pearce, David (1976). "The Limits of Cost-Benefit Analysis as a Guide to Environmental Policy". In: *Kyklos* 29(1):97–112.

Perelman, Michael (2003a). "Intellectual Property Rights and the Commodity Form: New Dimensions in the Legislated Transfer of Surplus Value". In: *Review of Radical Political Economics* 35(3):304–311.

——— (2003b). *The Perverse Economy. The Impact of Markets on People and the Environment.* New York: Palgrave Macmillan.

Phillips, Victoria F. (2007). "Commodification, Intellectual Property and the Women of Gee's Bend". In: *American Journal of Gender, Social Policy & the Law* 15(2):359–377.

Piketty, Thomas (2014). *Capital in the Twenty-First Century.* Cambridge (MA): The Belknap Press of Harvard University Press.

——— (2015). "About 'Capital in the Twenty-First Century'". In: *American Economic Review: Papers & Proceedings* 105(5):48–53.

——— (2019). *Capital et idéologie.* Paris: Seuil.

Polanyi, Karl ([1944] 2001). *The Great Transformation. The Political and Economic Origins of Our Time (1944).* Foreword by Joseph E. Stiglitz. Introduction by Frey Block. Boston (MA): Beacon Press.

Prigogine, Ilya (1993). "Time, Structure and Fluctuations. Lecture to the Memory of Alfred Nobel, December 8, 1977". In: *Nobel Lectures. Chemistry 1971–1980.* Singapore: World Scientific Publishing. Pp. 263–285.

Radin, Margaret Jane (1987). "Market-Inalienability". In: *The Havard Law Review* 100(8):1849–1938.

——— (1988). "The Liberal Conception of Property: Cross Currents in the Jurisprudence of Takings". In: *Columbia Law Review* 88(8):1667–1696.

——— (1996a). *Contested Commodities. The Trouble with Trade in Sex, Children, Body Parts, and Other Things.* Cambridge (MA): Havard University Press.

——— (1996b). "Property Evolving in Cyberspace". In: *Journal of Law and Commerce* 15(2):509–527.

Rayner, Steve (2003). "Democracy in the Age of Assessment: Reflections on the Roles of Expertise and Democracy in Public-Sector Decision Making". In: *Science and Public Policy* 30(3):163–170.

——— (2007). "The Rise of Risk and the Decline of Politics". In: *Environmental Hazards* 7:165–172.

Reid, Margaret G. (1934). *Economics of Household Production.* London: John Wiley & Sons.

Richard, Jacques (2012). *Comptabilité et Développement Durable.* Paris: Economica.

Rideau, Frédéric (2008). "Commentary on Diderot's Letter on the Book Trade (1763)". In: *Primary Sources on Copyright (1450–1900).* Ed. by L. Bently and M. Kretschmer. url: www.copyrighthistory.org.

Robbins, Lionel (1938). "Interpersonal Comparisons of Utility: A Comment". In: *The Economic Journal* 48(192):635–641.

Robinson, Joan (1953–1954). "The Production Function and the Theory of Capital". In: *The Review of Economic Studies* 21(2):81–106.

Romer, Paul M (1990). "Endogenous Technological Change". In: *Journal of Political Economy* 98(5 Part 2):S71–S102.

Rousseau, Jean-Jacques ([1789] 1897). *The Confessions*. Vol. II. London: Gibbings.

Ruddiman, William F. et al. (2015). "Defining the Epoch We Live In: Is a Formally Designated 'Anthropocene' a Good Idea?" In: *Science* 348(6230):38–39.

Ryle, Gilbert (2009). *The Concept of Mind*. London: Routledge.

Sahlins, Marshall (2008). *The Western Illusion of Human Nature: With Reflections on the Long History of Hierarchy, Equality, and the Sublimation of Anarchy in the West, and Comparative Notes on Other Conceptions of the Human Condition*. Chicago (IL): Prickly Paradigm Press.

Samuelson, Paul A. (1957). "Wages and Interest: A Modern Dissection of Marxian Economic Models". In: *The American Economic Review* 47(6):884–912.

——— (1967). *Economics*. New York: McGraw Hill.

Sassen, Saskia (2014). *Expulsions. Brutality and Complexity in the Global Economy*. Cambridge (MA): Belknap Press.

——— (2015). "'Es wird für alle enger.' Interview". In: *Der Freitag* 42 (October 16), p. 28.

Schäfer, Dieter (2004). "Unbezahlte Arbeit und Haushaltsproduktion im Zeitvergleich". In: *Alltag in Deutschland. Analysen zur Zeitverwendung*. Wiesbaden: Statistisches Bundesamt.

Scheffer, Marten et al. (2001). "Catastrophic Shifts in Ecosystems". In: *Nature* 423:591–596.

Schmid, Anne-Françoise (2001). *Que peut la philsophie des sciences?* Paris: Éditions Petra.

Scitovsky, Tibor de (1941). "A Note on Welfare Propositions in Economics". In: *The Review of Economic Studies* 9(1):77–88.

Screpanti, Ernesto and Stefano Zamagni (2005). *An Outline of the History of Economic Thought*. Second Edition. Oxford: Oxford University Press.

Self, Peter (1975). *Econocrats and the Policy Process. The Politics and Philosophy of Cost-Benefit-Analysis*. London: Macmillan.

Sen, Amartya K. (1970). "The Impossibility of a Paretian Liberal". In: *Journal of Political Economy* 78(1):152–157.

——— (1977). "Rational Fools: A Critique of the Behavioral Foundations of Economic Theory". In: *Philosophy and Public Affairs* 6(4):317–344.

——— (1982). "Just Deserts. Review of: P.T. Bauer, Equality, the Third World, and Economic Delusion". In: *The New York Review of Books* 29(3).

——— (1995). "Rationality and Social Choice". In: *American Economic Review* 85(1):1–24.

Serafy, Salah El (1998). "Pricing the Invaluable: The Value of the World's Ecosystem Services and Natural Capital". In: *Ecological Economics* 25:25–27.

Servet, Jean-Michel (2018). *L'économie comportementale en question*. Paris: Charles Léopold Mayer.

Servet, Jean-Michel and Bruno Tinel (2020). "The Behavioral and Neoliberal Foundations of Randomizations". In: *Strategic Change* 29:293–299.

Shiva, Vandana (2012). *Violent Economic ›Reforms‹, and the Growing Violence against Women*. Zcommunications. Url: https://zcomm.org/zcommentary/ violent-economic-reforms-and-the-growing-violence-againstwomen-by-vandana-shiva/.

Smith, Adam (1776). *An Inquiry into the Nature and Causes of the Wealth of Nations*. London: W. Strahan.

Sohn-Rethel, Alfred (2012). *Von der Analytik des Wirtschaftens zur Theorie der Volkswirtschaft. Frühe Schriften*. Ed. by Oliver Schlaudt and Carl Freytag. Freiburg: ça ira.

Solow, Robert M. (1956). "A Contribution to the Theory of Economic Growth". In: *The Quarterly Journal of Economics* 70(1):65–94.

—— (1994). "Perspectives on Growth Theory". In: *The Journal of Economic Perspectives* 8(1):45–54.

Stanovich, Keith E. (2013). "Why Humans are (Sometimes) Less Rational Than Other Animals: Cognitive Complexity and the Axioms of Rational Choice". In: *Thinking and Reasoning* 19(1):1–26.

Statistics Canada (1995). *Households' Unpaid Work: Measurement and Valuation*. Ottawa: Ministry of Industry.

Statistisches Bundesamt (2003). *Wo bleibt die Zeit? Die Zeitverwendung der Bevölkerung in Deutschland 2001/02*. url: https://www.destatis.de.

Steffen, Will et al. (2015). "Planetary Boundaries: Guiding Human Development on a Changing Planet". In: *Science* 347(6223):736.

Stehr, Nico and Marian Adolf (2015). *Ist Wissen Macht? Erkenntnisse über Wissens*. Weilerswist: Velbrück.

Steinhart, John S. and Carol E. Steinhart (1974). "Energy Use in the U.S. Food System". In: *Science* 184(4134):307–316.

Stern, David I. (2004). "The Rise and Fall of the Environmental Kuznets Curve". In: *World Development* 32(8):1419–1439.

Steuerle, Eugene et al. (2013). *Lost Generations? Wealth Building among Young Americans*. The Urban Institute. url: www.urban.org.

Stiglitz, Joseph E. (1991). *The Invisible Hand and Modern Welfare Economics*. Working Paper 3641. Cambridge (MA): National Bureau of Economic Research.

—— (2010). *Freefall. Free Markets and the Sinking of the Global Economy*. London: Allen Lane.

Stiglitz, Joseph E. and Andrew Weiss (1981). "Credit Rationing in Markets with Imperfect Information". In: *The American Economic Review* 71(3):393–410.

Strunz, Sebastian, Bartosz Bartowski, and Harry Schindler (2015). *Is There a Monetary Growth Imperative?* Discussion Paper 5. UFZ Helmholtz Zentrum für Umweltforschung.

Supiot, Alain (2017). *Governance by Numbers. The Making of a Legal Model of Allegiance*. Portland: Hart Publishing.

—— (2018). "Democracy laid low by the Market". In: *Jurisprudence* 9(3):449–460.

Syll, Lars Pålsson (2014). "Piketty and the Limits of Marginal Productivity Theory". In: *Real-World Economics Review* 69:36–43.

Toman, Michael (1998). "Why Not to Calculate the Value of the World's Ecosystem Services and Natural Capital". In: *Ecological Economics* 25:57–60.

Tomasello, Michael (2016). *A Natural History of Human Morality*. Cambridge (MA): Harvard University Press.

Trauger, David L. et al. (2003). *The Relationship of Economic Growth to Wildlife Conservation*. Technical Review 03-1. Bethesda (MD): The Wildlife Society.

Travis, Hannibal (2000). "Pirates of the Information Infrastructure: Blackstonian Copyright and the First Amendment". In: *Berkeley Technology Law Journal* 15(2):777–864.

Twain, Mark (1876). *The Adventures of Tom Sawyer*. Hartford: American Publishing Company.

United Nations, Department of Economic and Social Affairs, Population Division (2019). *World Urbanization Prospects 2018: Highlights (ST/ESA/SER.A/421)*. New York: United Nations. url: https://population.un.org/wup

Varoufakis, Yanis (2014). "Egalitarianism's Latest Foe: A Critical Review of Thomas Piketty's Capital in the Twenty-Frist Century". In: *Real-World Economics Review* 69:18–35.

Vatn, Arild (2000). "The Environment as a Commodity". In: *Environmental Values* 9:493–509.

Wahl, Peter (2009). *Food Speculation. The Main Factor of the Price Bubble in 2008.* Weed World Economy, Ecology & Development. url: http://www.weedonline.org/publikationen/2215521.html.

Wallerstein, Immanuel (2000). "Globalization or the Age of Transition? A Long-Term View of the Trajectory of the World-System". In: *International Sociology* 15(2):251–267.

——— (2004). *World-Systems Analysis. An Introduction.* Durham (NC): Duke University Press.

——— (2010a)."Ecology Versus Property Rights: Land in the Capitalist World-Economy". In: *Janus.net e-Journal of International Relations* 1(1):1–9.

——— (2010b). "Structural Crises". In: *New Left Review* 62:133–142.

——— (2011a). "Structural Crisis in the World-System: Where Do We Go from Here?" In: *Monthly Review* March 3:31–39.

——— (2011b). "The Gobal Economy Wont't Recover, Now or Ever". In: *Foreign Policy* 184:76.

Weber, Max (2012). *Collected Methodological Writings.* Ed. by Hans Henrik Bruun and Sam Whimster. Abingdon: Routledge.

Wenzlaff, Ferdinand, Christian Kimmich, and Oliver Richters (2014). *Theoretische Zugänge eines Wachstumszwangs in der Geldwirtschaft.* Discussion Paper 45. Hamburg: ZÖSS Zentrum für ökomische und soziologische Studien.

Wilde, Oscar (1995). *The Importance of Being Earnest and Other Plays.* Oxford: Oxford University Press.

Wildlife Society (2003). *The Relationship of Economic Growth to Wildlife Conservation.* Technical Review 03-1. Bethesda (MD): The Wildlife Society.

Windelband, Wilhelm ([1894] 1998). "History and Natural Science". In: *Theory & Psychology* 8(1):5–22.

World Economic Forum (2020). *The Global Risks Report 2020.* Insight Report. 15th Edition. url: https://www.weforum.org/reports/the-global-risksreport-2020.

Zelizer, Viviana (2005). *The Purchase of Intimacy.* Princeton (NJ): Princeton University Press.

Zerbisias, A. (2010). *Feminomics: Calculating the Value of 'Women's Work'.* url: http://www.thestar.com/news/insight/2010/10/30/feminomics_calculating_the_value_of_womens_work.html.

SUBJECT AND AUTHOR INDEX

Printed in the United States
by Baker & Taylor Publisher Services